FREE TRADE
UNDER FIRE

FREE TRADE
UNDER FIRE

DOUGLAS A. IRWIN

Copyright © 2002 by Princeton University Press

Published by Princeton University Press, 41 William Street, Princeton, New Jersey 08540

In the United Kingdom: Princeton University Press, 3 Market Place, Woodstock,

Oxfordshire OX20 1SY

All Rights Reserved

Library of Congress Cataloging-in-Publication Data

Irwin, Douglas A., 1962–

    Free trade under fire / Douglas A. Irwin.

      p. cm.

    Includes bibliographical references and index.

    ISBN 0-691-08843-8 (cl. : alk. paper)

    1. Free trade—United States.   2. United States—Commercial policy.

  3. Globalization.   I. Title.

    HF1756 .I68 2002

    382′.71—dc21   2001043159

British Library Cataloging-in-Publication Data is available

This book has been composed in ITC Garamond Light with Frutiger display

Printed on acid-free paper. ∞

www.pupress.princeton.edu

Printed in the United States of America

10 9 8 7 6 5 4 3 2 1

FOR MARJORIE, ELLEN, AND KATIE

Contents

_____Figures_

Tables

Acknowledgments

This book draws together part of the vast amount of economic research on international trade policy. I wish to acknowledge all of the scholars who have made contributions to this field in recent years, for it is their work that has inspired me. I would particularly like to thank Brink Lindsey, Michael Knetter, Anne Krueger, Nina Pavcnik, Phillip Swagel, and Alan Winters for providing valuable comments on earlier drafts of this manuscript. I am especially indebted to Meir and Becky Kohn. Meir convinced me to undertake the project and provided useful suggestions, while Becky helped to make significant improvements in the organization and clarity of the text. I also wish to thank my editor at Princeton University Press, Peter Dougherty, for his enthusiasm and good sense, both of which have encouraged and guided me through this process. Finally, I am grateful for the forbearance of my wife, Marjorie, and our daughters, Ellen and Katie. This book is for them.

Introduction

In 1824, the great British historian Thomas Babington Macaulay remarked that "free trade, one of the greatest blessings which a government can confer on a people, is in almost every country unpopular." The popularity of free trade has not changed much since Macaulay's day. The 1990s were a period of strong economic growth, expanding world trade, and the lowest U.S. unemployment in thirty years, and yet the decade began with fears of the "great sucking sound" of jobs lost due to the North American Free Trade Agreement (NAFTA) and ended with opponents of the World Trade Organization taking to the streets in the "Battle of Seattle," protesting the WTO's promotion of free trade.

While free trade has always been the subject of complaint, the rhetorical charges against it have stepped up in recent years, as the events in Seattle and elsewhere have made clear. Self-styled populists such as Ralph Nader and Pat Buchanan rail against free trade and the WTO as a system that serves the interests of corporations rather than people, harms workers, decimates manufacturing industries, sweeps aside environmental regulations, and undermines America's sovereignty. A wide range of groups, from environmentalists to religious organizations to human rights activists, have joined in the protests against free trade. The litany of complaints placed on the doorstep of free trade is quite impressive and goes well beyond the perennial objection that trade forces painful economic adjustments such as plant closings and layoffs of workers. Nader charges that "the Fortune 200's GATT and NAFTA agenda would make the air you breathe dirtier, and the water you drink more polluted. It would cost jobs, depress wage levels and make workplaces less safe. It would destroy family farms and undermine consumer protections." Buchanan chimes in with the claim that "broken homes, uprooted families, vanished dreams, delinquency, vandalism, crime— these are the hidden costs of free trade."[1]

Why was the economic prosperity of the 1990s accompanied by such hostility toward free trade? One view is that the rapid increase in international trade has unleashed a "globalization backlash." In this view, while beneficial to some groups, increased global integration has proven detrimental to the economic interests of others, who have redoubled their efforts to limit trade. Another view is that the reach of world trade rules has expanded beyond trade barriers to encompass internal regulatory policies regarding health, safety, and the environment. As a result, groups disturbed by this encroachment have raised concerns about sovereignty and whether the locus of decision making has shifted from elected representatives at home to faceless and unaccountable bureaucrats abroad.

Whatever the precise reason, the debate over trade policy has clearly intensified and shows little prospect of abating. It has raised many fundamental questions. Why is free trade considered to be a desirable policy? Do the most frequently made criticisms of free trade, such as its adverse impact on employment and the environment, have merit? Why did the United States break from its protectionist past and move to a policy of open trade after World War II? What is the World Trade Organization, and do world trade rules erode a country's sovereignty and undermine its health and environmental regulations?

This book aims to answer these basic questions for those seeking a better understanding of the ongoing debates over trade policy. These questions will be examined mainly through the lens of economics, but political and legal analysis is also required to understand many issues of policy.

Chapter 1, "The United States in a New Global Economy?" sets out basic facts about international trade and the U.S. economy. Information about the degree to which trade has increased in recent years pro-

---

[1] Nader 1993, 1; Buchanan 1998, 286. Ironically, a century ago populists railed against the inequities of protectionism, arguing that big business used tariffs to stifle competition and exploit consumers. Free trade was seen as a way of ensuring that competition would discipline the power of domestic monopolies and to prevent governments from using tariffs to give favors to special interests.

vides a context in which to consider trade policy. In addition, the chapter discusses the reasons for the increase in trade and the state of public opinion on the question of globalization.

Chapter 2, "The Case for Free Trade: Old Theories, New Evidence," examines the economic logic of free trade and recent empirical evidence reinforcing the case for it. Ever since Adam Smith and David Ricardo described the gains from trade in a systematic way, economists have stressed the benefits of improved resource allocation as the main advantage of trade. But economists have found mounting evidence that trade not only helps to allocate existing resources properly, but also makes those resources more productive. These productivity gains from trade, overlooked in the standard calculations, appear to be substantial. The welfare benefits of a greater variety of products as a result of trade have also been ignored until recently, and yet preliminary evidence suggests that they are quite important.

Chapter 3, "The Employment Rationale for Protection," focuses on the most frequent argument in favor of limiting trade: that jobs will be saved in industries that compete against imports. As we shall see, reducing trade saves those jobs only by destroying jobs elsewhere in the economy. Opponents of free trade have also argued that imports have replaced good, high-wage jobs with bad, low-wage jobs. The truth turns out to be quite the opposite: jobs in industries that compete against imports are mainly low-skill and consequently low-wage jobs. This chapter also evaluates government assistance to help workers displaced by imports.

Chapter 4, "Relief from Foreign Competition: Antidumping and the Escape Clause," describes the legal framework that allow firms to petition the government for the imposition of tariffs on competing imports. The antidumping law is the most heavily used measure to block so-called unfair imports. The government's definition of "dumping" is a lower price charged in the United States than in a foreign exporter's home market, but it is not clear that this is a problem requiring trade restrictions, or that the government calculates the price margin in a fair manner. This chapter also examines the case for providing domestic industries with temporary relief from imports so that they can adjust to the competition.

Chapter 5, "U.S. Trade Policy and the World Trading System," provides a historical look at how the United States came to embrace open trade policies around World War II. American trade politics had long been stacked in favor of protectionism, but a dramatic shift came as a result of the Reciprocal Trade Agreements Act of 1934. The RTAA fundamentally changed the politics of trade policy in the United States by strengthening domestic political support for freer trade. After the war, the United States played the leading role in creating a rules-based world trading system embodied in the General Agreement on Tariffs and Trade (GATT) and, after 1995, the World Trade Organization. This chapter examines the multilateral trading system, as well as preferential trade arrangements such as NAFTA.

Chapter 6, "The World Trade Organization and New Battlegrounds," focuses on the current controversies surrounding the WTO. Since its inception, the WTO has come under intense criticism from nongovernmental organizations (NGOs), which attack it as an antidemocratic institution that has struck down domestic environmental regulations by ruling them inconsistent with world trade laws. This chapter examines the WTO's rules and dispute settlement system, the leading trade and environmental cases that have come before it, and finally the arguments for including labor standards in future trade negotiations.

Macaulay long ago aptly summed up a fundamental incongruity about free trade: despite its palpable benefits, it is frequently the object of condemnation rather than approbation. That condemnation is often the result of misconceptions about the benefits of international trade, the structure of U.S. trade policy, and the role and function of the WTO. This book seeks to dispel these misconceptions and is offered in the modest hope that it may improve our understanding of the issues of trade policy that confront us.

1

The United States in a New Global Economy?

International trade has become an integral part of the U.S. economy over the past few decades. The United States imports toys from China, clothing from Costa Rica, and steel from Korea, and exports aircraft from Washington, wheat from Kansas, and machinery from Illinois. There is hardly a sector of the economy or a region of the country that is unaffected by international markets. As the twenty-first century begins, the United States may even have achieved a historically unprecedented degree of economic integration with the rest of the world. Perhaps it is not surprising, therefore, that the rapid growth of trade has been accompanied by a intensified debate over U.S. trade policy. To establish a context in which we can later examine current trade policy, this chapter briefly looks at the role of trade in the U.S. economy.

The Increasing Importance of Trade

How important is trade to the U.S. economy? The simplest way to answer this question is to look at its share in gross domestic product (GDP). In 2000, for example, merchandise exports amounted to about $773 billion, about 7.8 percent of GDP. At the same time, merchandise imports were about $1,223 billion, about 12.3 percent of GDP.[1]

By looking at these numbers in a historical perspective, we can determine whether they are high or low. Figure 1.1 presents U.S. mer-

[1] Joint Economic Committee and Council of Economic Advisers, *Economic Indicators*, April 2001. This standard indicator measures the numerator and denominator differently. Trade is measured as the gross value of goods crossing the border, while GDP is a value-added measure of goods and services produced in the country.

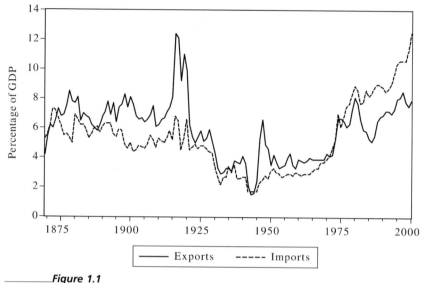

Figure 1.1

Merchandise exports and imports in the United States as a percentage of GDP, 1869–2000. (Data for merchandise trade 1869–1970 from U.S. Bureau of the Census 1975, and 1971–2000 from Council of Economic Advisers 2001, table B-103; GDP 1869–1928 from Balke and Gordon 1989, and 1929–99 from U.S. Bureau of Economic Analysis at http://www.bea.gov.)

chandise exports and imports as a share of GDP from 1869 to 2000. As the figure shows, merchandise trade was fairly stable at about 7 percent of GDP in the period just after the Civil War until the outbreak of World War I in 1914. Exports surged during the war, but the trade shares declined sharply during the interwar period from 1919 to 1939 and on through World War II. Between the world wars, many countries pursued inward-looking economic policies, including protectionist trade policies, restrictions on international labor migration, and limitations on international capital flows. These policies substantially reduced world economic integration. Many of these restrictions were relaxed after World War II, and thus in some sense the United States has gone back to the future, returning to the degree of integration that prevailed before World War I. Exports and imports were higher after World War II than before the war, but were then stable until they began to rise steadily in the early 1970s.

Economists have interpreted these data in two conflicting ways. One interpretation, that trade is about as important now as it was a century ago (the "fin de siècle déjà vu" view) points out that merchandise exports stood at about 7 percent of GDP in the late nineteenth century and are about 8 percent now, hardly a dramatic difference. A second interpretation (the "new global economy" view) stresses that the rapid rise in trade's share of GDP since the mid-1970s has put trade at a level unprecedented in recent history.[2] Further evidence will suggest that this second interpretation better identifies the crucial trends in trade.

Will the current trend toward a higher trade share continue? There is certainly no law in economics that dictates an inexorable rise in the ratio of trade to GDP over time. In fact, many economists, from Robert Torrens in the early nineteenth century to Dennis Robertson in the mid–twentieth century, have expounded a "law of diminishing international trade." They believed that the spread of industrial technology around the world would result in smaller differences in industrial efficiency across countries. Each country would eventually come to produce manufactured goods just as efficiently as any other, and so international trade would diminish. But this theory has been proven false: over time, the division of labor in manufacturing and in other sectors has become more refined, increasing trade even between those countries with similar technology. For example, the spread of industrial technology has enabled an increasing number of countries to produce automobiles. Rather than reducing international trade in cars, this development has increased trade in automobiles, especially in parts and components.[3]

A more plausible version of the idea of diminishing international trade is that the trade share would fall as countries grew richer because the composition of demand would shift away from traded goods (such as food, clothing, and manufactures) toward nontraded goods (such as housing, health care, education, and other services). And to some extent, this has taken place in the United States: the share of personal consumption expenditures devoted to services has risen steadily in recent decades at the expense of expenditures on durable and nondurable goods. This evolution of demand has contributed to a shift in the composition of

[2] Bordo, Eichengreen, and Irwin (1999) compare global integration now and a century ago and conclude that, despite similarities, the current period exhibits much greater integration.

[3] Furthermore, international differences in technology have not narrowed over time but have widened. See Clark and Feenstra 2002.

the U.S. economy away from the production of merchandise goods toward the production of services. (The more rapid productivity growth in
goods-producing sectors, which has reduced the price of goods relative
to services, has also contributed to this result.) As a result, the traded-
goods sectors of the economy—specifically, agriculture, mining, and
manufacturing—have declined from 33.5 percent of current-dollar GDP
in 1960 to 18.7 percent in 1999.[4] Other mostly nontraded sectors of the
economy, such as transportation and public utilities; wholesale and retail
trade; finance, insurance, and real estate; and government have grown
more rapidly than the traded-goods sectors.

Even though the merchandise goods share of the economy has
fallen, the merchandise trade share has not. The gradual rise in the share
of merchandise trade to GDP therefore masks the vastly increased importance of trade within the traded-goods sector. This is seen most
strikingly by comparing merchandise exports as a share of merchandise
production rather than merchandise exports to total GDP. As figure 1.2
indicates, merchandise exports as a share of merchandise production
soared from about 15 percent in 1970 to nearly 40 percent in 1999, while
the share relative to GDP has changed only modestly. This implies that
the increase in the size of the nontraded sector can sharpen the degree
to which countries specialize in the traded-goods sector and therefore
increase trade.[5] Thus, a close analysis of the merchandise trade figures
indicates that trade is substantially more important now than in the recent past for those sectors engaged in trade.[6]

The rise in trade relative to production is also evident in the case
of specific commodities. Table 1.1 compares exports as a share of domestic output and imports as a share of total supply (domestic output
plus imports minus exports) for selected commodities in 1960 and 1993.
Both the share of domestic production shipped to other markets and the
ratio of imports to domestic consumption are much more pronounced

[4] Council of Economic Advisers 2001, table B-12.

[5] This is precisely what the analysis of Flam (1985) predicted.

[6] See Irwin 1996a. Feenstra (1998) shows that this same trend is evident in other
OECD countries as well. As described in note 1, the export figures are measured on the
basis of gross value, while the production data (for agriculture, mining, and manufacturing)
from the national income accounts are based on value-added data. It would be therefore
incorrect to say that about 40 percent of U.S. merchandise production was exported in
1999.

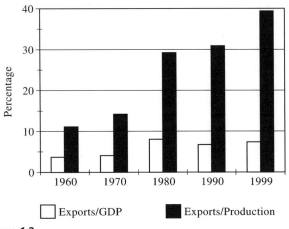

_____*Figure 1.2*
U.S. merchandise exports as a share of GDP and merchandise production, se-
lected years. (Data from Council of Economic Advisers 2001, tables B-12 and
B-103.)

today than just a few decades ago, especially for perishable products,
which only recently have become traded internationally.

Two final points should be made about U.S. merchandise trade.
First, the composition of both exports and imports has shifted toward
manufactured goods over the past few decades. Table 1.2 presents the
commodity composition of these exports and imports. The United States
is a net exporter of agricultural commodities and a net importer of fuels.
But the overwhelming majority (about 80 percent) of both exports and
imports are manufactured goods. Of course, they are different types of
manufactured goods. The leading manufactured exports consist of machinery (electrical, general industrial, power generating, and scientific),
office equipment, airplanes and parts, chemicals, and televisions and
VCRs. The major types of manufactured imports also include machinery,
televisions, and VCRs, but also clothing, iron and steel mill products, toys
and sporting goods, and footwear.

Second, most of this trade in manufactured goods is not in final
consumer goods, but rather in intermediate components and parts. The
Department of Commerce provides a closer look at the imports when it
attempts to classify them based on final actual use. Table 1.3 shows this
end-use classification of U.S. imports for three categories: consumer

_____Table 1.1

U.S. Exports and Imports of Perishable and Nonperishable Commodities as a Share of Domestic Output or Consumption

	1960		1993	
Commodity	Exports	Imports	Exports	Imports
Perishable				
Grapes	10	1	12	15
Broccoli			25	2
Tomatoes	3	9	7	18
Oranges	8	n.a.	21	2
Strawberries			11	31
Flowers and plants			4	9
Nonperishable				
Cotton	41	1	31	1
Wheat	36	0	63	3
Meat products	2	3	7	5
Coal	17	0	16	1
Cotton fabrics	5	3	9	19
Leather footwear	0	2	38	90
Pulp mill products	27	33	49	28
Blast furnace products	4	3	5	13
Radios, televisions, stereos, etc.	5	2	34	64
Machine tools	17	3	33	40
Passenger cars	2	3	16	40

Source: U.S. Bureau of Census 1963, 1995.
Note: Exports are expressed as a percentage of domestic shipments. Imports are expressed as a percentage of domestic consumption (domestic shipments minus exports plus imports).

_____Table 1.2

Composition of U.S. Trade, by Category of Commodity, 1960, 1980, 2000 (%)

	1960		1980		2000	
	Exports	Imports	Exports	Imports	Exports	Imports
Food, animals, etc.	16	23	14	8	6	4
Crude materials	16	20	12	5	4	2
Mineral fuels	2	11	4	33	2	11
Chemicals and manu-factured goods	32	36	31	30	36	38
Machinery and trans-port equipment	35	10	39	25	53	45

Sources: Organization for Economic Cooperation and Development 1981, 30–31; 2001, 32–33; United Nations 1962, 574–75.
Note: Commodities are grouped by SITC category. Columns may not total 100 percent because of rounding.

_____Table 1.3
U.S. Imports by Principal End-Use Category (%)

	Consumer Goods	Industrial Materials and Supplies	Capital Goods
1950	38	61	1
1960	42	52	4
1970	53	38	9
1980	24	52	25
1990	30	29	41
2000	30	25	45

Source: Lechter 1970, and http://www.ita.doc.gov.

Note: Consumer goods include foods, feeds, and beverages, assembled automobiles, and consumer durables and nondurables; industrial supplies and materials include crude and processed materials such as fuels and lubricants, paper, building materials, and the like; and capital goods include machinery, equipment, apparatuses, instruments, as well as parts, components, and accessories, including automobile engines, and parts.

goods, industrial supplies and materials, and capital goods. The most striking change is the rise of capital goods as a share of U.S. imports, especially since 1970. Capital goods include machinery, equipment, instruments, parts, and various other components to production. Over half of all imports are either intermediate components or raw materials. These imports are sold as inputs to domestic businesses rather than as goods consumed directly by households. As chapter 3 will explain, this fact has important implications for trade policy: protectionist policies will directly harm employment in other domestic industries by raising their production costs, in addition to forcing consumers to pay a higher price for the products they buy.

Though trade is more important than ever for the merchandise-producing sector, this is not necessarily the case for the overall economy. Production and employment have become much more based on nontraded services. In fact, only about 17 percent of American workers, those employed in agriculture, mining, and manufacturing, are directly exposed to international competition today, as opposed to 40 percent in 1960.[7] This means that a smaller part of the U.S. economy, in terms of output and employment, is directly affected by fluctuations in world trade.

At the same time, many previously nontraded services are now becoming more tradable. The major categories of services trade include shipping and tourism, royalties and fees (receipts from intellectual prop-

[7] Council of Economic Advisers 2001, tables B-46 and B-100.

erty rights, such as trademarks, patents, and copyrights), and military transfers. The most rapidly growing category of U.S. service exports are those listed as "other private services," which include education, finance, insurance, telecommunications, and business, professional, and technical services. In 2000, the value of these U.S. service exports (excluded from the merchandise trade figures considered so far) amounted to about $310 billion, nearly 40 percent of the value of merchandise exports. The United States is a large net exporter of services, having only imported $219 billion in 2000.

The addition of trade in services has raised the overall economic significance of trade. In 2000, the broader figure of exports of goods and services as a portion of GDP stood at 11.0 percent, of which merchandise exports were 7.9 percent and service exports were 3.1 percent. (In 1970, by contrast, service exports were only about 1 percent of GDP.) Also in that year, imports of goods and services stood at 14.7 percent of GDP, of which merchandise imports were 12.5 percent and service imports were 2.2 percent. As in the case of merchandise, service exports have risen as a share of services production. In 1960, the ratio of service exports to services value-added was 1.7 percent, but by 1999 that ratio had risen to 5.5 percent.[8] While small in comparison to the merchandise sector, this ratio has been rising rapidly and portends even greater trade in services in the future.

Yet even services that are not subject to trade are increasingly subject to international competition. This is because direct investments enable U.S. firms to enter foreign markets directly and allow foreign service providers to compete in the U.S. market. U.S. direct investment abroad increased from 6 percent of GDP in 1960 to 20 percent in 1996, and much of this investment was in the service sector. For example, in the 1990s the University of Chicago's Graduate School of Business built small campuses in Barcelona and Singapore to bring education services directly to Europeans and Asians who are not able to come to Chicago. Similarly, foreign direct investment in the United States increased from 1 percent of GDP in 1960 to 16 percent in 1996. For example, many foreign banks have established a presence in the U.S. market to provide financial services. In addition, domestic service firms are increasingly the

---

[8] Council of Economic Advisers 2001, table B-12.

target of mergers and acquisitions as foreign firms seek entry into the U.S. market. As an indication of the increased foreign presence in the U.S. economy, the foreign-owned affiliates' share of gross product originating in private industry in the United States increased from 2.3 percent in 1977 to 6.3 percent in 1998.[9]

As a result, firms have a choice in how they can sell products to foreign residents: either by exporting domestically produced goods, or by producing and selling directly in the foreign country. This gives us another way to look at international commerce. In 1998, U.S. companies sold $933 billion worth of goods to foreign consumers through exports and $2,810 billion through foreign affiliates. Meanwhile, foreign companies sold $1,100 billion to U.S. consumers through exports to the United States and $1,710 billion through sales by foreign-owned U.S. affiliates. Thus, worldwide sales by U.S. companies to foreign nationals exceeded sales by foreign companies to U.S. residents by $363 billion in that year.[10]

_____Trade and the Fragmentation of Production

Is the recent rise in the trade share misleading? The increased trade in intermediate components requires that we ask this question. Every time a component is shipped across a border, it gets recorded by customs officials as an export or an import. When components are repeatedly shipped across the border at different stages of production, the official recorded value of trade rises with each crossing, but there may be no more final goods output than before. Thus, the value of trade relative to production may be inflated if intermediate products cross national borders multiple times during the production process. For example, about 60 percent of U.S. auto exports to Canada are engines and parts, whereas 75 percent of U.S. auto imports from Canada are finished cars and trucks.[11] The increase in automobile trade between the United States, Canada, and other countries does not itself indicate that more and more cars are being built; rather, various parts and components that used to be

[9] See Bordo, Eichengreen, and Irwin 1999, 11; and Zeile 2000.
[10] Lowe 2001.
[11] Hummels, Rapoport, and Yi 1998, 84.

produced domestically are now produced in other countries and traded across international borders.

This phenomenon is known as *vertical specialization*. Vertical specialization refers to the fragmentation of the production process as intermediate goods and components become a greater part of world trade. According to one estimate, vertical specialization accounts for about a third of the increase in world trade since 1970.[12]

As the Canadian example suggests, a nonnegligible portion of the value of U.S. imports is simply the value of U.S. exports of domestically produced components that are shipped abroad for further processing or assembly and then returned to the United States for additional work before sale or export. Imports that incorporate U.S.-made components are often given duty-free or reduced-duty treatment under the "production sharing" provision of the tariff code.[13] In 1998, imports entering the United States under the production-sharing provision amounted to $74 billion, or 8.2 percent of total merchandise imports.[14] The value of U.S.-produced components in these imports was $25 billion, or 34 percent of the total value of imports entered under this provision. In other words, at least 3 percent of the value of U.S. imports actually represents the value of domestic products that have been exported and then returned to the United States.

This figure is a particularly striking aspect of U.S. trade with Mexico. In 1998, the United States imported $93 billion in goods from Mexico. Of this, $27 billion (36 percent) entered under the production-sharing provision, and $14 billion represented the U.S. content of these imports. Thus, 57 percent of the value of goods that entered under the production-sharing provision actually reflects the value of U.S.-made components.

These official figures significantly understate the magnitude of production sharing in U.S. trade. A majority of imports from Canada and

---

[12] Hummels, Ishii, and Yi 2001. See also Jones 2000.

[13] This provision of the tariff (chapter 98 of the Harmonized Tariff Schedule) dates back to 1964 and was designed to enable U.S. companies to reduce their costs by outsourcing labor-intensive assembly operations to neighboring countries, and thereby compete more effectively against European and Japanese companies, which take advantage of lower labor costs in Eastern Europe and Asia for assembly operations.

[14] The statistics in this paragraph come from the U.S. International Trade Commission (1999b).

Mexico incorporate U.S.-made parts but no longer enter the United States under the production-sharing provisions of the tariff code because they are already eligible for duty-free treatment under NAFTA. Nearly a third of U.S. imports from Canada, Mexico, and the Caribbean Basin consisted of motor vehicles, televisions, and apparel, the sectors in which production-sharing or outsourcing arrangements are extensive. This tariff provision, along with communication and transportation technology, has significantly deepened cross-border integration in North America and the Caribbean Basin, enabling firms to subcontract some operations to neighboring countries.

Such production sharing and outsourcing means that it is becoming difficult to determine the true origin of any particular product. For one particular car produced by an American manufacturer, for example, 30 percent of the car's value is due to assembly in Korea, 17.5 percent due to components from Japan, 7.5 percent due to design from Germany, 4 percent due to parts from Taiwan and Singapore, 2.5 percent due to advertising and marketing services from Britain, and 1.5 percent due to data processing in Ireland. In the end, 37 percent of the production value of this American car comes from the United States.[15] Similarly, one type of Barbie doll is manufactured with $0.35 in labor from China, $0.65 in materials from Taiwan, Japan, the United States, and China, $1.00 in overhead and management from Hong Kong. The export value from Hong Kong is $2.00, and, after shipping, ground transportation, marketing, and wholesale and retail profit, the doll is sold in American stores at $9.99.[16] Such specialization may account for the fact that world trade has grown much more rapidly than world output.

This outsourcing phenomenon is only partly related to the role that multinational firms have played in international trade during the postwar period. A significant part of U.S. trade is simply the exchange of goods between affiliated units of a multinational company: in 1994, such "intrafirm" transactions accounted for 36 percent of U.S. exports of goods and 43 percent of U.S. imports of goods.[17] However, this share has not changed much since the late 1970s, when the Commerce Department started collecting data. In fact, the share of U.S. trade accounted for by

[15] World Trade Organization 1998, 36.
[16] Tempest 1996.
[17] Zeile 1997.

multinationals has declined significantly. The overall share has been stable only because the intrafirm-share of the multinationals' trade has increased.

Thus, by simply looking at the sheer volume of goods leaving and entering the country, one can say that the United States engages in significantly more international trade today than in the recent or distant past. But the statistics on trade can also be misleading because a final good may be produced with inputs that cross national borders multiple times, each time getting recorded as an export or an import.

_____Why Is Commercial Integration Greater Today?

International trade has increased rapidly during the postwar period, particularly in the last two decades. What accounts for this growth in trade? One simple answer is that the costs previously inhibiting trade, and preventing exchanges from taking place, are now lower than before. These impediments to trade include transportation costs, transactions costs, and government policies.

Although the expansion of international trade in the late nineteenth century was propelled by a significant decline in shipping costs, the postwar period has apparently not experienced a comparable reduction in the costs of moving goods between markets.[18] Yet such costs have remained low and have changed in qualitative ways. Technological innovations have expanded the array of delivery mechanisms. Containerization, bulk shipping, and other innovations have cut loading times and resulted in more efficient transportation. The rise of air transport as a means of moving goods between countries has cut delivery times in ways that have brought an ever-increasing variety of perishable goods (cut flowers from Central America, lobsters from Maine) into world commerce.[19] According to one estimate, each day saved of shipping time is worth 0.5 percent of the value of the products. Trade in intermediate

[18] Hummels 1999.

[19] The share of U.S. imports that arrives via air has risen from about 9 percent in 1974 to nearly 20 percent in 1996. Similarly, nearly a third of U.S. exports (including aircraft) leave via air. Shipping via air has been largely a postwar phenomenon and has seen substantial cost reductions. Hummels (1999) finds that air cargo rates on long-distance routes have declined by about 15–20 percent (when deflated by U.S. import price index) over the 1975–93 period.

goods is the most time sensitive, and over the past fifty years faster methods of transport are equivalent to reducing tariffs from 20 percent to 5 percent.[20]

Other transactions costs are harder to quantify, but are lower in potentially important ways. These transactions costs are any expense that must be incurred to bring about exchange. The costs of acquiring information, for example, can limit the extent of market integration. A century ago, before the age of mass communications, obtaining information about distant markets was more difficult than today. Producers are now more likely to have better information about local tastes and demands than they did in the past, which makes them able to service demand in those markets more efficiently. In addition, consumers used to have good information only about the attributes of locally produced goods, but now they are likely to be equally as informed about the products of foreign firms.

Trade has also expanded because government trade restrictions have been reduced. Tariffs, import quotas, and exchange controls that originated in the interwar period have been gradually relaxed in the decades after World War II. Average tariffs on manufactured goods dropped from roughly 40 percent to less than 5 percent in most developing countries over the postwar period. Furthermore, whole geographic areas, such as Western Europe and North America, have abolished customs duties and become free-trade areas. Although some nontariff measures have been adopted to protect domestic producers from import competition, it is nonetheless true that overall trade barriers have fallen substantially over the postwar period.

Quantifying the precise contribution of these factors in the rapid growth in world trade is difficult. One study finds that about two-thirds of the postwar growth in the trade of countries belonging to the Organization for Economic Cooperation and Development (OECD) is due to income growth, a quarter to tariff reductions, and about 10 percent to transportation cost reductions.[21] This calculation, however, does not take into account production sharing or vertical specialization.

Even though world economic integration has increased rapidly

[20] Hummels 2000.
[21] Baier and Bergstrand 2001.

in recent decades, the world remains far from fully integrated. Within-country trade dominates between-country trade by an order of magnitude, suggesting that there is a strong "home bias" in the pattern of trade. The United States is more integrated with the rest of the world than in the recent past, but we are far from the point at which trade between New York and Rio de Janeiro is carried on as easily as trade between New York and Los Angeles.

One economist has used the following analogy to illustrate how far we are from perfect trade integration: if Americans were just as likely to purchase goods and services from foreign producers as from domestic producers, then the U.S. import-to-GDP ratio should equal the non-U.S. share of world GDP. In other words, the United States would spend as much on foreign products as the average foreign resident, or roughly 75 percent, which is about the non-U.S. share of world GDP. Since the current trade share is about 12 percent, while that hypothetical trade share would be 75 percent, one can conclude that we are only about one-sixth of the way to the point at which "it would literally be true that Americans did business as easily across the globe as across the country."[22]

Empirical models of bilateral trade (the so-called gravity equations) show that there are numerous factors that shape international trade: distance between countries; geographic location; language, currency, and political ties; and so on. In these empirical models, the mere presence of a national border acts as a powerful impediment to international trade. The implication is that even when countries share a common language and a common border, similar institutions and a similar culture, the mere existence of a national border creates a significant bias in favor of intranational trade as opposed to international trade even if trade barriers are low.[23]

[22] Frankel 2000.

[23] The most dramatic illustration of this effect is McCallum's (1995) study of trade flows between Canadian provinces and the United States. McCallum examined unique data that allowed him to compare trade between Canadian provinces and American states in 1985. He found that two Canadian provinces trade more than twenty times (2,200 percent) as much with each other than do a Canadian province and an American state, controlling for other factors such as distance, population, and economic size. More recent research has shown that taking the border effect from the perspective of the smaller economy exaggerates the impact of the border. Anderson and van Wincoop (2001) examine the border effect from the perspective of the United States and finds that it implies about a 45 percent drop in trade, after controlling for other factors.

_____Public Views on Globalization: The Trade Policy Controversy

What are the views of the American public on the "globalization" of the U.S. economy in general and on trade policy in particular? According to an exhaustive survey carried out by the University of Maryland's Program on International Policy Attitudes in 1999, Americans broadly favor global economic integration. A majority of 61 percent believe that the U.S. government should either "actively promote" globalization (28 percent) or "allow it to continue" (33 percent). Only 26 percent favored trying to "slow it down," and just 9 percent favored trying to "stop or reverse it." There is also strong public support for international trade. According to one, fairly representative poll taken in 1996, nearly 70 percent of Americans believe that trade is good for the U.S. economy.[24]

This support even carries over to reciprocal trade liberalization. In the University of Maryland study, when asked if the United States should reduce its trade barriers on goods from another country that lowers its trade barriers on U.S. exports, 64 percent of those polled agreed, while 29 percent disagreed. A strong majority also favor giving poor countries preferential access to the U.S. market and strengthening the World Trade Organization.

When the public is asked about specific trade policy initiatives, however, public support is considerably lower. The public is much more divided over NAFTA, normalized trade relations with China, and fast-track negotiating authority for the president than it is over international trade in general. Skepticism about trade initiatives is driven by the perception that businesses benefit more than workers from these trade agreements, leading to an increasing gap between rich and poor in the United States. While those in the University of Maryland survey were deeply skeptical about using trade barriers to protect workers from foreign competition, they gave overwhelming support to the idea of helping workers adjust to import competition through government programs for education and worker retraining. When asked whether measures protecting the environment and labor standards should be a part of trade agreements, nearly 80 percent of respondents answered yes.

These general findings were consistent across almost all demo-

[24] See Kull 2000; and Scheve and Slaughter 2001a.

graphic and socioeconomic categories.[25] The greatest variation in responses was linked to years of formal education: individuals with at least
some college education were much more likely to have positive attitudes
about globalization and trade than those with a high school degree only.[26]
As we will see in chapter 3, this association could arise because individuals with less education are more likely to be employed in sectors that
compete against imports, whereas those with greater education are likely
to benefit from increased trade.

Public opinion polls, therefore, reveal the following dichotomy:
there is a willingness to accept increased international trade driven by
the anonymous force of technology, but a hesitation to support integration driven by specific policy initiatives. Even though economists have
not untangled the precise degree to which recent trade integration has
been technology-driven or policy-driven, the public appears to view this
distinction as important. This is consistent with the finding that the public appears to care about jobs destroyed because of imports, but not care
as much about jobs destroyed due to the invisible hand of technological
change.

This divergence, support for trade in the abstract and skepticism
about trade policy in the particular, gets to the root of the controversy
over free trade. Trade policy has always been contentious, but trade
policy has come to involve complex economic, political, and legal factors, making it increasingly difficult to understand. This book aims to
examine how these factors affect U.S. trade policy. The appropriate
place to begin is with the economic case for free trade.

---

[25] Political affiliation and region made little difference in the responses. Women
were slightly more skeptical of the benefits of free trade and more sensitized to its costs
than men; younger people were more positive about globalization and trade than older
people; and minorities had a somewhat better view of trade than nonminorities (Kull 2000,
61–70).

[26] Kull (2000) reports this finding, and Scheve and Slaughter (2001a) provide a
more detailed analysis.

2

The Case for Free Trade: Old Theories, New Evidence

For more than two centuries, economists have pointed out the benefits of free trade and the costs of trade restrictions. As Adam Smith argued more than two centuries ago, "All commerce that is carried on betwixt any two countries must necessarily be advantageous to both," and therefore "all duties, customs, and excise [on imports] should be abolished, and free commerce and liberty of exchange should be allowed with all nations."[1] The economic case for free trade, however, is not based on outdated theories in musty old books. The classic insights into the nature of economic exchange between countries have been refined and updated over the years to retain their relevance to today's circumstances. More importantly, over the past decade economists have gathered extensive empirical evidence that contributes appreciably to our understanding of the advantages of free trade. This chapter reviews the classic theories and examines the new evidence, noting as well the qualifications to the case for free trade.

Specialization and Trade

The traditional case for free trade is based on the gains from specialization and exchange. These gains are easily understood at the level of the individual. Most people do not produce for themselves even a fraction of the goods they consume. Rather, we earn an income by specializing in certain activities and then using our earnings to purchase various goods and services—food, clothing, shelter, health care—produced by others. In essence, we "export" the goods and services that we produce with our

[1] Smith 1976, 511, 514.

own labor and "import" the goods and services produced by others that we wish to consume. This division of labor enables us to increase our consumption beyond that which would be possible if we tried to be self-sufficient and produce everything for ourselves. Specialization allows us to enjoy a much higher standard of living than otherwise and gives us access to a greater variety and better quality of goods and services.

Trade between nations is simply the international extension of this division of labor. For example, the United States has specialized in the production of aircraft, industrial machinery, and agricultural commodities (particularly corn, soybeans, and wheat). In exchange for exports of these products, the United States purchases, among other things, imports of crude oil, clothing, and iron and steel mill products. Like individuals, countries benefit immensely from this division of labor and enjoy a higher real income than countries that forgo such trade. Just as there seems no obvious reason to limit the free exchange of goods within a country without a specific justification, there is no obvious reason why trade between countries should be limited in the absence of a compelling reason for doing so. (Popular arguments for limiting trade will be examined later to see if they are persuasive.)

Adam Smith, whose magnificent work *The Wealth of Nations* was first published in 1776, set out case for free trade with a persuasive flair that still resonates today. Smith advocated the "obvious and simple system of natural liberty" in which individuals would be free to pursue their own interests, while the government provided the legal framework within which commerce would take place. With the government enforcing a system of justice and providing certain public goods (such as roads, in Smith's view), the private interests of individuals could be turned toward productive activities, namely, meeting the demands of the public as expressed in the marketplace. Smith envisioned a system that would give people the incentive to better themselves through economic activities, where they would create wealth by serving others through market exchange, rather than through political activities, where they might seek to redistribute existing wealth through, for example, legal restraints on competition. Under such a system, the powerful motivating force of self-interest could be channeled toward socially beneficial activities that would serve the general interest rather than socially unproductive activities that might advance the interests of a select few but would come at the expense of society as a whole.[2]

Free trade is an important component of this system of economic liberty. Under a system of natural liberty in which domestic commerce is largely free from restraints on competition, though not necessarily free from government regulation, commerce would also be permitted to operate freely between countries. According to Smith, free trade would increase competition in the home market and curtail the power of domestic firms by checking their ability to exploit consumers through high prices and poor service. Moreover, the country would gain by exchanging exports of goods that are dear on the world market for imports of goods that are cheap on the world market. As Smith put it:

> What is prudence in the conduct of every family can scarce be folly in that of a great kingdom. If a foreign country can supply us with a commodity cheaper than we ourselves can make it, better buy it of them with some part of the produce of our own industry, employed in a way in which we have some advantage. The general industry of the country . . . will not thereby be diminished . . . but only left to find out the way in which it can be employed with the greatest advantage. It is certainly not employed to the greatest advantage, when it is thus directed towards an object which it can buy cheaper than it can make.[3]

Smith believed that the benefits of trade went well beyond this simple arbitrage exchange of what is abundant in the home market for what is scarce on the world market. The wealth of any society depends upon the division of labor. The division of labor, the degree to which individuals specialize in certain tasks, enhances productivity. And productivity, the ability to produce more goods with the same resources, is

---

[2] Rosenberg (1960) provides an excellent discussion of this aspect of Smith's work.

[3] Smith 1976, 457. Free trade made this possible: "The interest of a nation in its commercial relations to foreign nations is, like that of a merchant with regard to the different people with whom he deals, to buy as cheap and to sell as dear as possible. But it will be most likely to buy cheap, when by the most perfect freedom of trade it encourages all nations to bring to it the goods which it has occasion to purchase" (464).

the basis for rising living standards. But, as he put it, the division of labor is limited by the extent of the market. Smaller, more isolated markets cannot support a high degree of specialization among their population and therefore tend to be relatively poor. Free trade enables all countries, but particularly small countries, to extend the effective size of their market. Trade allows such countries to achieve a more refined division of labor, and therefore reap a higher real income, than if international exchange were artificially limited by government policies.

Smith also issued a scathing attack on contemporary mercantilist policies that restricted trade for the ostensible purpose of promoting national wealth. Governments often justified trade restrictions as serving the public interest, but, as Smith pointed out, these restrictions did not benefit the public so much as the private interests of influential merchants who had captured government policy for their own advantage.[4]

Comparative Advantage

In 1799, a successful London stockbroker named David Ricardo came across a copy of *The Wealth of Nations* while on vacation and quickly became engrossed in the book. Ricardo admired Smith's great achievement, but thought that many of the topics deserved further investigation. For example, Smith believed that a country would export goods that it produces most efficiently and import goods that other countries produce most efficiently. In this way, trade is a mutually beneficial way of increasing total world output and thus the consumption of every country. But, Ricardo asked, what if one country was the most efficient at producing everything? Would that country still benefit from trade? Would disadvantaged countries find themselves unable to export anything?

To overcome this problem, Ricardo arrived at a brilliant deduction that became known as the theory of comparative advantage. Comparative advantage implies that a country could find it advantageous to

[4] Smith was critical of the influence of merchants on government policy because merchants always had a stake in narrowing the scope of competition. In his view, British trade regulations "may . . . be demonstrated to be in every case a complete piece of dupery, by which the interest of the State and the nation is constantly sacrificed to that of some particular class of traders" (Smith 1977, 272). However, Smith did believe trade restrictions could be justified in certain cases, such as protecting industries essential for national defense. See Irwin 1996b, 81–82.

import some goods even if it could produce those same goods more efficiently than other countries. Conversely, a country would be able to export some goods even if other countries could produce them more efficiently. In either case, countries would be able to benefit from trade. Ricardo's conclusions about the benefits of trade were similar to Smith's, but his approach contains a deeper insight.

At first, the principle of comparative advantage seems counterintuitive.[5] Why would a country ever import a good that it could produce more efficiently than another country? Yet comparative advantage is the key to understanding the pattern of international trade. For example, imagine a consulting firm hired to examine the factors explaining international trade in textiles. The consultants would probably start by examining the efficiency of textile production in various countries. If one country was found to be more efficient than another in producing textiles, the firm might conclude that this country would export textiles and other countries would import them. Yet because this single comparison is insufficient for determining the pattern of trade, this conclusion might well be wrong.

According to Ricardo and the other classical economists of the early nineteenth century, international trade is not driven by the *absolute* costs of production, but by the *opportunity* costs of production. The country most efficient at producing textiles might be even more efficient than other countries at producing other goods, such as shoes. In that case, the country would be best served by directing its labor to producing shoes, in which its margin of productive advantage is even greater than in textiles. As a result, despite its productivity advantage in textiles, the country would export shoes in exchange for imports of textiles. In the absence of other information, the absolute efficiency of one country's textile producers in comparison to another country's is insufficient to determine whether that country produces all of the textiles it consumes or imports some of them.

Put differently, a country can obtain textiles either directly

---

[5] When challenged by a distinguished mathematician to name "one proposition in all of the social sciences which is both true and non-trivial," Paul Samuelson (1972, 683) famously replied with the theory of comparative advantage. In a splendid essay entitled "Ricardo's Difficult Idea," Krugman (1998b) examines why many noneconomists have difficulty grasping the essential logic of comparative advantage.

through domestic production, or indirectly by producing something else and exporting it in exchange for imports of textiles. The most efficient way of getting textiles is whichever way yields the country the greatest quantity of such goods at the least cost. So when looking at the textile question, our consultants must first recognize that the real choice facing a country is whether it should devote its resources to producing textiles, or to producing other goods that can be exported in exchange for textiles. The efficiency of domestic and foreign textile producers alone is not the sole determining factor.[6]

Although the concept of comparative advantage can be counterintuitive when applied to countries, individuals base their actions on it every day. The neighborhood teenager may take three hours to mow your lawn when you could do it in one, but given the amount you have to pay the teenager for the chore, you might have a much better way to spend your time. Without information on alternative activities, your absolute efficiency in this one activity should not determine where you choose to direct your (scarce) labor time. Yet absolute efficiency is still frequently discussed as if it alone determines the pattern of international trade. Domestic steel and textile producers insist that they are the world's most efficient producers of their products, implying that something must be wrong or unfair because they are beset by competition from imports.

Figure 2.1, which compares industry-level productivity in the United States and Japan in 1990, provides an illustration of the concept. In comparison with the U.S. industry, Japan has an absolute advantage in producing steel, automobiles, and consumer electronics and an absolute disadvantage in producing computers, soap and detergent, and food. It should come as no surprise that Japan's export success has been greatest in steel, automobiles, and consumer electronics, and weakest in the other goods. But a few decades ago, there was *no* industry in which

---

[6] As James Mill, a close friend of Ricardo's, explained: "When a country can either import a commodity or produce it at home, it compares the cost of producing at home with the cost of procuring it from abroad; if the latter cost is less than the first, it imports. The cost at which a country can import from abroad depends, not upon the cost at which the foreign country produces the commodity, but upon what the commodity costs which it sends in exchange, compared with the cost which it must be at to produce the commodity in question, if it did not import it" (quoted in Irwin 1996b, 91).

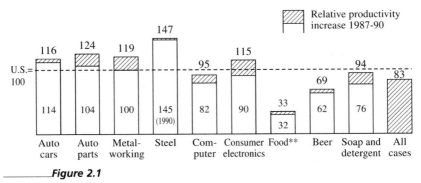

_____**Figure 2.1**
Relative productivity, United States and Japan, by industry, 1990. (*Source:* McKinsey Global Institute 1993, exhibit S-1.)

Japan's productivity exceeded that of the United States. For example, the figure indicates that in 1987 Japan's productivity in metalworking and consumer electronics, where Japan has been a strong exporter for many decades, was less than or equal to that of the United States. Although it lacked an absolute advantage in these goods, Japan still had a strong comparative (i.e., relative) advantage in exporting them in comparison to other goods.[7]

From the standpoint of the domestic industry, the trade patterns dictated by comparative advantage can sometimes seem unfair. Lee Iacocca, the charismatic chief of Chrysler in the 1980s, once admitted that American automakers had fallen behind their Japanese rivals in the past, but proudly proclaimed that the U.S. auto industry had met the competitive challenge and had finally matched the efficiency of Japanese producers. (This claim may stretch the truth, as figure 2.1 shows, but let us accept it for the sake of argument.)

Unfortunately, the theory of comparative advantage indicates that Iacocca has a problem: it may not be enough for an industry that competes with imports merely to match or even to exceed the productive efficiency of foreign producers to eliminate that competition and recapture market share. The reason is that Chrysler and other U.S. automakers were not really competing against Japanese automakers as much

_____
[7] Crude empirical tests of the Ricardian theory of comparative advantage show that it does a reasonably good job of explaining trade patterns. See Golub and Hsieh 2000.

as they were against those American industries that enjoyed an even greater productive superiority over their counterparts in Japan. U.S. auto producers might be able to match the productive efficiency of Japanese auto producers, but if American farmers and telecommunications equipment producers remain vastly more efficient than their Japanese counterparts, the United States will continue to export agricultural and telecom products to Japan in exchange for imports of automobiles.

It seems wrong that an American industry can be as efficient as any of its foreign competitors in absolute terms and yet fail to export—and even struggle against imports. But comparative advantage tells us that those sectors with the greatest *relative* efficiency advantage will be the ones that export with the greatest success. And the resulting trade will be mutually beneficial for the countries involved.

For developing countries, the theory of comparative advantage is good news as well. Even if a developing country lacks an absolute productive advantage in any field, it will always have a comparative advantage in the production of some goods. Other countries, from Korea to Bangladesh, are unable to match the productive efficiency of any U.S. industry and yet are still able to export some goods to the United States. Such countries will export goods where their relative disadvantage is least and use those export revenues to improve their standard of living by purchasing other goods from abroad, from fuel to capital equipment to medicine. There is no country whose economic circumstances prevent it from engaging in mutually beneficial trade with other countries.

An absolute productive advantage in any good is not required to participate in international trade and reap the benefits of trade. But an absolute productive advantage is enormously beneficial for another reason: it translates into higher per capita income. Even though the productivity of several Japanese manufacturing industries exceeds that of the United States, per capita income in Japan is only about 80 percent of that in the United States. As figure 2.2 indicates, this can be explained by looking at the employment-weighted average of Japanese productivity. Japan's weighted average productivity is only about 80 percent of that in the United States because it is dragged down by low productivity in the food sector. Japanese steel producers may be vastly more efficient than their American counterparts and hence be successful exporters (unless

RELATIVE PRODUCTIVITY LEVELS

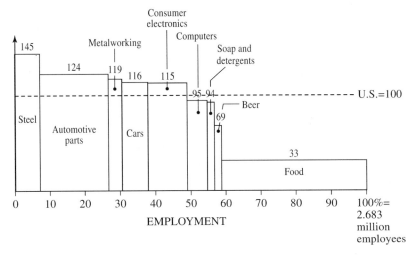

_____**Figure 2.2**

Employment-weighted relative productivity level, United States and Japan, 1990. (*Source:* McKinsey Global Institute 1993, exhibit S-2.)

the United States closes its market), but that advantage alone does not make Japan a rich country because that sector is a small part of the overall economy. Japan will match U.S. per capita income only when the average productivity of its overall workforce matches that of the United States.

_____**The Gains from Trade**

While the idea that all countries can benefit from international trade goes back to Smith and Ricardo, subsequent research has described the gains from trade in much greater detail. In the *Principles of Political Economy* (1848), John Stuart Mill, one of the leading economists of the nineteenth century, pointed to three principal gains from trade. First, there are what Mill called the "direct economical advantages of foreign trade." Second, there are "indirect effects" of trade, "which must be counted as benefits of a high order." Finally, Mill argued that "the economical benefits of commerce are surpassed in importance by those of its effects which are intellectual and moral."[8] What, specifically, are these three advantages of trade?

The "direct economical advantages" of trade are the standard gains that arise from specialization, as described by Smith and Ricardo. By exporting some of its domestically produced goods in exchange for imports, a country engages in mutually advantageous trade that enables it to use its limited productive resources (such as land, labor, and capital) more efficiently and therefore achieve a higher real national income than it could in the absence of trade. A higher real income translates into an ability to afford more of all goods and services than would be possible without trade.

These static gains from specialization are sizable. The classic illustration of the direct gains from trade comes from Japan's opening to the world economy. In 1858, as a result of American pressure, Japan opened its ports to international trade after decades of autarky (economic isolation). The gains from trade can be summarized by examining the prices of goods in Japan before and after the opening of trade. For example, the price of silk and tea was much higher on world markets than in Japan prior to the opening of trade, while the price of cotton and woolen goods was much lower on world markets. Japan therefore exported silk and tea in exchange for imports of clothing and other goods. With the introduction of trade, prices of those goods in Japan converged to the prices on the world market. Japan's terms of trade—the prices of the goods it exported relative to the prices of the goods it imported—improved by a factor of more than three and increased Japan's real income by as much as 65 percent.[9]

Unlike nineteenth-century Japan, most countries have been open to some international trade for centuries, making it difficult to measure the overall gain from free trade. However, economists can estimate the gains from increased trade as a result of the reduction in trade barriers. Computable general equilibrium models, which are complex computational models used to simulate the impact of various trade policies

---

[8] Mill 1909, 580ff.

[9] See Huber 1971; and Bernhofen and Brown 2000. Another example is the Jeffersonian trade embargo of 1807 to 1809, which cut off the United States from shipping for fourteen months. Irwin (2002) finds that the welfare cost of the embargo was about 8 percent of GNP, at a time when the ratio of trade to GNP was about 13 percent.

on specific industries and the overall economy, calculate the gains that arise from shifting resources between various sectors of the economy. Specifically, these models examine the shift of labor and capital away from industries that compete against imports toward those in which the country has a comparative advantage as a result of changes in trade policy.

For example, one study showed that the agreements to reduce trade barriers reached under the Uruguay Round of multilateral trade negotiations in 1994 would result in an annual gain of $13 billion for the United States, about 0.2 percent of its GDP, and about $96 billion in gains for the world, roughly 0.4 percent of world GDP.[10] Another recent study suggests that the gains from further global liberalization are even larger. If a new trade round reduced the world's tariffs on agricultural and industrial goods and barriers on services trade by one third, the welfare gain for the United States would be $177 billion, or 1.95 percent of GDP. Most of this gain comes from liberalizing trade in services. The gain for the world amounts to $613 billion, or about 2 percent of world GDP.[11]

As these examples indicate, the calculated welfare gains that emerge from these simulations are sometimes small as a percentage of GDP. Even some economists have interpreted these calculations to mean that trade liberalization is not especially valuable. But the small numbers arise partly because these agreements usually lead to modest policy changes for the United States. For example, what the United States undertook in signing the Uruguay Round or the North American Free Trade Agreement, essentially making already low import tariffs somewhat lower, cannot be compared to Japan's move from autarky to free trade. The numbers do not reflect the entire gains from trade, just the marginal gains from an additional increase in trade as a consequence of a partial reduction in trade barriers. A complete elimination of global barriers to trade in goods and services would bring much larger gains. According to the last study mentioned in the previous paragraph, removing all such barriers would generate $537 billion in gains for the United States (5.9

---

[10] Harrison, Rutherford, and Tarr 1996.
[11] Brown, Deardorff, and Stern 2001.

percent of GDP) and $1,857 billion in gains for the world (6.2 percent of world GDP).

More importantly, the reallocation of resources across industries as calculated in the simulation models does not take into account the other channels by which trade can improve economic performance. What are these other channels? One view is that greater openness to trade allows firms to sell in a potential larger market, and that firms are able to reduce their average costs of production by expanding the size of their output. The lower production costs resulting from these economies of scale are passed on to consumers and thereby generate additional gains from trade. In evaluating the impact of NAFTA through general equilibrium simulations, for example, moving from the assumption of constant returns to scale to increasing returns to scale boosted the calculated U.S. welfare gain from 1.67 percent to 2.55 percent of its GDP, Canadian welfare gain from 4.87 percent to 6.75 percent of its GDP, and Mexican welfare gain from 2.28 percent to 3.29 percent of its GDP, according to one study.[12]

These numbers are more impressive, but there are also reasons to be skeptical. Evidence from both developed and developing economies suggests that economies of scale at the plant level for most manufacturing firms tend to be small relative to the size of the market. As a result, most plants have attained their minimum efficient scale. Average costs seem to be relatively unaffected by changes in output, so that a big increase in a firm's output does not lead to lower costs, and a big reduction in output does not lead to higher costs. For example, many firms are forced to reduce output as a result of competition from imports, but these firms' production costs rarely rise significantly. This suggests that the importance of scale economies may be overstated, and yet the simulation models sometimes include them.[13]

There is much better, indeed overwhelming, evidence that free trade improves economic performance by increasing competition in the domestic market. This competition diminishes the market power of do-

---

[12] Roland-Holst, Reinhardt, and Schiells 1992.

[13] As Tybout and Westbrook (1995, 134) argue, "the simulation literature has created a mirage of large potential gains from unexploited scale economies by ignoring plant heterogeneity and, in some cases, by using market structure assumptions that lead to implausible adjustments in plant size." See also Tybout 2000; and Roberts and Tybout 1996.

mestic firms and leads to a more efficient economic outcome. This benefit does not arise because foreign competition changes a domestic firm's
costs through changes in the scale of output, as just noted. Rather, it
comes through a change in the pricing behavior of imperfectly competitive domestic firms. Firms with market power tend to restrict output and
raise prices, thereby harming consumers while increasing their own
profits. With international competition, firms cannot get away with such
conduct and are forced to behave more competitively. After Turkey's
trade liberalization in the mid-1980s, for example, price-cost margins fell
for most industries, consistent with a more competitive outcome.[14] Numerous studies confirm this finding in other countries, providing powerful evidence that trade disciplines domestic firms with market power. Yet
the beneficial effects of increasing competition are not always taken into
account in simulation models because they frequently assume that perfect competition already exists.

   Another problem with the standard estimates of the gains from
trade is that they largely overlook the benefits to consumers from exposure to a greater variety of goods. This neglect comes from the traditional emphasis on the easily calculated effects of trade on production,
whereas the gains to consumers from choice among a wider variety of
goods are more difficult to quantify. (Consumer utility is an amorphous
concept, and detailed product-level data are difficult to come by.) Yet
the few intriguing attempts to explore this benefit have suggested that it
is tremendously important. For example, one study suggests that tariffs
affect not just the amount but the range of foreign goods imported.[15]
When the selling of a product in a market has a fixed cost, a tariff reduces the size of the market and therefore the potential profits of engaging in trade. Because the smaller size would not allow firms to recoup
the fixed costs of selling in that market, some varieties of goods would
be excluded from it. In this way, barriers to trade can reduce the range
of goods available to an economy and limit the availability of specialized
consumer and producer intermediate goods.

   When restrictions reduce the number of traded goods, the welfare costs of trade restrictions are much larger than in the standard anal-

---

[14] Levinsohn 1993.
[15] Romer 1994.

ysis, where the number of traded goods is assumed to be fixed. The reason is this: if a tariff eliminates imports of a particular variety of good, then all the consumption benefits are lost with no offsetting gains. Although the standard computable models do not account for this loss, we know that variety is highly valued. For example, consider consumers in East Germany and Poland who, after the collapse of Communism, found exotic and affordable fruits such as bananas and oranges in the marketplace for the first time in their lives. Or consider their newfound ability to purchase apples and cabbages without worms and rot. The effect of such changes on aggregate output and income was minuscule, but the welfare gains from the availability of new and improved goods was not insignificant.[16]

If a tariff simply reduces the quantity of an imported good, the loss to consumers is a much smaller, second-order loss to overall welfare, because most of what consumers lose is transferred to producers or paid to the government in the form of tariff revenue. When a computable model assumes that a tariff just reduces the quantity of existing goods, when it actually reduces the range of imported goods, the welfare loss is understated—by as much as a factor of ten, according to some calculations.[17]

This welfare loss need not imply an enormous loss in national income: domestic output (measured GDP) may not change much as a result of the tariff. But the cost to consumer welfare is substantial when consumers value the consumption of different varieties of goods. To the extent that economists focus only on trade's effects on production or income, they understate the gains from trade.[18]

Variety is just as valuable for producers as it is for consumers.

---

[16] Economists are just beginning to estimate the gains from the introduction of new goods. Hausman (1997) estimated that the total consumer surplus generated by introducing Apple Cinnamon Cheerios was about $78 million per year, a substantial amount for a good for which many close substitutes already exist. Petrin (2001) finds that the total consumer welfare gain from the introduction of the minivan was $367 million in 1984, or $2.8 billion in consumer surplus over the 1984–88 period.

[17] See Romer 1994.

[18] This point was recognized some time ago by the Nobel laureate John Hicks: "The extension of trade does not primarily imply more goods; its main function is not to increase the quantity of goods produced, but to reshuffle them so that they are made more useful. The variety of goods available is increased, with all the widening of life that that entails. This is a gain which 'quantitative economic history,' which works with index numbers of real income, is ill-fitted to measure, or even to describe" (1969, 56).

Free trade expands the range of intermediate goods available for domestic firms to use as inputs. The availability of different specialized inputs can increase the productive efficiency of the industry that produces the final goods. For example, the use of new inputs by Korean business groups *(chaebol)* helped to promote total factor productivity growth at the industry level, even after controlling for other factors such as research-and-development expenditures.[19]

Is there systematic evidence that tariffs reduce the range of consumer and intermediate varieties available to an economy? Can we be sure that this reduction in variety is costly to economic welfare? A study of detailed import data from Costa Rica, which liberalized its trade policy in the mid-1980s, found a strong negative relationship between the product-level tariff and the number of countries that Costa Rica imported that product from. A 1 percent increase in the tariff rate resulted in the importation of 0.34 percent fewer varieties of intermediate goods and 0.73 percent fewer varieties of consumer goods. Taking account of the expanded variety of goods made available by trade increased the standard welfare gains from reducing tariffs by 50 percent.[20] By overlooking effects on variety, the standard calculations of gains from trade clearly understate the true advantages of international commerce.

Productivity Gains

Trade improves economic performance not only by allocating a country's resources to their most efficient use, but by making those resources more productive in what they are doing. This is the second of John Stuart Mill's three gains from trade, the one he called "indirect effects." These indirect effects include "the tendency of every extension of the market to improve the processes of production. A country which produces for a larger market than its own can introduce a more extended division of labour, can make greater use of machinery, and is more likely to make inventions and improvements in the processes of production."[21]

In other words, trade promotes productivity growth. The higher is an economy's productivity level, the higher is that country's standard

---

[19] Feenstra, Markusen, and Zeile 1992.

[20] Klenow and Rodríguez-Clare 1997. Since even detailed import data do not reveal product characteristics, they use the number of countries from which Costa Rica purchased specific imports as a proxy for variety.

[21] Mill 1909, 581.

of living. International trade contributes to productivity growth in at least two ways: it serves as a conduit for the transfer of foreign technologies that enhance productivity, and it increases competition in a way that stimulates industries to become more efficient and improve their productivity, often by forcing less productive firms out of business and allowing more productive firms to expand. After neglecting them for many decades, economists are finally beginning to study these productivity gains from trade more systematically.

The first channel, trade as a conduit for the transfer of foreign technologies, operates in several ways. One is through the importation of capital goods. Imported capital goods that embody technological advances can greatly enhance an economy's productivity. For example, the South Carolina textile magnate Roger Milliken (an active financier of anti-free-trade political groups) has bought textile machinery from Switzerland and Germany because domestically produced equipment is more costly and less sophisticated.[22] This imported machinery has enabled his firms to increase productivity significantly. Between a quarter and half of growth in U.S. total factor productivity may be attributed to new technology embodied in capital equipment. To the extent that trade barriers raise the price of imported capital goods, countries are hindering their ability to benefit from technologies that could raise productivity. In fact, one study finds that about a quarter of the differences in productivity across countries can be attributed to differences in the price of capital equipment.[23]

Advances in productivity are usually the result of investment in research and development, and the importation of foreign ideas can be a spur to productivity. Sometimes foreign research can be imported directly. For example, China has long been struggling against a devastating disease known as rice blast, which in the past destroyed millions of tons of rice a year, costing farmers billions of dollars. Recently, under the direction of an international team of scientists, farmers in China's Yunnan province started planting a mixture of two different types of rice in the same paddy. By this simple technique of biodiversity, farmers nearly eliminated rice blast and doubled their yield. Foreign R&D enabled the Chinese farmers to increase

[22] Lizza 2000.
[23] Eaton and Kortum 2001.

yields of a staple commodity and to abandon the chemical fungicides they had previously used to fight the disease.[24]

At other times, the benefits of foreign R&D are secured by importing goods that embody it. Countries more open to trade gain more from foreign R&D expenditures because trade in goods serves as a conduit for the spillovers of productive knowledge generated by that R&D. Several studies have found that a country's total factor productivity depends not only on its own R&D, but also on how much R&D is conducted in the countries that it trades with.[25] Imports of specialized intermediate goods that embody new technologies, as well as reverse-engineering of such goods, are sources of R&D spillovers. Thus, developing countries, which do not conduct much R&D themselves, can benefit from R&D done elsewhere because trade makes the acquisition of new technology less costly. These examples illustrate Mill's observation that "whatever causes a greater quantity of anything to be produced in the same place, tends to the general increase of the productive powers of the world."

The second channel by which trade contributes to productivity is by forcing domestic industries to become more efficient. We have already seen that trade increases competition in the domestic market, diminishing the market power of any firm and forcing them to behave more competitively. Competition also stimulates firms to improve their efficiency; otherwise they risk going out of business. Over the past decade, study after study has documented this phenomenon. After the Côte d'Ivoire reformed its trade policies in 1985, overall productivity growth tripled, growing four times more rapidly in industries that became less sheltered from foreign competition.[26] Industry productivity in Mexico increased significantly after its trade liberalization in 1985, especially in traded-goods sectors.[27] Detailed studies of India's trade liberalization in 1991 and Korea's in the 1980s reached essentially the same conclusion: trade not only disciplines domestic firms and forces them to behave more like a competitive industry, but helps increase their productivity.[28]

[24] Yoon 2000.
[25] See Helpman 1997; Keller 2000, 2001.
[26] Harrison 1994.
[27] Tybout and Westbrook 1995.
[28] Kim 2000; Krishna and Mitra 1998.

Competition can force individual firms to adopt more efficient production techniques. But international competition also affects the entry and exit decisions of firms in a way that helps raise the aggregate productivity of an industry. In any given industry, productivity is quite heterogeneous among firms: not all firms are equally efficient. Trade acts to promote high-productivity firms and demote low-productivity firms. On the export side, exposure to trade allows more productive firms to become exporters and thereby expand their output. In the United States, plants with higher labor productivity within an industry tend to be the plants that export; in other words, more efficient firms are the ones that become exporters.[29] The opportunity to trade, therefore, allows more efficient firms to grow.

On the import side, competition forces the least productive firms to reduce their output or shut down. For example, when Chile began opening up its economy to the world market in the 1970s, exiting plants were, on average, 8 percent less productive than plants that continued to produce. The productivity of plants in industries competing against imports grew 3 to 10 percent more than in non-traded-goods sectors. Protection had insulated less productive firms from foreign competition and allowed them to drag down overall productivity within an industry, whereas open trade weeded out inefficient firms and allowed more efficient firms to expand.[30] Thus, trade brings about certain firm-level adjustments that increase average industry productivity in both export-oriented and import-competing industries.

The impact of the U.S.-Canada Free Trade Agreement on Canadian manufacturing is also suggestive. Tariff reductions helped boost labor productivity by a compounded rate of 0.6 percent per year in manufacturing as a whole and by 2.1 percent per year in the most affected (i.e., high tariff) industries. These are astoundingly large effects. This amounts to a 17 percent increase in productivity in the post-FTA period in the highly affected sectors, and a 5 percent increase for manufacturing overall. These productivity effects were not achieved through scale effects or capital investment, but rather due to a mix of plant turnover and

[29] Bernard and Jensen 1999. Clerides, Lach, and Tybout (1998) show that this selection mechanism operates in developing countries (such as Mexico, Columbia, and Morocco) as well. See also Bernard et al. 2000.

[30] Pavcnik 2000.

rising technical efficiency within plants. By raising productivity, the FTA also helped increase the annual earnings of production workers, particularly in the most protected industries.[31]

To sum up, traditional calculations of the gains from trade stress the benefits of shifting resources from protected industries to those with an international comparative advantage. But new evidence shows that, because large productivity differences exist between plants within any given industry, shifting resources between firms within an industry may be even more important. Trade may affect the allocation of resources among firms within an industry as much as, if not more than, it affects the allocation of resources among different industries.[32] In doing so, trade helps improve productivity.

While difficult to quantify, these productivity effects of trade may be an order of magnitude more important than the standard gains. Countries that have embarked upon the course of trade liberalization over the past few decades, such as Chile, New Zealand, and Spain, have experienced more rapid growth in productivity than previously. Free trade contributes to a process by which a country can adopt better technology and exposes domestic industries to new competition that forces them to improve their productivity. As a consequence, trade helps raise per capita income and economic well-being more generally.

_____Can We Measure the Gains from Trade?

We have seen that trade raises aggregate income through a variety of mechanisms. But can this be empirically verified in studies using cross-country data? Do countries engaging in more trade also have a higher per capita income? This question may seem straightforward, but the issue is deceptively difficult. Until recently, empirical analysis of it was unsatisfactory. The usual approach was to examine the statistical relationship between trade (typically measured by the ratio of exports to GDP) and income across many countries. Although studies usually uncovered a positive correlation between trade and income, the meaning of this result is uncertain. Perhaps countries that trade more have higher incomes, or perhaps countries with higher incomes engage in more

---

[31] Trefler 2001.
[32] Melitz (1999) provides a theoretical model of this phenomenon.

trade, because they have better ports and other infrastructure that supports trade or because they have better economic policies in general.

Fortunately, creative research by Jeffrey Frankel and David Romer has overcome this ambiguity.[33] They have shown that greater trade is not associated with greater income because high-income countries simply trade more. Indeed, the effect of trade on income is strikingly higher once the part of trade that is not driven by income is isolated: the standard estimates suggest that a 1 percent increase in the trade share increases per capita income by about 0.8 percent, but using only geographic determinants of trade raises the estimated effect to about 2 percent (although this is imprecisely estimated). Frankel and Romer find that the effect of trade on income works mainly through higher productivity, but also by increasing the capital stock.

Although these results are suggestive for trade policy, differences in trade resulting from policy may not affect income the same way as differences resulting from geography. One study therefore used dozens of statistical specifications to examine the link between indicators of a country's trade policy and its per capita income. Almost invariably, more open trade policies are associated with higher per capita income, although the magnitude and significance of the relationship varied considerably.[34]

Then there is the question of the relationship between trade and economic growth. Recent empirical research has uncovered an indirect

---

[33] The problem is that trade affects income and income affects trade. To isolate the effect of trade on income, a measure of trade that is unrelated to income must be found. Noting that distance from trade partners is a key determinant of trade but is unrelated to income, Frankel and Romer (1999) used a country's geographic attributes to identify the relationship between trade and income. Using a cross-section of countries in 1985, they found that the effect of trade on income is considerably higher in instrumental variables estimation than in an ordinary regression. Irwin and Terviö (2002) confirm that the Frankel-Romer findings are not unique to 1985, but hold in most periods from 1913 to 1990. Rodríguez and Rodrik (2001) suggest that the Frankel-Romer result disappears once one controls for distance from the equator, but other research, such as Hall and Jones (1999), finds that the inclusion of latitude does not undermine the positive effect of trade on income.

[34] Jones 2001. Rodríguez and Rodrik (2001) have countered that this finding may be afflicted with reverse causality, that richer countries generally choose to have lower trade barriers.

link between trade and growth: the share of investment in GDP is positively correlated with growth in per capita income, and trade is positively correlated with investment. This means that while trade may not be directly correlated with growth, it may stimulate growth indirectly through investment.[35]

A related question concerns the relationship between trade policy and economic growth. In most theories, freer trade leads to higher income or higher consumer welfare, but not necessarily to a higher growth rate. While several studies have a found positive relationship between lower trade barriers and more rapid economic growth in the postwar period, others have questioned these results.[36] One obstacle that hampers these empirical studies is the absence of a single variable that accurately measures trade policy.[37] The relationship between trade policy and economic growth may be hard to pin down in the context of cross-country growth regressions, partly because trade policy is poorly measured, and partly because the effects of trade policy may be swamped by other factors that are difficult to measure.

Once again, however, there is evidence of an indirect relationship that operates through investment. Trade policies that increase the domestic relative price of imported capital goods can prove harmful to investment and therefore to growth as well. Tariffs and other trade barriers that raise the domestic price of capital goods mean that each investment dollar buys less capital, reducing the efficiency of investment spending. Empirical evidence tends to support the idea that the free importation of intermediate and capital goods is an effective way of promoting investments that increase growth.[38]

---

[35] Levine and Renalt 1992.

[36] Sachs and Warner 1995 is notable for finding that open economies grow faster than closed economies. Rodríguez and Rodrik (2001) have dissected this and other studies and suggest that many results are not robust.

[37] There is no single metric that ideally describes the stance of a country's trade policy. Import tariffs can be measured imperfectly, but they are not necessarily the most important feature of trade policy today. Nontariff barriers are an even more important impediment to trade in many countries, but cannot be measured precisely.

[38] See, for example, Wacziarg 2001. Lee (1995) finds that the ratio of imported to domestically produced capital goods is significantly related to growth in per capita income, particularly in developing countries, and Mazumdar (2001) reaches a similar conclusion.

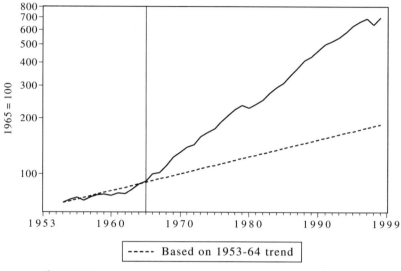

_____ Based on 1953-64 trend

_____Figure 2.3

Per capita GDP in South Korea, 1953–99. Major trade reform was initiated in 1964–65. (Data from International Monetary Fund 2000.)

Thus, despite shortcomings in method and measurement, cross-country studies of growth suggest that economies with more open trade policies tend to perform better than those with more restrictive trade policies. Additional, striking evidence comes from individual countries. These event studies clearly dramatize the benefits of deregulating imports. Consider three examples: South Korea, which liberalized its trade policies in the 1960s, Chile, which liberalized in the 1970s, and India, which liberalized in the 1990s.

In the mid-1960s, Korea's trade policy changed sharply. The number of items that were automatically approved for import went from zero in June 1964 to 63 percent by December 1965. Korea's currency (the won) was devalued by nearly 50 percent, and a unified exchange rate was adopted. In 1967, many import quotas were abolished and tariffs were sharply reduced. The effective tax on imports fell from nearly

De Long and Summers (1991) and others have found that investment in machinery and equipment is robustly correlated with growth. Jones (1994) shows that the relative price of capital goods is much lower in developed than in developing economies and that this relative price is correlated with growth even after controlling for initial income.

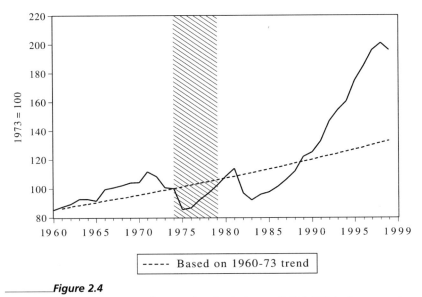

_____**Figure 2.4**

Per capita GDP in Chile, 1960–99. The shaded area (1974–79) indicates major trade reforms. (Data from International Monetary Fund 2000.)

40 percent in 1960 to 8 percent by 1967.[39] Figure 2.3 shows the results: a marked acceleration in Korea's growth of per capita income from around the time of these reforms.

In the mid-1970s, Chile also sharply changed its trade policy. Between 1975 and 1979, Chile eliminated all quantitative restrictions and exchange controls and reduced import tariffs from over 100 percent to a uniform 10 percent.[40] Although it suffered a severe economic recession due to a banking crisis in the early 1980s, Chile continued to liberalize trade after the recovery began. By the late 1980s, the payoff materialized in terms of higher per capita income, as figure 2.4 illustrates.

Finally, India announced sweeping trade liberalization measures in 1991. Tariffs were reduced from an average 85 percent to 25 percent, a rigid and complex system of import controls was dismantled, and the rupee was devalued and made convertible. Growth of per capita income began to pick up in the late 1980s when some initial, tentative steps

[39] Frank, Kim, and Westphal 1975, 75.
[40] Edwards and Lederman 1998.

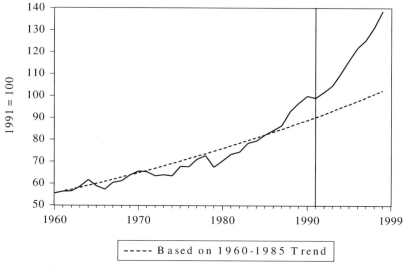

_____Figure 2.5

Per capita GDP in India, 1960–99. The vertical line in 1991 indicates major
trade reform. (Data from International Monetary Fund 2000.)

toward reducing import barriers were taken, but figure 2.5 shows a
marked acceleration in growth after 1991.

Three different countries on three different continents chose to
liberalize in three different decades, and yet the outcomes were similar.
They provide a dramatic illustration of the improvement in economic
circumstances that can result when poor economic policies are replaced
with better ones, particularly with respect to international trade.[41] Higher
per capita incomes translate into tangible improvements in the well-
being of millions of people. Because of the economic opportunities
opened up after the 1991 reforms, millions of Indians have become a
part of the middle class. With higher incomes, families can afford more
nutritional foods, better medicines and health care, and better schooling.

This improvement in well-being cannot be measured in terms of
dollars and cents alone, but in the lives that are saved as a result of

_____

[41] To be sure, other policy reforms were undertaken in these countries at the
time trade policy was liberalized, but the changes in trade policy were among the most
important.

moving people away from the knife edge of poverty, where a bad harvest or the loss of a job can spell malnourishment or even death. Hunger and malnutrition, illiteracy, and infant mortality persisted for decades after India received political independence in 1947. One Indian has called the failure to undertake economic reforms during those years a "great betrayal," arguing passionately that "by suppressing economic liberty for forty years, we destroyed growth and the future of two generations."[42]

Additional Benefits of Trade

The economic gains from trade are substantial, but they are not the only benefits that come to countries with a policy of open trade. John Stuart Mill's third and final claim was that "the economical advantages of commerce are surpassed in importance by those of its effects which are intellectual and moral."[43] Mill did not elaborate, but he may have been referring to the idea of *deux commerce*, exemplified by Montesquieu's observation in *The Spirit of the Laws* (1748) that "commerce cures destructive prejudices."[44] Trade brings people into contact with one another and, according to this view, breaks down the narrow prejudices that come with insularity. Commerce can also force merchants to be more responsive to customers, as greater competition gives consumers a wider choice. This may be one margin on which producers compete for the patronage of consumers.

For example, a recent study on the effects of McDonald's on Asian culture noted that rest rooms in Hong Kong previously had the reputation for being unspeakably filthy. When McDonald's opened in the mid-1970s, it redefined standards, setting a new, higher benchmark for cleanliness that other restaurants were forced to emulate.[45] In Korea, McDonald's established the practice of lining up on first-come, first-serve

---

[42] Das 2001, 175.

[43] "It is hardly possible to overrate the value . . . of placing human beings in contact with persons dissimilar to themselves, and with modes of thought and action unlike those with which they are familiar," Mill continues, because "there is no nation which does not need to borrow from others, not merely particular arts or practices, but essential points of character in which its own type is inferior" (1909, 581).

[44] Montesquieu 1989, 338.

[45] Watson 1997.

basis to purchase food, rather than the rugby scrum that had been the norm. When McDonald's first opened in Moscow, a young woman with a bullhorn stood outside its doors to explain to the crowd that the servers smiled not because they were laughing at customers but because they were happy to serve them. Sanitation, queuing, and friendly service have their advantages and surely make for more pleasant living, whatever your opinion of McDonald's food.[46]

There is also a long-standing idea that trade promotes peace among nations. Many Enlightenment philosophers in the eighteenth century and classical liberals in the nineteenth century expressed this view. Montesquieu argued that "the natural effect of commerce is to lead to peace" because "two nations that trade with each other become reciprocally dependent."[47] In his essay "Perpetual Peace," Immanuel Kant suggested that durable peace could be built upon the tripod of representative democracy, international organizations, and economic interdependence. A burgeoning political science literature now examines whether economic interdependence mitigates conflict between nations. Most of that work affirms that there is indeed a positive link between trade and peace.[48]

While the link between trade and peace is intriguing, there are also reasons for being skeptical of any attempt to establish a statistical relationship between them.[49] The methodological obstacles include making political concepts operational and representing them numerically, as well as establishing causal relationships. For example, countries that are

[46] Some globalization critics revile McDonald's for destroying local cuisine and foisting homogenous, processed, lowest-common-denominator food on the public. Yet Watson (1997) points out that McDonald's restaurants located in foreign countries are locally owned and highly attuned to local culture and tastes (particularly in Asia).

[47] Montesquieu 1989, 338.

[48] Oneal and Russett (1997), for example, examined Kant's hypothesis concerning the effect of democracy, trade, and membership in international institutions on the use of military force using a data set that spans country-pairs for the years 1950 to 1985. They find that each of these three factors independently contributes to more peaceful relationships with other countries. See also Oneal and Russett 2000. While most research supports their findings, the results are not always uniform over time; see Barbieri 1996. For the recent state of play, see the articles by Barbieri and Schneider and Oneal and Russett in the July 1999 issue of the *Journal of Peace Research.*

[49] See Gates, Knutsen, and Moses 1996.

at peace with one another are also more likely to be trading partners; which is the cause and which is the effect? Countries that are less aggressive are probably more likely to join international institutions, raising the same question. One must avoid reading too much into these findings. After all, on the eve of World War I, Norman Angell proclaimed that, in view of the extensive trade that existed between Germany and Britain and France, economic interdependence had rendered war obsolete.

If the trade-peace link is plausible though uncertain, a stronger finding is that democracies are more peaceful than autocratic countries. While we do not know whether democratic regimes are inherently more peaceful than other types of government, overwhelming evidence shows that democracies rarely go to war against one another. Does increasing trade contribute to peace indirectly, by promoting political reform and democratization? This view of nineteenth-century classical liberals has new support: as Chile, Taiwan, South Korea, and Mexico have been integrated into the world economy, they have moved toward a more democratic political system.

The link between trade liberalization and political liberalization was a contentious issue in the debate over extending Permanent Normalized Trade Relations (PNTR) to China in early 2000. Proponents of normalized trade argued that expanding commerce would enhance the power and influence of the private sector in China at the expense of the government. Opponents disagreed. Those opposed to U.S. economic sanctions against Cuba believe that greater trade with that country would increase the prospects of political reform there too.

While we cannot, at this time, provide statistical proof of the relationships between trade, peace, and democracy, the apparent links make us consider political reform as a leading noneconomic benefit of trade.[50] Even if trade fails to generate a movement toward democracy, it can still promote better performance among other domestic institutions. For example, countries that are more open also tend to be less corrupt, a

---

[50] Arriving at a definitive statistical test of the link between trade and political reform pushes the limits of quantitative social science. Constructing a clean test is difficult enough, let alone dealing with all of the causality issues. Trade may indeed promote democracy, but democracies are also more likely to pursue open trade policies and therefore trade more, as Mansfield, Milner, and Rosendorff (2000) demonstrate.

finding that holds even after accounting for the fact that less corrupt countries may engage in more trade.[51]

In sum, Mill's observations about the noneconomic benefits of trade appear valid, even if they have not been systematically proven by economists.

_____Free Trade and the Environment

Among the most vocal critics of free trade are those who worry about its effect on the environment. Some environmentalists believe that freer international trade will lead to more economic activity, and more economic activity will lead to greater environmental degradation. In other words, with trade comes more logging, more fishing, more soil erosion, more industrial pollution, and so on. But what, in fact, is the relationship between trade and the environment? Must trade lead to environmental damage, or might it in some ways actually benefit the environment?

To answer these questions, we must recognize that the link between trade and the environment is indirect. The greatest environmental disasters in recent years have taken place in Eastern Europe and the former Soviet Union. The horrible air pollution caused by state-run, coal-burning, capital-intensive industries and the killing of lakes and streams with toxic chemicals owe nothing to free trade but resulted from a system of centralized decision-making that valued resources less wisely than a system of decentralized markets with well-established property rights and prudent government regulation. In other countries as well, trade is not the underlying cause of environmental damage. The burning of the Amazon rain forests is largely motivated by local inhabitants clearing land for their own use, not international trade. And simple observation demonstrates that more trade and commerce does not always create more pollution: air quality in Delhi and Mexico City is much worse than in most industrialized countries, even though those cities have fewer cars and generate less electricity.

Environmental damage results from poor environmental policies, not poor trade policies. Environmental damage results from the in-

---

[51] Ades and Di Tella 1999. This finding makes sense for several reasons. Trade restrictions can foster corruption, particularly when bureaucrats are responsible for allocating import licenses among those who wish to import goods.

appropriate use of our natural resources in the land, sea, and air. The overuse of these resources is commonly related to the lack of well-defined property rights. When property rights are not well established, that is, when no one has ownership rights and control over a resource, then open access to the resource frequently leads to its exploitation beyond the socially optimal level. For example, if ownership of a forest is not well defined, then anyone can chop down trees for his or her own use without paying the costs associated with utilizing the resource. If control of the forest were established through property rights, then the owners would regulate and charge for the use of the timber. Obviously, the ownership and overuse problems are particularly acute for the air and ocean, where government regulation of the right to use the resource, reflecting public ownership of it, may be called for.

In many such cases, because environmental problems stem from the failure to clearly establish and enforce private or public property rights, trade policy is not the first-best means by which to achieve environmental objectives. Trade is only indirectly related to environmental problems, and therefore trade policy is an indirect, inefficient, and often inefficacious way of addressing environmental problems. Fortunately, the objectives of free trade and the environment do not always conflict; in fact, they often work together. Many government policies that are harmful to the environment are also those that international trade negotiators are attempting to limit. Three cases provide an illustration: fisheries, agriculture, and forestry trade.

Ocean fishing is a classic example of a common resource that is overutilized, and yet fishing is a heavily subsidized activity. The Food and Agriculture Organization estimates that world fishing subsidies are on the order of $54 billion annually, nearly 80 percent of the total value of the world's harvested fish.[52] Many of these subsidies have led to excess capacity in fishing fleets, which in turn promotes overfishing. In this way, such subsidies directly harm efforts to conserve fishing stocks and promote sustainable development. Clearly there is no trade-off in eliminating fishing subsidies and preserving the environment. In fact, the United States, Iceland, Australia, and New Zealand have pressed the membership of the World Trade Organization to discuss an international

---

[52] Milazzo 1998.

agreement to limit or abolish fishing subsidies, not just because such subsidies distort trade, but to prevent further depletion of ocean resources.

In the agricultural sector, import restrictions, domestic price supports, and export subsidies are widespread among the industrialized countries. These trade barriers and price subsidies tend to intensify agricultural production in countries that do not have a comparative advantage in such goods. As figure 2.6 indicates, the more a country protects its domestic agricultural producers, the more those producers rely on pesticides and fertilizers. Korea, Japan, Switzerland, and, to a lesser extent, the European Union heavily protect agriculture and must rely on chemicals to boost yields because these regions are not particularly well suited for all types of agricultural production.[53] As a result, trade barriers and production subsidies have "intensified land use, increased applications of agrochemicals, [and caused] adoption of intensive animal production practices and overgrazing, degradation of natural resources, loss of natural wildlife habitats and bio diversity, reduced agricultural diversity, and expansion of agricultural production into marginal and ecologically sensitive areas."[54] Countries that have a comparative advantage in agriculture, whether they are industrialized, such as Canada and Australia, or developing, such as Argentina and Brazil, do not depend as heavily on fertilizers and pesticides to maintain output.

Liberalizing trade in agricultural products would therefore benefit the environment by allowing countries with a comparative advantage in agriculture to expand production and forcing countries with a comparative disadvantage to contract output. One economist has noted that "an international relocation of cropping production from high-priced to low-priced countries would reduce substantially, and quickly, the use of chemicals in world food production."[55] In addition, the relocation of

[53] As Anderson (1998, 74) notes, "land-scarce Western Europe and Japan crop twice as much of their total land area as does the rest of the world on average, so the extent of contamination of their soil, water, and air from the use of farm chemicals is even greater" than figure 2.6 suggests. Thus, "the relocation of crop production from densely populated protectionist countries to the rest of the world would cause a much larger reduction in degradation in the former compared with any increased degradation in the latter, where chemical use would expand from a low base and to still-modest levels."

[54] Sampson 2000, 55.

[55] Anderson 1992, 163.

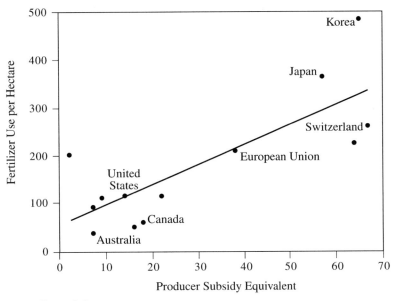

_____*Figure 2.6*
Protection of producers and use of fertilizers in agriculture, 1998. (Data from
Organization for Economic Cooperation and Development 2000a, table III.5;
Food and Agriculture Organization 1998, table 14.)

meat and milk production from intensive grain-feeding enterprises in
densely populated rich countries to pasture-based enterprises in relatively lightly populated poorer countries would reduce the use of growth
hormones and medicines for animals.

With regard to forest products, the United States sought without
success to eliminate all tariffs on forest products in recent multilateral
trade negotiations. Environmental critics have charged that liberalizing
trade in forest products will merely accelerate an unsustainable rate of
deforestation around the world. Yet trade in timber and timber products
is a minor cause of deforestation in tropical countries. Almost all the
annual logging in developing countries is for the domestic production of
fuel and charcoal—for the simple reason that fuel and charcoal are the
cheapest source of energy for poor people. About 77 percent of forest
timber production in Asia, 70 percent in South America, and 89 percent
in Africa is for domestic fuel and charcoal.[56] As with all open-access re-

[56] World Resource Institute 1999, table 11.3.

sources, better forestry management is the key to reducing the rate of deforestation.

In fact, not only are policies that reduce trade in forest products ineffective in reducing deforestation, limiting trade in forest products may exacerbate the problem. Without the timber trade, which raises the value of forests by providing external demand for its products, the investment value of these forests would fall. This smaller value would give local users less of an incentive to conserve the resource. In addition, eliminating trade restrictions would directly improve the efficiency of wood use. For example, Indonesia maintains high export taxes on logs to promote domestic forest-based industrialization. These export taxes have generated a large but inefficient domestic lumber industry. Every cubic meter of Indonesian plywood produced requires the cutting of 15 percent more trees than if plywood mills elsewhere in Asia had processed the logs. Indonesia's policy of protecting plywood mills has not only failed to reduce total log demand, but gross operational inefficiencies have also led to a much higher rate of logging than if log exports were allowed.[57] Thus, a ban on imports of raw tropical forest lumber by developed countries would not only fail to counter the underlying cause of deforestation, but might accelerate it due to the inefficiency of local processors.

Finally, there is the issue of whether free trade exacerbates industrial pollution. Once again, trade itself is not a direct cause of pollution, so one must examine the indirect links. Numerous studies have traced the relationship between pollution emissions and a country's per capita income. They have generally found a relationship shaped like an inverted U: as per capita incomes rise from low levels, pollution increases, but beyond a certain point, further increases in income tend to diminish pollution. The initial increase in pollution is due to industrialization, while the decrease is due to more effective environmental regulation and cleaner production technologies that come with higher incomes. Both Delhi and New York City have traffic jams, for example, but the locally made cars and scooters in developing countries tend to belch out worse fumes than the cleaner exhaust systems in the United States.

A recent study examined three channels by which trade can af-

[57] Barbier et al. 1995, 419.

fect sulfur dioxide (SO_2) emissions: the scale effect (increases in economic activity increase SO_2 emissions), the technique effect (increases in
income lead to cleaner production methods and reduce emissions), and
the composition effect (trade alters the composition of activity and hence
the average pollution intensity of national output). The authors were
surprised to conclude that free trade is good for the environment because, as an empirical matter, the technique effect outweighs the scale
and composition effects.[58] The effect of income growth on pollution depends largely on the underlying source of growth: growth achieved
through capital accumulation tends to raise pollutants, while growth
achieved by trade and technological change appears to reduce pollutants. This could also account for the inverted-U-shaped relationship of
pollution to income—developing countries tend to achieve growth
through (dirtier) capital accumulation, whereas growth in developed
countries is based on human capital accumulation and technology
(cleaner methods).

Controversy about the environmental impact of free trade was
particularly intense during the debate over NAFTA in 1993. There are
several reasons to expect that, with time, NAFTA will lead to environmental improvements. One study found that pollutant emissions increase
until per capita income reaches about five thousand dollars and diminish
thereafter. Because Mexico is near that watershed, NAFTA will improve
the environment if it increases Mexico's income.[59] Because Mexico has a
comparative advantage in unskilled labor-intensive goods rather than in
capital-intensive goods, freer trade may force dirtier capital-intensive industries in Mexico to contract as a result of competition. With protective
tariffs eliminated, these industries are forced to shut down or adopt better technology to stay in business. Furthermore, the "dirty industry migration" hypothesis, that polluting industries will migrate to developing
countries where environmental regulations are lax, has received no empirical support. There is no "race to the bottom" in environmental standards because the costs of abating pollution are not a significant determi-

---

[58] Antweiler, Copeland, and Taylor 2001. Their empirical estimates of the scale
effect indicate that a 1 percent increase in the scale of economic activity increases SO_2
emissions by 0.3 percent, but that the technique effect suggest that a 1 percent increase in
income decreases emissions by 1.4 percent.

[59] Grossman and Krueger 1993.

nant of industries' location, and consequently not a significant determinant of trade flows.[60]

The mainstream environmental community recognizes that free trade and the environment can go hand in hand. For example, once the environmental side agreements to NAFTA were negotiated, environmental groups that represented approximately 80 percent of the membership of the entire environmental community agreed to support the agreement.[61] Smaller and more militant organizations, such as the Sierra Club, Friends of the Earth, Greenpeace, and Public Citizen, continued to oppose NAFTA. But these groups generally oppose any growth-oriented trade policy, regardless of its environmental provisions. Steward Hudson of the National Wildlife Foundation testified before Congress that "a fair and objective reading of the NAFTA leaves you with one uncompromising conclusion: the environment is far better off with this NAFTA than without . . . . those who want to kill NAFTA are hiding behind the environment. The environmental critics of NAFTA, those who would forever be holding out for more, even at the expense of making progress on the environment in dealing with problems that concern all of us, are out to kill trade. . . . No amount of fine tuning or renegotiation will satisfy these opponents of NAFTA. The bar will continue to be raised because the goal is to kill NAFTA."[62]

This evidence should not be taken as minimizing the importance of taking effective measures to improve the environment. But free trade and a cleaner environment are not incompatible. Because trade in itself is not a driving force behind pollution, a policy of free trade rarely detracts from such goals, and in many instances may help. (This link between world trade rules and environmental regulation is considered in chapter 6.)

---

[60] See Jaffe et al. 1995; and Kahn 2000.

[61] These groups included the World Wildlife Fund, the National Wildlife Federation, the Environmental Defense Fund, the National Audubon Society, and others (Audley 1997, 90).

[62] U.S. House of Representatives 1994, 368–70. In the end, the major congressional critics of NAFTA, such as Richard Gephardt, David Bonior, and Marcy Kaptur, made no reference to the environment in their floor speeches against the agreement, but rather focused on job loss in the United States (Audley 1997, 106). The more extreme opponents of NAFTA were prone to exaggeration and hyperbole. The Sierra Club, for example, said that NAFTA would be "a major step toward ending democracy" in America.

_____**The Costs of Protection**

When considering the benefits of free trade, we also have to take into account the costs of protectionist policies. Such policies include tariffs, quotas, voluntary restraint agreements, and other means of blocking imports or impeding exports. When a country imposes trade restrictions, it forgoes the gains from specialization. Specifically, when imports of a certain good are restricted, it becomes more scarce in the domestic market. Scarcity drives up the price, benefiting domestic producers of the product because consumers are forced to pay more for it.

As a result, import restrictions redistribute income from domestic consumers to domestic producers. This redistribution is hard to justify. For example, because of restrictions on imports, the U.S. price of sugar is roughly twice that on the world market. Domestic sugar producers reap about $1 billion annually as a result of this policy. However, 42 percent of the total benefits to sugar growers went to just 1 percent of all farms.[63] The rationale for rewarding a few large sugar producers with hundreds of millions of dollars at the expense of consumers has never been made clear.

Even worse, protectionist policies distort prices and therefore economic incentives. This distortion leads to wasted resources, known as a deadweight loss. As import restrictions push the domestic price of a good above the world price, domestic firms produce more, while consumers reduce their overall purchases and suffer a real income loss as a result of the higher prices. The inefficiency associated with these distortions of incentives imposes a deadweight loss on the overall economy. The income transfer from consumers to producers is therefore inefficient, akin to taking ten dollars from one group while giving only eight dollars to another, resulting in a two-dollar loss to the economy as a whole. The sugar policy benefited producers of sugar to the tune of $1 billion, but it imposed far greater costs (about $1.9 billion, according to the General Accounting Office) on consumers, resulting in a net (or deadweight) loss to the economy of $900 million.

Economists can make rough estimates of the income transfers and the deadweight losses associated with trade barriers. The U.S. Inter-

[63] U.S. General Accounting Office 2000a; 1993, 32–33.

national Trade Commission calculated that the net cost—that is, the deadweight loss—of existing U.S. trade barriers was about $12.4 billion in 1996.[64] An older estimate using a different method arrived at the figure of $10.4 billion in net gains if protection were eliminated in twenty-one leading sectors in 1990. This calculation also suggested that the total consumer cost of protection was about $32 billion.[65]

U.S. import restrictions on textiles and apparel are by far the most costly of all sectoral measures. The Multifiber Arrangement (MFA) has been called the biggest piece of protectionist cholesterol blocking the arteries of world trade today. The MFA restricts imports of foreign textiles and apparel through a complex maze of country- and product-specific quotas. As of the early 1990s, the United States maintained more than three thousand separate quotas on imports from more than forty nations. The narrowly defined quotas include cotton diapers from China, men's and boys' cotton coats from Sri Lanka, women's and girls' wool coats from Czech Republic, women's bras from Mexico, men's trousers from Guatemala, women's and girls' man-made-fiber woven blouses from the United Arab Emirates, and so on. In 1989, the Treasury Department's Customs Service prohibited the import of thirty thousand tennis shoes from Indonesia because the boxes contained an extra pair of shoelaces, which were, it was decided, to fall in a separate import quota category.[66] The result is severely distorted trade and significantly higher prices of clothing for U.S. consumers.[67]

[64] U.S. International Trade Commission 1999a. This computational estimate is generated by using a complex general equilibrium model that, as previously noted, includes only the static costs of protection on resource allocation across sectors and fails to capture the losses due to forgone variety and productivity.

[65] Hufbauer and Elliot 1994. They use a computationally simpler, partial equilibrium method of estimating the costs of protection by specifying supply-and-demand relationships in each industry and calculating the costs to consumers and the gains to producers from the higher domestic prices that result from the trade barriers. This industry approach neglects the indirect effects of protection on other sectors of the economy.

[66] Customs later decided that extra pair of shoelaces would be permitted so long as they were laced into the shoes and color-coordinated with the shoes; Bovard 1991, 45. See also Faini, de Melo, and Takacs 1995.

[67] The restrictiveness of the MFA varies considerably across commodity products, ranging from an implicit export tax of 0.2 percent in nonwoven fabrics to 19.9 percent in apparel made from purchased materials (1993 estimates). The International Trade Commission estimates for 1996 were substantially lower in range, from 0.2 to 6.0 percent.

Under the Uruguay Round trade agreement of 1994, the United States and other countries have vowed to abolish the MFA by the year 2005. Like most trade reforms, the reduction in trade barriers is phased in over time. Unfortunately, the phase-in is "back-end loaded," meaning that most of the reforms take place late in the transition period. (This is akin to a diet plan that calls for losing twenty pounds over twelve months: none in the first ten months and then ten pounds in each the last two months.) Such plans are often difficult to implement. Many developing countries see the MFA abolition as a test case: they are anxious to see the United States follow through on its commitment to open its markets in textiles and apparel without coming up with some excuse to extend the transition period or otherwise postpone the elimination of the MFA. Because the United States frequently calls upon other countries to open their markets, a failure by the United States to abolish the MFA would be a serious blow to the cause of open trade.

And yet, according to virtually every study on the matter, the economic benefits to the United States from eliminating the MFA are enormous. A consensus figure is that the net deadweight losses associated with the textile and apparel import restrictions are over $10 billion a year.[68] The direct consumer cost of this protection amounts to $24.4 billion in 1990, a burden of over $260 per household. The tax is generally believed to be quite regressive, because lower-income households devote a greater share of their expenditures to clothing than those with higher incomes.[69]

The costs of the MFA are so high not just because of the import limits are restrictive but because the MFA transfers large amounts of income from domestic consumers to foreign exporters. When the United States imposes a tax on imports, the government collects as tariff revenue the difference between the world price and the higher, tariff-inclusive domestic price charged to consumers. But when a country limits the quantity of imports with a quota, the difference between the world price and the higher domestic price becomes a scarcity rent rather than tariff

---

[68] The U.S. International Trade Commission (1999a) estimates a net gain of $10.4 billion (1996 data), Harrison, Rutherford, and Tarr (1996) estimate $10.1 billion (1992 data), de Melo and Tarr (1992) estimate $10.4 billion (1984 data), and Hufbauer and Elliot (1994) estimate $8.6 billion (1990 data, using partial equilibrium methods).

[69] This has been questioned by Hanson and Reinert (1997).

revenue. This scarcity rent is captured by foreign exporters as a markup if they have obtained the right to export a certain amount under the quota in the import-restricting market, where they get to charge a higher price than on the world market.

The transfer of quota rents is a national loss because money is taken from consumers and handed to foreign firms (in the form of a higher markup) instead of the government (in the form of tax revenue), as would have happened if a tariff had been imposed. According to one study, of the $8.6 billion net cost of the MFA, the quota rent transfer amounts to $6.1 billion and the deadweight efficiency loss to $2.5 billion.[70] The transfer of quota rents also distorts the incentives of the exporters, particularly in developing countries. When the United States imposes an import quota, foreign governments are usually responsible for determining which exporters will be allowed to sell in the U.S. market (and thus receive the quota rent) and which exporters will be prohibited from exporting. The allocation of quota rights, except when those rights are auctioned off, is inherently arbitrary and increases the power of government bureaucrats, thereby fostering corruption. The politically well-connected firms, who perhaps are not averse to sharing the quota rents with the bureaucrats, are most likely to obtain export licenses, whereas other firms are shut out. This gives entrepreneurs in developing countries the wrong signal: the way to get rich is to invest in political influence, not to invest in productive efficiency.

As the MFA example indicates, the quota rents can be extremely valuable. In other cases, the quota rent received by foreign producers helps them compete against American firms. For example, when the United States limited the quantity of Japanese black-and-white televisions sold in the U.S. market in the early 1970s, the quota rent transfer is said to have given Japanese electronics producers the financial resources to enter the market for color televisions and videocassette recorders more quickly. When the United States persuaded Japan to limit its automobile exports in 1981, Japan's auto exporters were able to raise the average price of their cars by about one thousand dollars, part of which they invested in product improvements that enabled them to compete

[70] Hufbauer and Elliot 1994.

even more effectively against their American rivals.[71] Another example comes from the mid-1980s, when the United States mandated that Japan maintain high minimum prices on its semiconductor exports. Some of Japan's electronics producers were pleased that the American government, acting to help domestic semiconductor producers, was also helping them raise their prices in the U.S. market. Japan's exporters reaped billions of dollars in higher profits as a result. According to one account, Japanese companies producing 1 megabyte dynamic random access memories (DRAMs) took in $1.2 billion in profits in 1988 alone because of the U.S. trade intervention.[72]

The textiles and apparel industry is not the only sector of the U.S. economy that is protected by special import barriers. As already noted, the United States assists the domestic sugar industry through price supports and import restrictions in the form of a tariff-rate quota. Under a tariff-rate quota, sugar-exporting countries are given a certain (small) quantity that they can sell in the United States at the regular tariff, and any exports beyond that specified quantity are subject to a tariff rate of nearly 150 percent. As already noted, the sugar import restrictions and price supports cost domestic users of sweeteners $1.9 billion in 1998. Domestic sugar beet and sugarcane producers reaped $1 billion as a result of these policies, with most of the benefit accruing to sugar beet growers. The net loss to the economy is $900 million annually, $500 million due to economic inefficiency bred by the policy and $400 million in the transfer of quota rents to foreign exporters.

The United States maintains other protectionist policies. The steel industry, among others, has succeeded in getting high antidumping duties imposed on imports. According to an estimate discussed in chapter 4, the welfare cost of antidumping actions amounted to $4 billion in 1993. The Jones Act restricts trade in maritime services and cargo shipments within the United States and is estimated to have a welfare cost of $1.3 billion in 1996.[73] A 1996 softwood lumber agreement between the United States and Canada imposed high duties on any imports of Canadian lumber above a certain threshold and, according to one study,

---

[71] Feenstra 1988.

[72] Flamm 1996, 277.

[73] See U.S. International Trade Commission 1999a, 85ff.; and Francois et al. 1996.

raised the average cost of a new home by eight hundred to thirteen hundred dollars and thus pricing some three hundred thousand families out of the housing market.[74] Although the agreement expired early in 2001, the lumber industry has requested that import duties as high as 70 percent be imposed on Canadian imports.

Yet simply documenting the economic costs of protection often has a limited impact on policy. One reason could be that the calculated welfare gains from additional trade liberalization are quite small as a share of GDP. The International Trade Commission's estimate of $12.4 billion in gains from unilaterally removing U.S. import restraints in 1996, for example, amounts to only 0.16 percent of that year's GDP. To be sure, this is not a trivial sum—it is equivalent to an extra $320 pay for a worker who earns $20,000 a year—and it is an annual gain that accrues in perpetuity. (In other countries, particularly many developing countries, trade barriers are much more pervasive and restrictive, and therefore the potential gains from liberalization are much more substantial.[75])

But as we already know, such estimates understate the true costs of trade barriers, in part because they fail to consider the productivity and variety benefits of trade. The estimates are also understated because they do not take into account the resources devoted to political pressure. These expenditures on campaign contributions and lawyer fees may generate private benefits for those making the expenditures, but they can be socially unproductive because they aim at redistributing wealth rather than creating it.

A recent study pointed out how the impact of trade barriers can be understated if the political determinants of those barriers is not taken into account. A standard statistical method of gauging the effect of trade restraints on imports is to examine the determinants of import demand, such as the relative price of imports, domestic income, and other explanatory variables. To the extent that trade restrictions increase the price of imports, the detrimental effect on the volume of trade can be calculated.

---

[74] Lindsey, Groombridge, and Loungani 2000.

[75] Messerlin (2001) reports that the costs of protection in the European Union are equivalent to about 6 to 7 percent of the EU's GDP, or about the same as the annual economic output of Spain. The net cost of trade protection in Japan (circa 1989) has been estimated to be anywhere from $8 billion to $17 billion, according to Sazanami, Urata, and Kawai (1995).

But this approach ignores the simultaneity of imports and protection: higher tariffs may reduce imports, but more imports also lead to greater political pressure for higher tariffs. This confounds any attempt to isolate the effect of tariffs on imports and, unless corrected for, leads one to understate the effect of tariffs on imports. When one economist confronted this problem by examining the political-economic determinants of trade barriers in the United States and using the results to help explain imports, the statistical coefficient representing the negative impact of nontariff barriers (such as quantitative restrictions) on imports was increased by a factor of ten.[76] The conventional estimate suggests that removing nontariff barriers would increase manufactured imports by $5.5 billion (in 1985), whereas after controlling for the political determinants of those barriers, the impact was estimated to be closer to $50 billion.

Even when we can accurately state the welfare costs of trade barriers, the resulting numbers have a surreal magnitude that makes them hard to fathom. It is questionable whether these welfare costs have much political significance: if welfare losses were to double or triple, would that make any difference to policy? Exposing the seamier details of the protectionist racket might create more of a stir.

The sugar program is a classic example. Sugar imports are restricted to maintain domestic price supports for sugar beet and cane producers. The benefits of these restrictions are highly concentrated because Congress has not limited the amount of support that large firms can receive. For example, one farm received over $30 million in benefits from the sugar program in 1991, and just 0.2 percent of all sugarcane farms—thirty-three in total—received 34 percent of the entire program benefits.[77] The family of Alfonso Fanjul single-handedly supplies the United States with about 15 percent of its sugarcane through its land holdings in south Florida and the Dominican Republic, collecting somewhere between $52 to $90 million in benefits from the price supports on U.S. production and the quota rents on Dominican sugar exports.[78] Not surprisingly, the Fanjul family could afford to make nearly three hundred thousand dollars in campaign contributions in 1988. At the same time, the Fanjul farms were being investigated for chronic violation of U.S. labor laws. Government

[76] Trefler 1993.
[77] U.S. General Accounting Office 1993.
[78] Mayer and de Cordoba 1991.

support for the sugar industry has also harmed the environment because chemical runoff from the intensive farming of sugarcane in south Florida has seeped into the Everglades.

The sugar program is not just an economic, political, and environmental inequity, but it prevents desperately poor sugar-producing countries from exporting to the United States. Countries such as Colombia and Guatemala are deprived of valuable foreign exchange earnings that could be spent on food, fuel, and medicine. Congressional opponents of the sugar policy have suggested that Andean farmers, prevented from selling their sugar in major markets such as the United States, have turned their cropland toward the production of coca used in cocaine production and other illegal drugs. The Caribbean and Latin American farmers who find themselves cut out of the American sugar market may be forced to turn to illegal crops as a way to make a living.

When examined up close, trade policy is not a pretty sight. Steel industry lobbyists, for example, have induced members of Congress to change U.S. trade laws for the benefit of the industry, which has received pension bailouts, loan guarantees, environmental exemptions, decades of trade restrictions—and continues to push for more.[79] When a politician intervenes on behalf of an industry, the story is often an ugly one.

_____Is Protection Ever Beneficial?

The theory and evidence reviewed thus far have failed to indicate any instances in which import restrictions are economically beneficial.[80] However, trade protection can, under certain conditions, improve welfare. Broadly speaking, trade measures can be beneficial when they are used to improve the terms of trade, to promote industries with positive externalities, or to capture rents in international markets.[81]

If a country has the ability to influence the prices of its exports and imports on the world market, then trade restrictions can potentially raise national income by improving the country's terms of trade, the ratio

---

[79] Barringer and Pierce 2000.

[80] Adam Smith fully conceded that there are sound noneconomic rationales for restricting trade, such as protecting industries essential for national defense.

[81] Irwin (1996b) explores the debate among economists about various cases in which protection is thought to be economically justifiable.

at which a country exchanges exports for imports. An improvement in the terms of trade, either through higher export prices or lower import prices, increases the purchasing power of exports in terms of the imports they procure. This translates into higher income because the country can acquire more imports for the same amount of exports.

The power to influence the world market price is usually held by a country that dominates production of a certain good. For example, the United States produced 80 percent of the world's cotton prior to the Civil War. Southern cotton producers collectively had a significant impact on the world price, but each producer alone had no particular influence. The United States might have been better off if producers had formed a cartel to restrict exports or, barring that, if the government had imposed an export tax to force up the world price of cotton.[82] The Organization of Petroleum Exporting Countries (OPEC) has with some success set the world price of oil by limiting production, and the member countries have enriched themselves as a result. (Of course, it is always difficult for such cartels to prevent smaller members from cheating and to prevent nonmembers from arising.)

Except in such special cases, the terms-of-trade motive for trade restrictions has little relevance for most countries' policies. Few countries have the ability to manipulate their terms of trade, and most policymakers probably have little idea what the terms of trade are or what conditions would have to be met for tariffs to be set optimally.[83] To the extent that countries can influence the price of their exports, the appropriate response is an export tax, something that is unlikely to be popular. In addition, any gains from such a policy could evaporate if competing suppliers emerged or if other countries imposed retaliatory duties. Finally, such a trade restriction is not desirable from the standpoint of world welfare and global efficiency. An improvement in the exporting country's terms of trade implies a deterioration in the importing country's terms of trade and actually leaves the world as a whole worse off.

[82] There is an "optimal" reduction in exports beyond which a country is worse off because the cost from reducing trade more than offsets the gain from a higher world price for its exports. If the domestic producers are aware of their market power, they can appropriately determine the price of their exports with less need for government interference. See Rodrik 1989.

[83] See Panagariya, Shah, and Mishra (2001) for evidence that developing countries are price-takers on world markets.

Another situation in which trade interventions can, in principle, yield economic benefits is when they serve as a second-best measure to promote industries that generate positive externalities. In the case of positive externalities, the private costs of production are higher than the social costs of production because producers do not take into account the benefits of their actions for other sectors of the economy. As a result, the domestic industry produces less of a good than is socially desirable. These benefits can be captured if the private and social costs of production are properly aligned, which can sometimes be achieved through domestic subsidies. If subsidies cannot be used, there may be a second-best case for promoting the industry through protection. Recent theoretical cases have considered optimal trade policy for industries in which there are static or dynamic external economies, such as learning-by-doing or R&D spillovers, in which the production experience or research of one firm benefits others in the industry, as is alleged to be the case in certain high-technology industries. In theory, circumstances can arise in which some government promotion may be appropriate.

But as a practical matter, using trade policy to correct for such market failures is problematic. Correctly identifying these externalities is, by their very nature, extremely difficult.[84] Even if the externality can be identified, the first-best policy of a subsidy has to be ruled out. Using tariffs to promote a targeted industry has been likened to acupuncture with a fork: the relevant market failure may be corrected, but at the cost of introducing a by-product distortion, such as a higher price for domestic consumers. Finally, the relevant externality must be external to the firm and internal to the country. The R&D or learning benefits could spill over between countries, particularly if foreign firms maintain a presence in the domestic market or have an ownership stake in the domestic firms, or when the knowledge cannot be limited geographically. In this

---

[84] Industrial policy advocates propose various criteria for determining which industries are better than others and therefore deserve promotion. One proposed criteria was industries with high valued added per worker, but as Krugman (1994) notes, these are really just capital-intensive industries. This would lead one to support the cigarette industry and the oil pipeline industry. Sometimes it is argued that the presence of external economies of scale is demonstrated by geographically concentrated industries. Just because most U.S.-made carpet comes from one county in Georgia, to use a commonly cited example of this phenomenon, does not mean that the carpet industry deserved to be subsidized at its inception or deserves to be subsidized now.

case, any promotion scheme benefits all firms around the world and not just domestic ones, significantly narrowing the cases in which intervention would produce purely a national advantage instead of simply providing an international public good.[85] It is particularly difficult for the United States, in which policy is largely producer-driven and lawyer-determined, to impartially discern which industries exhibit such dynamic externalities and which do not, let alone the degree to which the knowledge spills over to foreign firms.

Many industries that are expected to create positive externalities fail to do so. For example, in the late 1980s and early 1990s, high-definition television (HDTV) was widely believed to be a "technology driver" for the high-technology industry: if the United States failed to dominate the underlying technology, it would lose its competitive position in commercial applications and in related industries, such as semiconductors and workstations. Whichever country invested in the "right" technology first was expected to have a strategic advantage over latecomers in what was projected to be a lucrative new market. To this end, Europe and Japan moved quickly to subsidize their producers. Japan invested nearly $1.2 billion in HDTV research (much of it from the Ministry of International Trade and Industry and the state broadcaster, NHK), while taxpayers in the European Community spent about $1 billion on HDTV research through 1991.[86]

Fearing the United States would be left behind, in 1989 the American Electronics Association proposed that Congress appropriate $1.35 billion in direct subsidies and loan guarantees to support HDTV research. Congress authorized $30 million in research grants through the Defense Department and promised more, but the Bush administration opposed the funding. The ensuing stalemate prevented any further spending. Yet gridlock not only saved American taxpayers millions of dollars, it proved to be the best policy. The European and Japanese technologies were developed first, but they settled on an analog standard that was soon viewed as obsolete. Meanwhile, frustrated by the impasse

[85] Irwin and Klenow (1994) studied memory chip production in the semiconductor industry and concluded that international learning-by-doing spillovers were about as substantial as within country spillovers. In the case of R&D spillovers, Branstetter (2001) suggests that the domestic component is stronger than the international component.

[86] Hart 1994; and Dai, Cawson, and Holmes 1996.

in Washington, American firms set to work themselves on HDTV research and, by entering the field somewhat later, were able to improve upon foreign research. Ultimately, American firms created a digital system that was later selected as the industry standard by the Federal Communications Commission. Moreover, HDTV has not yet become the driving or profitable technology that many influential commentators thought it would.

The final rationale for trade intervention is to capture rents or profits in the international market. To understand this process, consider a firm that is competing against a single foreign rival in an imperfectly competitive market (i.e., one in which there are above-normal profits) in a third country. In this case, a government export subsidy for the firm could induce the foreign rival to cut its output, thereby shifting profits from the foreign to the domestic firm. This practice is known as strategic trade policy, in which the government undertakes a precise, strategic intervention on behalf of domestic firms in a way that increases national welfare.[87] While there was much enthusiasm for this idea in the 1980s, numerous theoretical and practical objections have diminished its appeal.

First, successful intervention depends crucially upon key parameters in the market's structure that make it difficult for governments to determine the best policy. For example, one study showed that if the firms competed by setting prices rather than quantities, then the optimal policy would switch from an export subsidy to an export tax.[88] The introduction of asymmetric information between the firms and the government further increases the range of possible outcomes and makes clear-cut predictions even more difficult. Setting aside theoretical issues, calibrated simulation models of strategic trade policy reveal that the potential gains from implementing the optimal policy are exceedingly small.[89] When the right policy is excruciatingly difficult to determine in the first place and depends upon getting parameters of industry structure and competitive interaction exactly right, the small potential payoff suggests that such interventions are not worthwhile, especially when the potential outlays are high.

Theoretical work on optimal trade interventions is usually devel-

[87] Brander (1995) provides a comprehensive survey of this literature.
[88] Eaton and Grossman 1986.
[89] Krugman and Smith 1994.

oped in the context of an omniscient government that has full information and the capability of setting policy in an optimal manner. In the real world, governments are neither omniscient nor immune to external pressure. Do the theoretical results stand up when the government is confronted with political pressure to use policy on behalf of certain industries? Not surprisingly, the answer is no. Research has shown that the case for such interventions is substantially weakened when government policy is subject to strategic manipulation by politically active firms.[90] Thus, there are many reasons to be skeptical about whether a government can determine where strategic intervention will be worthwhile among the many industries competing for government assistance, especially in a representative democracy, where trade policy is often driven by the interests of politically active domestic producers.[91]

The three theoretical possibilities for trade intervention discussed here depend upon particular circumstances in special cases and require constant adjustment to changing market conditions. Free trade is a much simpler policy because it does not need changing when the underlying economic conditions change. Furthermore, any government that undertakes large, systematic sectoral interventions creates a great deal of concentrated political and economic power, not just to do good but also to make costly mistakes.

_____Free Trade in Perspective

The benefits of free trade appear to be substantial, although precise quantification of those benefits is sometimes difficult. In extreme cases, governments that force their citizens to forgo the advantages of interna-

---

[90] Grossman and Maggi (1998) examine whether a welfare-maximizing government should pursue a program of strategic trade intervention or instead commit itself to free trade when domestic firms have the opportunity to manipulate the government's choice of the level of intervention. Domestic firms, for example, may overinvest in physical and knowledge capital in a regime of strategic intervention in order to influence the government's choice of subsidy. They find that this manipulation can make a commitment to free trade desirable even in settings where profit-shifting opportunities are available.

[91] Krueger (1990, 21) argues that "in the real world of scarce information, uncertainty, and pervasive rent seeking, policymakers will inevitably miss the crucial and subtle distinctions between profits that are high because of rents and those that are high because of risk; between wages that are high because of rents, and those that are high because of skills; and between sectors that provide inputs, and those that result in spillover externalities."

tional trade, particularly in developing countries, do not sacrifice just a couple of percentage points of national income, but risk impoverishing their people. The higher real income that comes with trade is valuable not just to allow the consumption of more goods for crass material reasons, but to help people afford food and medicine. With free trade comes higher income, which gives people access to better health care, better education, and better technologies that will help improve the environment. Regrettably, the United States imposes stiff import barriers on labor-intensive manufactured goods, such as clothing and leather, and on agricultural products, in which developing countries have a comparative advantage. This not only harms consumers in the United States, but reduces the income of people in developing countries as well.

But several caveats should be offered. Free trade may be beneficial because it allows a country to take advantage of the opportunity to trade, but it is not the only—or even the most important—determinant of whether a country's achieves economic prosperity. Free trade is not a "magic bullet" that can solve all economic problems. The real and substantial gains from free trade should not be exaggerated when other fundamental economic problems are pressing. The rule of law and the protection of property rights that enable the market mechanism to provide the right incentives for investment and commerce, in addition to stable macroeconomic policies, are preconditions for reaping the full benefits of international trade.[92] As Macaulay stated in 1845, "It is not one single cause that makes nations either prosperous or miserable. No friend of free trade is such an idiot as to say that free trade is the only valuable thing in the world; that religion, government, police, education, the administration of justice, public expenditure, foreign relations, have nothing whatever to do with the well-being of nations."[93]

At the same time, restricting trade entails real economic costs. These losses may appear to be abstractions, but they are in fact harm for

---

[92] According to Adam Smith, "Commerce and manufactures can seldom flourish long in any state which does not enjoy a regular administration of justice, in which the people do not feel themselves secure in the possession of their property, in which the faith of contracts is not supported by law, and in which the authority of the state is not supposed to be regularly employed in enforcing the payment of debts from all those who are able to pay. Commerce and manufactures, in short, can seldom flourish in any state in which there is not a certain degree of confidence in the justice of government" (1976, 910).

[93] Macaulay 1900, 89.

real individuals. And yet protectionist policies are maintained, and new ones are proposed. This is because most trade restraints have a superficially plausible justification for their existence. These rationales are often more apparent than real, however, and the next two chapters will address them.

3

The Employment Rationale for Trade Protection

Economic analysis has long established free trade as a desirable economic policy. This conclusion has been reinforced by mounting empirical evidence on the benefits of free trade, and yet protectionism is far from vanquished in the policy arena. Of course, this is nothing new: as Adam Smith observed more than two hundred years ago, "not only the prejudices of the public, but what is much more unconquerable, the private interests of many individuals, irresistibly oppose" free trade.[1] Industries that compete against imports will always actively promote their own interests by seeking trade restrictions. But, as Smith acknowledges, the general public also has concerns about foreign competition. The argument that resonates most strongly with the public and with politicians is that imports destroy jobs. Is this an accurate view of trade as a whole? And if so, are import restrictions the remedy? This chapter examines the relationship between trade and employment, and the hidden costs of intervening in trade to protect jobs.

____Does Free Trade Affect Employment?

The claim that trade should be limited because imports destroy jobs has been trotted out since the sixteenth century.[2] And imports do indeed destroy jobs in certain industries: for example, employment in the Maine shoe industry and in the South Carolina apparel industry is lower to the extent that both industries face competition from imports. So we can

---

[1] Smith 1976, 471.
[2] See Viner 1937, 51–52; and Irwin 1996b, 36ff.

understand why the plant owners and workers and the politicians who represent them prefer to avoid this foreign competition.

But just because imports destroy some jobs does not mean that trade reduces overall employment or harms the economy. After all, imports are not free: in order to acquire them, a country must sell something in return. Imports are usually paid for in one of two ways: the sale of goods and services or the sale of assets to foreign countries. In other words, all of the dollars that U.S. consumers hand over to other countries in purchasing imports do not accumulate there, but eventually return to purchase either U.S. goods (exports) or U.S. assets (foreign investment). Both exports and foreign investment create new jobs: employment in export-oriented sectors such as farming and aircraft production is higher because of those foreign sales, and foreign investment either contributes directly to the national capital stock with new plants and equipment or facilitates domestic capital accumulation by reducing the cost of capital.

Thus, the claim that imports destroy jobs is misleading because it ignores the creation of jobs elsewhere in the economy as a result of trade. Similarly, while trade proponents like to note that exports create jobs, which is true, they generally fail to note that this comes at the expense of employment elsewhere. Export industries will certainly employ more workers because of the foreign demand for their products, but exports are used to purchase the very imports that diminish employment in other domestic industries.

Since trade both creates and destroys jobs, the pertinent question is whether trade has a *net* effect on employment. The public debate over NAFTA consisted largely of claims and counterclaims about whether it would add to or subtract from total employment. NAFTA opponents claimed that free trade with Mexico would destroy jobs: the Economic Policy Institute put the number at 480,000. NAFTA proponents countered with the claim that it would create jobs: the Institute for International Economics suggested that 170,000 jobs would be created.[3]

In fact, the overall effect of trade on the number of jobs in an economy is best approximated as zero. Total employment is not a function of international trade, but the number of people in the labor force. As figure 3.1 shows, employment in the United States since 1950 has

---

[3] Orme 1996, 107.

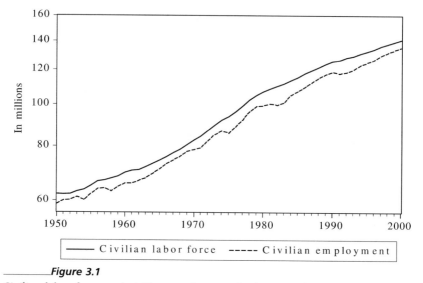

_____Figure 3.1

Civilian labor force and civilian employment in the United States, 1950–2000.
(Data from Council of Economic Advisers 2001, table B-35.)

closely tracked the number of people in the labor force. And while there
is always some unemployment, represented by the gap between the two
series, this is determined by the business cycle, demographics, and labor
market policies rather than changes in trade flows or trade policy. For
example, unemployment rose in the early 1980s and the early 1990s
because the economy fell into a recession, not because of the behavior
of imports.

How can we be sure that the number of jobs destroyed by imports is matched by the number of jobs created by exports and foreign
investment? The enormous turnover in the American labor market makes
it is impossible to identify the precise reasons for changes in an individual's job status. But figure 3.1 shows us that, in the aggregate, the process of job creation and of job destruction is roughly matched over time.
This is partly because any imbalance in those forces is offset by an adjustment of wages or by a change in macroeconomic policy. If imports
begin rolling in and trigger widespread layoffs, for example, the unemployment rate begins to rise. If the unemployment rate rises, and with it
the risks of a recession, the Federal Reserve Board is likely to ease monetary policy and reduce interest rates, other things being equal. This ac-

tion not only stimulates the economy in the short run, but also leads to a depreciation of the dollar on foreign exchange markets, which in turn makes U.S. exports less expensive to foreign consumers and imports more expensive to U.S. consumers. As a result, employment goes back up and returns to its long-run relationship with the labor force.[4]

Yet there remains a deep-seated inclination to frame the trade policy debate in terms of its impact on employment. This has motivated many attempts, however futile, to quantify the overall employment effects of trade. Analysts at several Washington think tanks (both favorable and unfavorable to NAFTA) have settled upon the rule of thumb that every $1 billion in exports generates or supports thirteen thousand jobs (implying conversely that every $1 billion in imports eliminates thirteen thousand jobs) as a way of evaluating the employment effects of trade agreements. Some NAFTA proponents argued that, because Mexico was to eliminate relatively high tariffs against U.S. goods while U.S. tariffs against Mexican goods were already very low, the agreement would generate more exports to than imports from Mexico. Using the rule of thumb, it was therefore reasoned that NAFTA would result in net job creation. Anxious to sell NAFTA to a wary Congress, Mickey Kantor, the Clinton administration's trade representative, claimed that two hundred thousand jobs would be created by 1995 as a result of the agreement.[5]

Such formulaic calculations were publicized to fight the dire forecasts that thousands of jobs would be lost as a result of NAFTA. But even if tariff reductions are asymmetric, exports may not grow more rapidly than imports. Trade agreements themselves have little effect on any bilateral trade balance or the overall trade balance, as we will see

[4] The adjustments can work the other way too. NAFTA opponents argue that the agreement kept the unemployment rate higher than it otherwise would have been. If this claim is true, then the unemployment rate would have been even lower if NAFTA had not been enacted. The unemployment rate fell from 6.1 percent in 1994 (when Congress passed NAFTA) to 4.0 percent in 2000. But an even lower unemployment rate would probably have caused the Federal Reserve Board to push interest rates higher in an effort to slow the economy, harming employment in interest-sensitive sectors such as housing and probably keeping the unemployment rate about where it was anyway.

[5] Hufbauer and Schott (1993, 14), for example, conclude that NAFTA and Mexican economic reforms "will create about 170,000 net new U.S. jobs in the foreseeable future. . . . Our job projections reflect a judgment that, with NAFTA, U.S. exports to Mexico will continue to outstrip Mexican imports to the United States."

shortly. And it is a mistake to think that changes in the trade balance translate into predictable changes in employment; a booming economy with low unemployment may be accompanied by a growing trade deficit because people have more money to spend on imports. Thus, any attempt to isolate the portion of the change in overall employment that is due to changes in trade is immediately suspect: it is bound to rest on implausible and arbitrary assumptions, and the predictions are ultimately unverifiable. In addition, stressing the positive employment effects of trade gives the false impression that achieving a higher level of employment is the principal motivation for pursuing more open trade policies. As we saw in chapter 2, the reason for pursuing more open trade policies is not to increase employment but to facilitate the more productive employment that comes with mutually beneficial exchanges that raise aggregate income.

Misleading claims for the job-creation benefits of free trade oversell these agreements and can even boomerang when underlying economic conditions change. For example, when the peso collapsed in late 1994, for reasons that had nothing to do with NAFTA, imports from Mexico surged and the U.S. trade surplus evaporated. NAFTA opponents then argued, using the rule-of-thumb formula, that thousands of jobs had been lost as a result of trade with Mexico because the trade surplus had become a trade deficit. An analyst at the Economic Policy Institute, for example, claimed that the trade deficit with Mexico and Canada destroyed 440,172 American jobs between 1994 and 1998.[6] While this number should be disregarded, as should any other purporting to show the employment impact of a change in trade flows, this episode demonstrates the precariousness of taking the position that overall employment will rise with the expansion of trade, or worse yet that employment will rise because exports will expand faster than imports. However seductive it may be for proponents of trade agreements to make such an argument, the logic can be turned against them if circumstances change.

Thus, even if free trade leads to greater imports, it is not the case that overall employment will suffer. Any effort to reduce imports may succeed in increasing employment in industries that compete with im-

---

[6] Scott 1999.

ports, but employment in other industries, such as export industries, will decrease. This effect is far from obvious and deserves some explanation.

_____*How Protection Harms Exports*

Imagine taking a poll of Americans and asking: "Should the United States impose tariffs on foreign goods to prevent imports from low-wage countries from harming American workers?" A sizable fraction of the respondents would surely answer "yes." If asked to explain their position, they would probably reply that import tariffs would create jobs for Americans and thereby reduce unemployment. Now suppose you then asked those same people: "Should the United States levy an export tax on domestically produced goods such as aircraft, grains, computers, software, and the like?" The answer would probably be a resounding and unanimous "no!" After all, they would argue, export taxes would destroy jobs and harm important industries (in addition to being unconstitutional under Article 1, section 9 of the Constitution).

Yet according to an important proposition known as the Lerner symmetry theorem, these two policies are fundamentally equivalent in their economic effects.[7] The Lerner symmetry theorem holds that a tax on imports is equivalent to a tax on exports. In other words, any restriction on imports also acts as a restriction on exports. This theorem helps us understand how import tariffs destroy jobs in export industries.

Some participants in the debate on trade tend to believe that a country's exports and imports are independent of one another, and therefore one can reduce imports without having an adverse effect on exports. In fact, exports and imports are the flip side of the same coin. Exports are the goods a country must give up in order to acquire imports. Exports are necessary to generate the earnings to pay for imports. The past century illustrates the close relationship between export and

[7] The theorem is named after Abba Lerner, who published a short but brilliant paper on the subject as a graduate student at the London School of Economics in 1936. Lerner's paper established the formal truth of the proposition, but it had been a feature of trade policy debates long before then. The converse proposition, that an export subsidy is equivalent to an import subsidy, does not exactly hold except under certain circumstances (Casas 1991). It remains the case that when a government undertakes policies to expand exports, it cannot help but expand imports as well.

imports in the United States. Looking back at figure 1.1, which plots U.S. merchandise exports and imports as a percentage of GDP from 1869 to 2000, we see that exports and imports are highly correlated.[8] (The trade deficit will be discussed shortly.)

Additional evidence of the Lerner symmetry theorem comes from the recent experience of developing countries. Figure 3.2 depicts exports and imports as a percentage of (GDP for two years (1970 and 1998) for Chile and Brazil. These countries pursued quite different types of commercial policies over this period. Chile undertook an extensive liberalization of its trade policy in the 1970s, dramatically cutting its import tariffs. This change in policy helped Chile's imports surge from about 15 percent of GDP in 1970 to 30 percent of GDP in 1998. And yet this period also witnessed a surge in exports on the same order of magnitude: the import expansion was matched by an export expansion. Other countries that have significantly reduced trade barriers, such as South Korea in the 1960s and India in the early 1990s, also have seen sharp rises in both exports and imports as a share of GDP. As in the case of other countries, Chile's experience also suggests that export diversification is an additional benefit that comes with lifting the implicit export tax that is inherent in import tariffs.[9]

By contrast, Brazil has pursued "import substitution" policies since the 1960s. These policies aimed to promote industrialization by severely restricting imports. In 1970, Brazil's exports and imports amounted to about 7 percent of its GDP. Brazil's trade policy did not change dramatically in the subsequent twenty-eight years, and thus, Bra-

---

[8] Trade policy revisionists often complain that the postwar period was marked by a one-sided opening of the U.S. market and that foreign trade barriers and unfair practices have been tolerated far too long. Yet to the extent that other countries have blocked trade in this way means not only that U.S. exports to those market will be lower, but that U.S. imports from those markets will be lower as well.

[9] By reducing import tariffs, a country is lifting an implicit tax on the export sector. The lifting of this tax constraint allows marginal exports, previously squelched by that tax, to become profitable. As a result, countries do not simply export more of the same things, but other goods that were previously unprofitable to export. This implies that trade liberalization allows exports to become more rather than less diversified, thereby reducing the risk of adverse export price shocks. Chile, for example, reduced its export dependence on metals (principally copper) from 64 percent of its exports in 1980 to 46 percent in 1996.

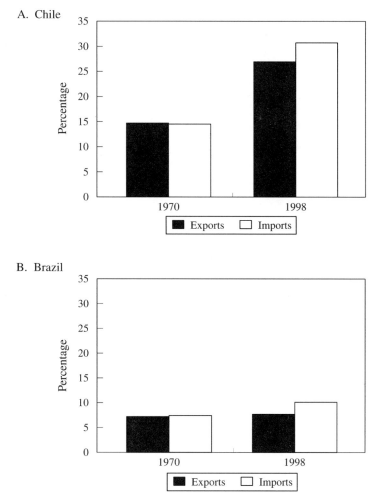

A. Chile

B. Brazil

_____*Figure 3.2*

Exports and imports as a share of GDP, Chile and Brazil, 1970 and 1998. (Data from International Monetary Fund 2000.)

zil's exports and imports remained at 7 percent of GDP in 1998 despite the tremendous growth in world trade over this period. The Brazilian government has made great efforts to expand exports, but substantial import barriers have indirectly constrained exports and undermined those efforts.

At one level, the idea that import restraints will reduce exports is straightforward. If foreign countries are blocked in their ability to sell their goods in the United States, they will be unable to earn the dollars they need to purchase U.S. goods. The mechanisms that link a country's exports and imports to one another are complex and not always readily apparent, but can be illustrated by focusing on the foreign exchange market. If the United States unilaterally reduces its tariff on Japanese goods, for example, one would expect U.S. demand for Japanese goods to increase. To make these purchases, consumers in the United States will (indirectly) have to sell dollars on the foreign exchange market to purchase yen. In response to the increased demand for yen from those holding dollars, the value of the dollar will fall in terms of yen, or conversely the yen's value will rise in terms of dollars. This change tends to raise the price of Japanese goods in the United States, dampening demand for those goods.

But here is the flip side: although it was the United States that lowered its tariffs while Japan left its tariffs unchanged, Japan will now purchase more goods from the United States. This is because the cheaper dollar tends to lower the yen price of U.S. goods, stimulating Japanese demand for them. Therefore, the foreign exchange market is one of several mechanisms that link exports and imports, ensuring that a country's exports increase when it unilaterally reduces its own import tariffs.[10]

The pattern of U.S. exports and imports shown in figure 1.1 also illustrates this relationship. The ratio of exports and imports to GDP was fairly stable in the 1950s and 1960s, but in the early 1970s and again in the late 1970s there was a pronounced jump in both of these ratios. These jumps coincide with large increases in world oil prices. (As late as 1980, almost 30 percent of U.S. imports by value were mineral fuels.) The big increase in the import bill is seen in the higher ratio of imports to GDP, but—since those imports must be paid for with something—the export ratio rose as well in each case. In both instances the increase in exports was brought about by a depreciation in the value of the dollar.

This link between exports and imports also explains why the employment effects of trade intervention tend to cancel each other out.

---

[10] A change in the exchange rate is only one of several mechanisms by which symmetry will hold; for example, it still holds for countries with fixed exchange rates or in single-currency areas such as Europe.

Throughout U.S. history, large tariff increases have failed to stimulate greater employment because any increase in employment in import-competing industries is offset by a decrease in employment in export-oriented industries. The Smoot-Hawley tariff of 1930, for example, significantly reduced imports but failed to create jobs overall because exports fell almost one-for-one with imports, resulting in employment losses in those industries.

Thus, the connection between imports and exports cannot be overlooked when evaluating trade policy. Governments that undertake policies to reduce imports will find themselves reducing exports also. This reduction in imports may expand employment in industries that compete with them, but the reduction in exports can also contract employment in export-oriented industries. Recognizing the effect of the Lerner symmetry theorem is particularly important when assessing the argument that import tariffs have a beneficial effect on employment.

_____*How Protection Can Destroy Jobs*

Not only do import restrictions reduce the number of jobs required to produce exports, but they also directly destroy jobs in downstream industries that use the imports. Recall from table 1.2 that the majority of U.S. imports are not final consumer goods, but intermediate goods used by domestic firms in their production processes. Any trade restriction that raises the price of an intermediate good directly harms downstream user industries and thus adversely affects employment in those industries. In other words, when domestic firms have to pay a premium on their productive inputs, particularly when they are competing with foreign rivals who do not pay those high prices, employment in those industries suffers.

Restrictions on imported sugar, for example, have reduced employment in such industries as sugar refining and candy making. After all, if food manufacturers who produce sugar-intensive products must pay a higher price for sugar than their foreign rivals, their competitive position suffers. In 1990, Brachs Candy Company announced that because of the high domestic price of sugar, it would close a factory in Chicago that employed three thousand workers and expand production in Canada, which does not artificially inflate the price of sugar. In 1988, the Department of Commerce estimated that the high price of domestic sugar cost almost nine thousand jobs in food manufacturing (because of increased imports of cheaper sugar-containing products) and three thousand jobs in the sugar-refining industry (due to lower demand for sugar). At the time of the Commerce study, sugar-producing farms employed about thirty-five thousand workers, but the sugar-processing sector employed about eight thousand workers, and industrial users of sugar (soft drink, baking, confectioneries industry) employed over seven hundred thousand workers. A great many workers in the sugar-using industries were put at risk to save the jobs of the few workers in the sugar-producing industry.[11]

There are numerous examples of the adverse effect that trade restrictions have on employment in related industries. In 1991, the United States imposed antidumping duties on imported flat panel displays, used by domestic manufacturers of laptop computers: specifically, 62.67 percent duties on active matrix LCD displays and 7.02 percent duties on electroluminescent displays. Producers of laptops could no longer afford to purchase the expensive displays in the United States and still compete effectively against overseas rivals, who could buy the same displays at much lower prices on the world market and then export their laptops freely to the United States. To avoid the higher domestic prices, several manufacturers decided to shift production abroad. Immediately after the imposition of the antidumping duties, Toshiba announced that it would cease production of laptops in California and shift production to Japan, Sharp announced that it would cease production of laptops in Texas and move production to Canada, and Apple announced that it would relocate its assembly of laptops from California to Ireland or Singapore.[12] Similarly, after the United States imposed price floors on Japanese DRAM semiconductors, computer manufacturers shifted their assembly operations outside of the United States to take advantage of the

---

[11] See U.S. Department of Commerce 1988. Of course, when the domestic price of sugar is forced up, jobs are created in producing sugar substitutes, such as high fructose corn syrup. But even if the overall effect on employment is zero, we have to ask: is it good government policy to reshuffle employment so much in this sector, creating jobs in the sugar industry but destroying them in the confectioneries industry, creating jobs in the HFCS industry but destroying them in the baking industry?

[12] Hart 1993.

lower prices for memory chips in other markets. In these and numerous other cases, import restrictions benefiting one industry have only harmed another industry.

When the purchasers of imported intermediate goods organize politically, they can alter the debate over the desirability of protection on employment grounds. In the case just mentioned, firms that used semiconductors (particularly computer manufacturers, IBM, Hewlett-Packard, Sun Microsystems, and others) formed a coalition to oppose the renewal of the price floors on Japanese memory chips. As a result of this consumer coalition, U.S. trade officials no longer heard a single voice—that of semiconductor producers—regarding America's trade policy. The government did not know how to deal with the sharply conflicting domestic interests, so it simply let the price floor agreement expire.[13]

The same political process played out in the steel industry. In 1984, the United States negotiated voluntary restraint agreements (VRAs) that limited steel imports from all major foreign suppliers. The VRAs raised the domestic price of steel and helped steel producers, but harmed the production, employment, and exports of the far more numerous domestic users of steel, including the automobile, machine tool, and construction industries. To fight the VRAs, these downstream industries formed the Coalition of American Steel-Using Manufacturers (CASUM), led by Caterpillar, the manufacturer of heavy earthmoving equipment, and by the Precision Metalforming Association, a small business group whose members process raw steel for industrial users such as the automobile industry.

As in the case of semiconductors, the VRAs were allowed to expire in part because CASUM posed an extremely difficult question to government officials: How are Caterpillar, John Deere, and other domestic steel-using firms supposed to compete at home and abroad against such foreign competitors as Komatsu when they are forced to pay a hefty premium for the steel they must purchase?[14] If Caterpillar laid off

---

[13] Irwin 1996c.

[14] As Moore (1996, 111–12) notes, "the overall strategy of CASUM was to turn the debate away from the actions of foreign firms and governments and away from an argument about free trade versus protection. Instead, CASUM tried to direct the discussion toward the VRA's effects on U.S. manufacturing interests, especially exporters and small businesses. This was a highly effective tactic since both have broad political support."

workers because higher domestic steel costs led to sales being lost to foreign producers, those workers could justifiably ask whether the government believed that jobs in the steel industry were more important to the economy than jobs in the equipment-manufacturing industry.

The protectionist steel industry has kept the steel-consuming industries busy as they battle for political influence in Washington. When the steel industry filed massive antidumping suits in 1998–99, steel-using groups formed the "40-to-1" coalition, referring to the fact that the fewer than two hundred thousand steelworkers are outnumbered by 8 million employees in steel-using industries, particularly in construction, metal fabrication, heavy machinery, and transportation equipment. The jobs of workers in steel-using industries would be at risk if steel prices were artificially increased. General Motors, which purchases over 7 million tons of steel annually, warned that imposing tariffs on imported steel would make GM's domestic operations "less competitive in the international marketplace to the extent that those operations are subjected to costs not incurred by offshore competition, and to the extent that U.S. import barriers impede access to new products and materials being developed offshore, or remove the competitive incentives to develop new products in the United States."[15]

In 1999, the steel industry managed to get the House of Representatives to pass a bill restricting steel imports. The bill failed in the Senate, but steel interests continued to introduce legislation that would block imports. Once again, the steel users coalition—this time, the Consuming Industries Trade Action Coalition, or CITAC—was forced to respond. According to one study, import quotas in the Steel Revitalization Act, introduced in Congress in March 2001, would protect 3,700 steel jobs but cause the loss of anywhere from 19,000 to 32,000 jobs in the steel-consuming sector. Over five years, steel consumers would be forced to pay anywhere from $6.8 billion to $14.5 billion in higher prices, amounting to as much as $732,000 per steel job protected.[16] Once

---

Moore also noted that "CASUM also appealed indirectly to protectionist elements in Congress by emphasizing that VRAs rewarded unfair traders through the transfer of quota rents," that is, foreign exporting firms reaped high profits by selling at higher prices in the U.S. market.

[15] Quoted in Lindsey, Griswold, and Lukas 1999, 7.

[16] Francois and Baughman 2001.

again, in deciding whether to limit steel imports, the government faced the choice of protecting jobs in the steel industry or protecting jobs in automobiles, commercial building, wire products, electronic equipment, heavy machinery, oil and gas drilling, and other steel-using industries.

These examples demonstrate the first lesson of economics: there is no such thing as a free lunch. Every action involves a trade-off of some sort. Higher sugar prices increase employment in sugar production, but reduce employment in food-manufacturing industries. Higher semiconductor prices increase employment in the semiconductor industry, but decrease employment in the computer industry. Higher steel prices increase employment in the steel industry, but decrease employment in the equipment industries. When a domestic industry asks the government to impose trade barriers that would raise the domestic price above the world price, the choice means trading off jobs in one sector of the economy for jobs in another sector, not creating or losing jobs overall.

Why do policymakers usually fail to see themselves as facing such a trade-off? For one thing, if downstream consumers do not organize politically, indirect effects of trade barriers may never get brought to legislators' attention. And the nature of the political process gives members of Congress and officials in the executive agencies responsible for trade policy a strongly biased view of the effects of trade. Constituents who lose their jobs in import-sensitive industries, such as steel, do not fail to contact their representatives and the responsible agencies to complain about foreign competition. Legislators cannot be so impolitic as to tell these voters to go away, and it is hard to resist the temptation to help by "doing something" about the situation, even if that imposes hardship on others who are often silent. Meanwhile, those who owe their jobs and high wages to exports or to industries that depend upon inexpensive intermediate goods almost invariably fail to express their appreciation to policymakers for not interfering in the process of trade. As a result, those seeking to limit trade tend to be more vocal than those who benefit from open markets.

_____*Employment and the Trade Deficit*

Does the trade deficit injure domestic industries and have adverse effects on employment? In every year since 1976, the value of goods and ser-

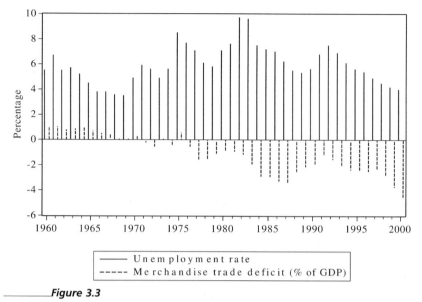

_____**Figure 3.3**

Unemployment and the trade deficit in the United States, 1960–2000. (Data from Council of Economic Advisers 2001, tables B-1, B-35, and B-103.)

vices imported into the United States has exceeded the value of goods and services exported. Should the trade deficit be a matter of concern and reversing it an objective for trade policy?[17]

The connection between the trade deficit and employment is much more complex than the simple view that jobs are lost because imports exceed exports. As figure 3.3 shows, the correlation between the merchandise trade deficit and the unemployment rate is actually negative: the trade deficit has risen during periods of falling unemployment and has fallen during periods of rising unemployment. As noted earlier, the business cycle may be driving this relationship: a booming economy in which many people are finding employment is also an economy that sucks in many imports, whereas a sluggish economy is one in which expenditures on imports slacken.

[17] To investigate the causes and consequences of the trade deficit, Congress set up the Trade Deficit Review Commission, which issued its report in November 2000. Unfortunately, the commission split along partisan lines: Democrats viewed the deficit as malign (a serious threat employment in trade-affected industries), while Republicans viewed the deficit as benign (as reflecting the good state of the economy). The commission's report is available at http://www.ustdrc.gov.

A deeper understanding of the trade deficit, however, requires some familiarity with balance-of-payments accounting. Balance-of-payments accounting may be a dry subject, but it helps lift the fog that surrounds the trade deficit. That accounting also suggests which remedies are likely to be effective in reducing the deficit, should that be considered desirable.

The balance of payments is simply an accounting of a country's international transactions. All sales of U.S. goods or assets to nonresidents constitute a receipt to the United States and are recorded in the balance of payments as a positive entry (credit); all purchases of foreign goods or assets by U.S. residents constitute a payment by the United States and are recorded as a negative entry (debit). The balance of payments is divided into two broad categories of transactions: the current account, which includes all trade in goods and services, plus a few smaller categories; and the capital account, which includes all trade in assets, mainly portfolio and direct investments.

The first accounting lesson is that the balance of payments always balances. By accounting identity, which is to say by definition, the balance of payments sums to zero. This implies that

current account + capital account = 0.

Because the overall balance of payments always balances, a country with a current account deficit must have a offsetting capital account surplus. In other words, if a country is buying more goods and services from the rest of the world more than it is selling, then the country must also be selling more assets to the rest of the world than it is purchasing.[18]

To make the link clearer, consider the case of an individual. Each of us as individuals export our labor services to others in the economy. For this work, we receive an income that can be used to import goods and services produced by others. If an individual's expenditures exactly match his or her income in a given year, that person has "balanced trade" with the rest of the economy: the value of exports (income) equals the value of imports (expenditures). Can individuals spend more

---

[18] A country therefore cannot experience a "balance-of-payments deficit" unless one is using the old nomenclature that considers official reserve transactions (an important component of the balance of payments under fixed-exchange-rate regimes) as a separate part of the international accounts.

in a given year than they earn in income, in other words, can a person import more than he or she exports? Of course, by one of two ways: either by receiving a loan (borrowing) or by selling existing financial assets to make up the difference. Either method generates a financial inflow—a capital account surplus—that can be used to finance the trade deficit while also reducing the individual's net assets. Can an individual spend less in a given year than that person earns in income? Of course, and that individual exports more than he or she imports, thereby running a trade surplus with the rest of the economy. The surplus earnings are saved, generating a financial outflow—a capital account deficit—due to the purchase of financial investments.

What does this mean in the context of the United States? In 2000, the United States had a merchandise trade deficit of about $450 billion and a services trade surplus of $80 billion. The balance on goods and services was therefore a deficit of about $370 billion, but owing to other factors (net income payments and net unilateral transfers) the current account deficit was nearly $435 billion, or 4.4 percent of that year's GDP. This implies that there must have been a capital account surplus of roughly the same magnitude. Sure enough, in that year U.S. residents (corporations and households) increased their ownership of foreign assets by just over $550 billion while foreigners increased their ownership of U.S. assets by over $950 billion. Therefore the capital account surplus was approximately $400 billion. In other words, foreigners increased their ownership stake in U.S. assets more than U.S. residents increased their holdings of foreign assets, the mirror image of the current account deficit.[19]

The balance of payments "balances" in the sense that every dollar we spend on imported goods must end up somewhere. Here's another way of thinking about it: in 2000, the United States imported almost $1,440 billion in goods and services from the rest of the world, but the rest of the world only purchased $1,070 billion of U.S. goods and services. What did the other countries do with the rest of our money? They invested it in the United States. In essence, for every dollar Americans handed over to foreigners in buying their goods (our imports), foreigners used seventy-five cents to purchase U.S. goods (our exports) and

[19] Joint Economic Committee and Council of Economic Advisers, *Economic Indicators*, April 2001, 36–37.

the remaining twenty-five cents to purchase U.S. assets. What assets are foreign residents purchasing? Some are short-term financial assets (such as stocks and bonds) for portfolio reasons; some are direct investments (such as mergers and acquisitions) to acquire ownership rights; and some are real assets (such as buildings and land) for the same reasons. In developing countries, foreign investment sometimes includes large amounts of short-term government debt, denominated in a foreign currency. It is misleading to compare these debts to the foreign purchase of U.S. assets by saying that the United States is borrowing from other countries. Borrowing implies a specific payback schedule, hence the repayment problems that developing countries sometimes encounter. In the U.S. case, foreign investors are simply choosing to purchase dollar-denominated assets from the owners of those assets. The investors often wish to take a direct, long-term ownership stake in the United States that they do not intend to reverse. The current account deficit is sustainable for as long as foreign investors desire to hold more U.S. assets. In the mid-1980s, many commentators feared that the current account deficit was unsustainable and that the economy would face a hard landing once foreign capital stopped flowing into the United States. These fears proved to be misplaced: the economy did not suffer a hard landing when capital inflows slowed in the late 1980s, and the current account deficit was sustained through the 1990s.

In running a current account deficit, the United States is selling assets to the rest of the world. These foreign purchases of domestic assets allow the United States to finance more investment than it could through domestic savings alone. In essence, the United States is supplementing its domestic savings with foreign investment and thus is able to undertake more investment than if it had relied solely on domestic savings. The equation that expresses this relationship is

current account = savings − investment.

Once again, this equation is an identity, meaning that it holds by definition. A current account deficit (the capital account surplus) implies that domestic investment exceed domestic savings. Conversely, countries with current account surpluses have domestic savings in excess of domestic investment, the excess being used to purchase foreign assets via foreign investment (capital account deficit).

Figure 3.4 illustrates this point by presenting the U.S. current

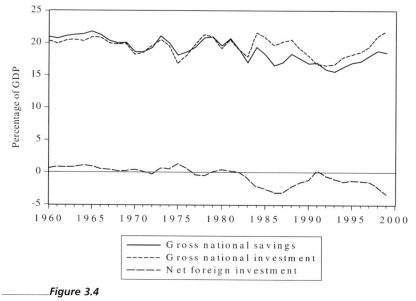

_____**Figure 3.4**

Savings and investment in the United States as a percentage of GDP, 1960–99.
(Data from Council of Economic Advisers 2001, table B-32.)

account as a percentage of GDP from 1950 to 1999, along with the evolution of savings and investment. The current account registered a slight
surplus during the 1960s, indicating that the United States was making
net foreign investments in the rest of the world. In the 1980s and 1990s,
however, domestic investment was greater than domestic savings, and
net foreign investment was negative, meaning that the United States was
a net recipient of foreign investment.

    That the U.S. current account was roughly balanced in the 1960s
and 1970s is no coincidence. The ability of a country to run a current
account surplus or deficit depends upon the degree to which capital is
allowed to move between countries, which in turn is a function of the
international monetary system and the exchange rate regime. In the absence of international capital mobility, domestic savings must equal domestic investment and therefore the current account will be balanced.
Under the Bretton Woods system of fixed exchange rates, which lasted
from just after World War II until 1971, governments maintained fixed
exchange rates by imposing controls on capital movements. As a result,
capital flows were minimal by present-day standards. When the interna-

tional monetary system suppresses capital account transactions, the capital account balance must be close to zero, and therefore the current account balance must also be close to zero.

The Bretton Woods system collapsed in 1971, and since then international capital movements have been deregulated. With the return of international capital mobility, relatively large current account imbalances also began to emerge. The United States became a magnet for capital from the rest of the world, particularly after the early 1980s. For example, after Japan eased restrictions on the holding of foreign assets in 1980, Japanese investors took part of their large pool of capital (invested in its domestic market as a result of its high savings rate) and sought higher rates of return in foreign capital markets, particularly in the United States. Now that they were free to buy U.S. assets as well as U.S. goods, Japanese residents chose to allocate some of the dollars they earned in selling products in the United States to buying U.S. assets rather than U.S. goods.

Because the United States is a net recipient of foreign investment, it is difficult to say much about the impact of the trade deficit on the number of jobs in the economy. The Economic Policy Institute, a Washington think tank aligned with organized labor, regularly issues reports stating that the trade deficit has destroyed American jobs. So why has the unemployment rate fallen during periods of large trade deficits? In recent years, they have argued that job losses due to trade has been more than offset by job creation due to consumer spending and business investment.[20] And yet that higher business investment is made possible precisely because of foreign capital inflows, the flip side of the current account deficit. If the United States took action to reduce the trade deficit (supposedly reducing the number of jobs lost to trade), those capital inflows would necessarily fall. Then domestic investment would have to be financed by domestic savings, implying higher interest rates, which would reduce the number of jobs created by business investment. In the end, a lower trade deficit's positive impact on employment would be offset by the negative impact of lower domestic investment and higher interest rates.

So what are the implications for trade policy? The current ac-

[20] See, for example, Scott and Rothstein (1998).

count is fundamentally determined by international capital mobility and the gap between domestic savings and investment. The main determinants of savings and investment are macroeconomic in nature. Current account imbalances have nothing to do with whether a country is open or closed to foreign goods, engages in unfair trade practices or not, or is more "competitive" than other countries. If net capital flows are zero, the current account will be balanced. Japan's $11 billion current account deficit in 1980 grew to a $87 billion current account surplus in 1987 not because it closed its market, or because the United States opened its market, or because Japanese manufacturers suddenly become more competitive on international markets. The surplus emerged because of financial and macroeconomic reasons in Japan and the United States.[21]

Trade policy cannot directly affect the current account deficit because trade policy has little influence on the underlying determinants of domestic savings and investment, the ultimate sources of the current account. If a country wishes to reduce its trade deficit, then it must undertake macroeconomic measures to reduce the gap between domestic savings and investment. Long ago it was believed that restrictions on imports would reduce the trade deficit. But that result would follow only if exports remained unaffected, an assumption that is false under the Lerner symmetry theorem. Adam Smith saw through such policies of restriction: "Nothing, however, can be more absurd than this whole doctrine of the balance of trade, upon which, not only these restraints, but almost all the other regulations of commerce are founded."[22]

Trade and Industry Wages

We have seen that framing trade policy in terms of employment is ultimately an empty exercise: blocking imports may protect jobs in industries that compete against imports, but it harms employment in export-

[21] Japanese exporters became more price competitive in the U.S. market due to the appreciation of the dollar in the early to mid-1980s, but this appreciation was driven by capital flows into the United States. While trade policy cannot directly affect the current account deficit, the deficit does affect trade policy. A large trade deficit puts a competitive squeeze on both exporting and import-competing industries resulting mainly from the exchange rate appreciation that usually accompanies the rising deficit. This pressure fuels protectionist sentiment, as seen by the experience of the early and mid-1980s.

[22] Smith 1976, 488.

oriented and import-using industries. Yet trade has important implications for employment in particular sectors of the economy. Even those
who agree that the overall effect of trade on employment is essentially
zero may oppose free trade because they believe that it shifts jobs into
less desirable sectors.

The gravest of such concerns is that in the last three decades
good jobs in manufacturing have been traded for bad jobs in services. In
the United States, employment in manufacturing fell from 19.4 million
workers in 1970 to 18.5 million in 1999. Manufacturing's share of total
employment fell even more sharply, from 27 percent in 1970 to 14 percent in 1999.[23] At the same time, real manufacturing output has increased
significantly, by nearly 40 percent in the 1990s alone, and has declined
only slightly as a share of GDP when measured at constant prices.
Growth in productivity has allowed manufacturing to achieve vastly increased output with roughly the same number of workers, or alter-
natively to maintain its share of constant-dollar GDP with a much smaller
share of the workforce. Like agriculture starting in the mid–nineteenth
century, manufacturing has been a victim of its own improving productivity. On the other hand, the relatively poor performance of the service
sector in improving productivity has meant that increasing output there
(to keep up with the rapidly growing demand for finance, health care,
and education) requires shifting a greater share of the labor force into
those occupations.[24]

Has trade contributed to this sectoral shift? The problem with
blaming trade for the relative decline in manufacturing employment is
that the United States is both a big exporter and a big importer of manufactured goods, as table 1.2 shows. The trade deficit in manufactured
goods is smaller than the overall trade deficit, because the United States
is a large net importer of mineral fuels. The trade deficit in manufactured
goods is also a small percentage of GDP. Thus, even if the United States
had had balanced trade in manufactured goods after 1970, the effect on
output and employment in manufacturing would have been modest.
Manufacturing output as a share of current-dollar GDP fell from 25.0

[23] Council of Economic Advisers 2001, table B-46.

[24] This is not a uniquely American phenomenon, but one that has taken place
(sometimes to an even greater extent) in most developed countries. See Burtless et al.
1998, 54.

percent in 1970 to 18.4 percent in 1990, whereas the share would have fallen to 19.2 percent if the United States had balanced trade in manufactured goods over this period.[25] In other words, even with balanced trade, the share of manufacturing in GDP would have continued to decline, but just slightly less than it actually did.

But an even more basic point must be stressed: the perception that imports destroy good, high-wage jobs in manufacturing is almost completely erroneous. It is closer to the truth to say that imports destroy bad, low-wage jobs in manufacturing. This is because wages in industries that compete against imports are well below average, whereas wages in exporting industries are well above average. The United States tends to import labor-intensive products, such as apparel, footwear, leather, and goods assembled from components. Comparable domestic industries in these labor-intensive sectors tends to employ workers who have a lower than average educational attainment, and who therefore earn a relatively low wage. For example, in 1999 average hourly earnings of Americans working in the apparel industry were 36 percent less than in manufacturing as a whole. Average hourly earnings were 30 percent lower in the leather industry and 23 percent lower in the textile industry than in the average manufacturing industry.[26]

By contrast, the United States tends to export more skill-intensive manufactured products, such as aircraft, construction machinery, engines and turbines, and industrial chemicals. Workers in these industries earn relatively high wages. For example, in 1999 average hourly earnings in the aircraft industry were 42 percent above the average in manufacturing, 8 percent higher in industrial machinery, and 24 percent higher in pharmaceuticals. One study reports that even "after being adjusted for skill differences, wages in export-intensive industries are 11 percent above average, whereas wages in import-intensive industries are 15 percent below average."[27]

As a result, any policy that limits overall trade by reducing both

[25] According to the calculation in Krugman and Lawrence 1994.

[26] U.S. Bureau of the Census 2001, 429.

[27] Katz and Summers 1989, 264. Similarly, Bernard and Jensen (1995, 71) find that wages at exporting plants pay a premium of 7 to 11 percent over nonexporting plants, after controlling for various other factors. Labor economists use educational attainment as a proxy for skill level because education is observable, whereas skill is not. This is not quite satisfactory because one can be a very skilled artisan in the textile and apparel industry, for example, and yet still receive a relatively low wage.

exports and imports tends to increase employment in low-wage industries and reduce employment in high-wage industries. Restricting trade would shift American workers away from things that they produce relatively well (and hence export and earn relatively high wages in producing) and toward things that they do not produce so well (and hence import and earn relatively low wages in producing) in comparison with other countries. Employment gains for the low-wage textile machine operators in the factory mills would be offset by employment losses for the high-wage engineers in aircraft and pharmaceutical plants.

Some people justify import restrictions as a way of slowing the movement of workers out of industries in decline because of structural shifts in the economy. And while trade barriers can raise employment (or slow the decline of employment) in industries that compete against imports, two points should be recognized: jobs are "saved" in the industry only by destroying jobs elsewhere, as we have already seen, and protection is a costly and inefficient jobs program. The Multifiber Arrangement for example, is a costly method of keeping more people employed in the textile and apparel industry than would otherwise be the case. The consumer cost per job saved as a result of trade restrictions can be calculated by dividing the total cost of protection to the consumer (due to the higher prices that they pay) by the number of jobs that protection maintains in the industry. In the textile and apparel industry, for example, trade restrictions cost consumers about $24 billion annually and prevent the loss of roughly 170,000 jobs in the industry. To preserve one job in the textile and apparel industry, therefore, consumers pay $140,000 a year.[28] This is a stiff price for society to pay merely to keep workers employed in relatively low-wage occupations. The cost per job saved is even higher in the industries typically associated with high-paying manufacturing jobs, such as the machine tool industry ($350,000 per job) or the sugar industry ($600,000 per job).

This general finding—industries that compete against imports tend to be low-wage—has two important exceptions: steel and automobiles. Wages are high in these two industries, and yet they confront competition from imports and are relatively unsuccessful in exporting.[29]

---

[28] Hufbauer and Elliot 1994, 12–13.

[29] As Katz and Summers (1989, 264) note, "the widely cited examples of automobiles and steel, where very high wage industries face substantial import penetration and

Not coincidentally, they also have strong labor unions. Could protecting these unionized manufacturing industries be justified on the basis of preserving high-wages jobs? Some researchers suggest yes, arguing that the existence of wage premiums in such industries justifies government support.[30]

But the case for protecting these industries to preserve the wage premium is extremely dubious. First, it not even clear that these wage premiums, which are the large unexplained variation in the interindustry wage structure and which some economists attribute to labor market rents, should be explained on that basis.[31] If the variation is unexplained, we cannot be certain of what it represents, which makes it a questionable target for intervention. Second, even if workers in certain industries earn a wage premium, the case for promoting those industries depends on those premiums being taken as given. If instead the wage premium is determined by the behavior of labor unions, then using protection to promote the industry might enhance the union's ability to raise wages above the competitive level and exacerbate the wage premium without significantly increasing employment.

Unions strive to attain a combination of higher wages and greater employment for their members. If imports are restricted and the demand for steelworkers increases as domestic firms expand their pro-

---

are almost completely unable to export, appear to be atypical. As a rule export-intensive industries are the ones that have substantial wage premiums."

[30] Katz and Summers (1989, 264) argue that this generally would imply export promotion schemes, since "as a rule export-intensive industries are the ones that have substantial wage premiums," but the automobiles and steel industries are the atypical import-competing sectors in which wages are above average. They argue that the abnormally high wages reflect the high marginal product of workers, which they take to be indicative of an economic distortion that results in too few workers being employed in such industries. In principle, therefore, policies to increase employment in these industries would capture these rents for the economy, offset the underlying distortion, and thereby improve national welfare.

[31] The unexplained variation could reflect unobserved worker characteristics such as productivity. In an incisive comment published along with the Katz and Summers article (1989), Robert Topel notes that the sorting of individuals based on their productivity (e.g., people who work in the communications industry may be more productive than private household workers) and certain job characteristics (e.g., miners earn more than restaurant waiters) cannot be captured by statistical data and yet provides an alternative explanation for the high wages. There remains much debate about this point. See, for example, Gibbons and Katz 1992.

duction, the union can focus more on obtaining higher wages and less on increasing employment. Several studies show that this response, in which unions increase their pressure to raise wages, can ultimately undermine the policy's aim of increasing employment and capturing wage premiums.[32] In this case, a protectionist policy exacerbates rather than ameliorates the underlying distortion, the union's ability to raise wages above the competitive level. In this way, the policy negates the benefits that it aimed to capture and imposes costs on other industries.[33]

_____*Trade and Income Distribution*

Because exports increase the number of workers in relatively more productive, high-wage industries, and imports reduce the number of workers in relatively less productive, low-wage industries, the overall impact of trade in the United States is to raise average wages. Yet many people are concerned that international competition, particularly with low-wage developing countries, will unleash a "race to the bottom" in which wages are cut to match lower labor costs elsewhere.

Such fears are misguided because high American wages are based on the high productivity of U.S. workers. Foreign competition cannot take away the advantages that give rise to this high productivity, namely, the use of sophisticated technology, a substantial investment in education and human capital, and the many other advantages of operating in the U.S. market. Furthermore, the growth in a country's average wages is determined by the growth of a country's productivity. As figure 3.5 shows, the growth of worker compensation (deflated by the producer price index) tracks growth in productivity almost perfectly.[34] Foreign competition does not suppress this growth. Rather, as chapter 2

[32] See de Melo and Tarr 1993; and Swagel 2000.

[33] Dickens (1995) also points out that workers who will fill the high-wage vacancies are themselves likely to come from fairly high wages jobs. This undercuts the ability of activist policies to capture labor rents. There is also the issue of equity. By restricting imports, the government is implicitly forcing workers in other industries earning average wages or below to pay more for automobiles and steel products so that already highly paid workers in those industries can earn even more.

[34] Thus, workers have been compensated for the growth in output per worker in terms of the revenue received by firms. When compensation is deflated by the consumer price index, however, the growth in real wages is lower because consumer prices (which include items such as the cost of housing) have risen more rapidly than producer prices.

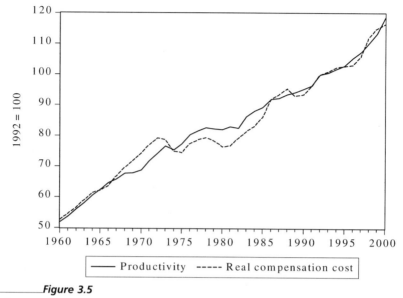

Figure 3.5

Labor productivity and labor compensation costs in the United States, 1960–2000. Productivity is output per hour of all persons in the business sector. Real compensation is compensation per hour divided by the producer price index of total finished goods. (Data from Council of Economic Advisers 2001, tables B-49, B-65.)

described, trade can foster growth in productivity through several channels.

Furthermore, firms that compete against imports cannot cut wages because they do not determine what those wages will be. Those firms must pay the prevailing market wage as determined by the productivity of workers. An increase in competition from imports does reduce employment in competing domestic industries, but does not drive down wages in them.[35] This makes sense: if a firm tried to cut wages, the best workers would leave because they have skills that give them oppor-

[35] In a careful study, Revenga (1992) examined the impact of changes in import prices (a good measure of import competition) on industry wages and employment. She found that industry employment is sensitive to import prices and that a rise (fall) in import prices would increase (reduce) industry employment. The relationship between import prices and industry wages was also positive, but the magnitude was minuscule. This evidence suggests that industries adjust to import competition primarily by altering employment, not wages.

tunities elsewhere in the economy. The least desirable workers would stay because they have no attractive alternatives. Rather than cut wages, firms adjust to competition by reducing employment, because then they can choose which workers to keep and which to lay off.

Although average wages are determined by the underlying attributes that make American workers productive, trade can affect the *distribution* of wages in an economy. This is implicit in what we have discussed: trade creates jobs in high-wage industries in which the United States exports (aircraft, machinery), and reduces jobs in low-wage industries in which the United States imports (apparel, footwear). In a classic article published in 1941, economists Wolfgang Stolper and Paul Samuelson connected the distribution of wages to the relative prices of various goods. They reached the unambiguous conclusion that some factors of production will receive an absolute gain as a result of free trade, while other factors will suffer an absolute loss. For example, if we consider only skilled and unskilled labor, a rise in the relative price of skill-intensive goods increases the real wage of skilled workers and decreases the real wage of unskilled workers. While the precise relationship between product prices and factor rewards depends upon many other factors, such as the degree to which labor can move between sectors, the essential conclusion is unmistakable: trade can have sharp consequences for income distribution.

The impact of trade on the wage distribution has always been a key source of the controversy surrounding trade. Some economic interests are bound to be harmed by free trade and therefore will seek to keep imports out of the domestic market. Because there are overall gains from trade, however, the benefits of free trade to some workers exceeds the losses to other workers. Given this imbalance, we might think it sensible to compensate the losers from free trade, making them just as well off as they were before, while still having the winners keep some of their gain. If such compensation actually took place, and assuming that compensation really buys off opposition to the policy, there should be no resistance to free trade based on economic interests. Yet, as we will discuss shortly, actual compensation is rarely sufficient to make up for all of the losses suffered by those adversely affected. So while free trade is beneficial to the economy overall, it carries some costs that may be concentrated in certain segments of society.

Has international trade contributed to the increasing wage inequality in the United States? Over the past three decades, the wage premium for college-educated workers relative to workers with less education (high school degree or dropout) has risen substantially and then leveled off. There is evidence of an absolute decline in the real wages of workers with very little education. The consensus of researchers seems to be that the increased demand for educated workers due to technological changes has produced the rising wage premium. By contrast, the role of trade in generating wage inequality appears to be modest.

How has this conclusion been reached? If trade had been driving the changes in relative wages in the United States during the 1980s, then Stolper and Samuelson's work suggests that the price of unskilled labor-intensive goods should have fallen relative to the price of skilled labor-intensive goods. But after closely examining the data, economists failed to detect any such decline.[36] In addition, they found that manufacturing firms were consistently choosing to employ more skilled labor relative to unskilled labor, despite the rising cost of hiring those skilled workers. This evidence is consistent with an increase in the demand for educated workers.[37]

Another way of looking at the question examines the quantities of imports of labor-intensive goods as a factor that may cause the displacement of less educated workers and reduce their wages. That is, the volumes of traded goods, rather than their prices, is the focus. This approach yields essentially the same conclusion. Examining the period from 1980 to 1995, one study finds that the wages of college graduates rose 21 percent relative to high school graduates. At the same time, trade and immigration accounted for only about 10 percent of this change.[38] The relatively small contribution of trade is related to the fact that imports of manufactured goods from developing countries, presumably the

---

[36] The pioneering work here was done by Lawrence and Slaughter (1993).

[37] These findings stimulated an enormous amount of research on the impact of trade on wages, but subsequent work has not fundamentally altered this basic conclusion. See the papers in Collins 1998 and Feenstra 2000 for an overview. Some economists have dissented from this general verdict. Feenstra and Hanson (2002), for example, link outsourcing to lower relative wages for production workers.

[38] Borjas, Freeman, and Katz 1997. However, they found that these factors are somewhat more important in explaining the wage gap between high school graduates and high school dropouts.

primary source of unskilled labor-intensive goods, rose from just 1.0 percent of GDP in 1970 to 3.2 percent in 1990, hardly a dramatic increase in light of the spectacular increase in the labor market return to education during this period.

Trade, then, does not appear to be primarily responsible for increased wage inequality. Evidence instead suggests that technological change has raised the demand for more highly educated workers. For example, the advent of ATM machines and personal computers reduced the demand for bank tellers and secretaries and increased the demand for skilled technicians and highly educated personnel. Whereas international trade would shift the demand for skills between sectors of the economy, skill-biased technical change would increase the demand for skilled workers in all sectors. One study found that nearly three-quarters of the overall shift in labor demand (for nonproduction workers) was a change in demand within industries rather than between industries.[39] Furthermore, the relative wage of educated workers in many developing countries has been increasing as well, a pattern that can be explained by skill-biased technical change but not by international trade.

But if trade has contributed even modestly to increased wage inequality, we can understand why those workers affected would oppose free trade. Survey evidence indicates that workers with less educational attainment, those whose wages have suffered the most, are also the most skeptical of the benefits of free trade.[40] Although these workers have a legitimate economic interest in preventing trade, it does not make sense to deal with their concerns by harming the overall economy. It is no more reasonable to help them by imposing barriers to trade than it would be to ban ATM machines or word processing so as to increase the demand for bank tellers and secretaries. This might help them in the short run, but would also reduce economic opportunities for others now and for their children in the future. The more constructive response is to encourage workers to make investments in education and, where possible, cushion the blow for those who are adversely affected by trade. One reason the debate over trade policy is never-ending, however, is that policies to cushion the blow are poorly designed.

[39] Berman, Bound, and Griliches 1994.
[40] Scheve and Slaughter 2001a.

_____Displaced Workers and Trade Adjustment Assistance

Although free trade is good for the economy as a whole, some workers will be displaced from their jobs in sectors that compete against imports. Without some policy to help these workers, opposition to free trade will always be politically potent. But how important a factor in workers' displacement has trade been? How should these displaced workers be helped? And do we need special policies for trade-displaced workers apart from workers displaced for other reasons?

In any rapidly changing economy, jobs are continuously created and eliminated. Changes in consumers tastes, domestic competition, growth in productivity, and technological innovation, in addition to international trade, all contribute to the churning of the labor market. It is virtually impossible to disentangle all of the reasons for job displacement because they are interdependent; for example, technological change may be stimulated by domestic or foreign competition. Yet to the extent that such attributions can be made, the available evidence suggests that trade is a small factor in the displacement of labor. According to the Bureau of Labor Statistics, import competition was responsible for only 1.5 percent of the total employment separations due to mass layoffs during the period 1996 to 1999.[41]

One of the biggest fears about NAFTA was that liberalizing trade with Mexico would cause a great loss of jobs in the United States. Yet the "great sucking sound" of jobs migrating south that Ross Perot so famously predicted has not been heard.

> By any reasonable measure, even the gross job turnover induced by the agreement has been slight. According to the Department of Labor, over the nearly four years from January 1994 through mid-August 1997, 220,000 workers had petitioned for adjustment assistance (cash and training allowances) under the legislation enacted when the trade deal was signed. Of this total, 136,000—an average of about 40,000 workers per year—

[41] Such data are available from the BLS website, http://www.bls.gov/datahome. htm. Displaced workers are those who face involuntary separations due to plant closings, mass layoffs, etc., and do not include those who lose their jobs due to temporary layoffs or voluntary separations.

were certified as eligible for assistance (under both the more general trade adjustment assistance program and that created as part of NAFTA). Even this figure overstates NAFTA's true impact, because to be eligible under both programs workers only need to show that "imports" have contributed to their losses, but not specifically as a result of NAFTA. By way of comparison, the gross monthly turnover of jobs in the United States exceeds 2 million. Since NAFTA, overall employment in the United States has risen by more than 10 million.[42]

Even when judged by the liberal standards of the NAFTA assistance program, only 2.4 percent of displaced workers on permanent layoff required assistance for being harmed by the agreement.[43]

Study after study has confirmed that the trade-induced turnover in U.S. labor markets is small in comparison with the overall turnover.[44] Trade is only slightly related to cross-industry variation in worker displacement rates. Although industries with high displacement rates are often import-sensitive, not all import-sensitive industries have high displacement rates. This conclusion should not come as a great surprise because, as noted in chapter 1, merchandise trade directly affects only 17

[42] Burtless et al. 1998, 57.

[43] Schoepfle 2000, 115. Another study estimates that the total employment impact in the United States from 1990 to 1997 due to imports from Mexico would be an average of thirty-seven thousand workers per year and from Canada fifty-seven thousand workers per year. They note that this is exceedingly small in an economy in which four hundred thousand workers separate from their jobs every *month* and that has created over two hundred thousand jobs per *month*. See Hinojosa-Ojeda et al. 2000.

[44] See Addison, Fox, and Ruhm 1995. Kletzer (1998b, 455) similarly concludes that "increasing foreign competition across industries accounts for a small share of job displacement" across industries because there are "high rates of job loss for industries with little trade." Davis, Haltiwanger, and Schuh (1995, 48–49) find that there is "no systematic relationship between the magnitude of gross job flows and exposure to international trade. . . On balance, the evidence is highly unfavorable to the view that international trade exposure systematically reduces job security." They also find that there is a higher rate of gross job destruction in very high import penetration industries, but that this disappears after controlling for industry wages. "This evidence indicates that import-intensive industries exhibit greater gross job flows because their workers have relative low levels of specific human capital—not because foreign competition subjects these industries to unusually large and volatile disturbances" (49). Simply put, workers who lack industry-specific skills are more apt to switch jobs and are less apt to remain in any given industry than workers who have industry-specific skills.

percent of the labor force that is employed in agriculture, mining, and manufacturing.

Even so, who are the displaced workers in import-competing industries and what is being done to help them? Workers in high import-share industries tend to be younger, have less education, and have shorter job tenure and are more likely to be female than workers in medium and low import-share industries.[45] The two most salient of these characteristics are gender and relatively low levels of education. These underlying characteristics tend to determine the labor market experiences of these workers, not the fact that they are employed in industries that compete against imports.

For example, workers displaced from high import-share industries are less likely to find new employment within a certain time period. This fact could be interpreted as indicating that the reemployment prospects of workers who have been laid off from industries that compete against imports are worse than average. But this correlation disappears once one controls for the higher proportion of female workers in those industries. In other words, women in general tend to have lower reemployment rates after being laid off any job. They may opt to leave the labor force, for example, or take more time off between jobs than men do. It is this characteristic, rather than anything special about import-competing industries per se, that accounts for the lower reemployment rate of workers displaced from high import-share industries. As one researcher concludes, "Trade-displaced workers may have more difficult labor market adjustments, but the source of the difficulty is their otherwise disadvantaged characteristics, not the characteristics of their displacement industry."[46]

What about the wage losses suffered by workers thrown out of work as a result of imports? As it turns out, workers displaced from industries in which import penetration was increasing rapidly had lower earnings losses than other displaced workers.[47] In general, the size of the earnings losses depends largely on how long the workers had been employed in the jobs from which they were displaced (the longer they were employed, the greater the earnings loss) and whether the workers found reemployment in the same industry or in a different industry (if reem-

---

[45] Kletzer 1998b, 450.
[46] Kletzer 2000, 375. See also Kletzer 1998b.
[47] Addison, Fox, and Ruhm 1995.

ployed in a different industry, then the earnings losses are greater). Because workers in import-sensitive sectors tend to be low-wage workers with shorter job tenures, workers displaced from industries that compete with imports generally have lower earnings losses than the average displaced worker.

The textile and apparel industry, in which employment declined nearly 40 percent from 1973 to 1996 (due to technological change, as well as imports), illustrates this phenomenon. As shown in tables 3.1 and 3.2, about 90 percent of textile and 86 percent of apparel workers in North Carolina who lost their job as a result of layoffs or plant closings between 1986 and 1991 were reemployed by 1992, a slightly lower percentage than those in other manufacturing industries. But in contrast to displaced workers in other manufacturing industries, who experienced an average 10 percent drop in wages after finding new employment, displaced apparel workers who found new jobs actually received higher wages, while textile workers experienced little change in their wages. The explanation is that apparel workers receive very low wages in the first place and that over 60 percent of laid-off apparel workers found reemployment in another manufacturing industry.

Table 3.3 presents more recent data for the entire United States. Workers displaced from jobs in the textile and apparel sector were much more likely to drop out of the labor force than workers in manufacturing overall. Particularly in the apparel industry, displaced workers tend to be older women who never earned a high school diploma, and therefore are more likely to have difficulty finding new employment or to leave the labor force. But because workers in the textile and apparel industry are paid much less than the average worker in manufacturing, those that later find employment are likely to earn the same or somewhat higher wages than they originally had.

_____*Table 3.1*
Labor Market Outcomes for Displaced Workers in North Carolina, 1986–1992

	Textiles	*Apparel*	*Other Manufacturing*
Percentage reemployed	90.6	86.4	93.9
Duration of unemployment (quarters)	2.1	2.3	1.9
Ratio of new to old wage	0.99	1.22	0.90

Source: Field and Graham 1997.

_____Table 3.2
Reemployment within Same or Another Industry, Displaced Workers in North Carolina, 1986–1992

	Reemployed in Same Industry		Reemployed in Another Industry	
	Proportion	New/Old Wage Ratio	Proportion	New/Old Wage Ratio
Textiles	50%	1.003	50%	0.969
Apparel	38%	1.049	62%	1.336
Other manufacturing	64%	0.972	36%	0.761
All other sectors	83%	1.026	17%	0.967

Source: Field and Graham 1997.

While most workers displaced from industries that compete against imports eventually find employment in the same industry, in related manufacturing industries, or in the nontraded service sector, they almost never find employment in export-oriented industries. A worker laid off from the apparel industry, for example, is extremely unlikely to find employment in the aircraft industry, because a different skill mix is required. This pattern creates a problem for policymakers: workers harmed by imports will not reap the benefits of new employment opportunities in export-oriented industries. Telling these workers that rising employment in export industries will offset the decline in their own is not likely to persuade them that free trade is a good thing.

The plight of displaced workers should not be trivialized; numerous studies have shown that their earnings losses are generally siz-

_____Table 3.3
Status (as of February 2000) of Workers Displaced from Full-Time Jobs between January 1997 and December 1999

	Labor Market Outcome (percentage distribution)			Of Those Reemployed			
	Reem-ployed	Unem-ployed	Not in Labor Force	At Lower Wage	At Same or Higher Wage	Ratio of New/ Old Wage	Median Weekly Earnings in Lost Job
Textiles	57	11	32	35%	64%	1.07	$363
Apparel	41	21	38	26%	74%	0.98	$288
Manufacturing	73	12	15	40%	60%	0.91	$632

Source: Displaced Workers Survey, Bureau of Labor Statistics, August 9, 2000 press release available at http://stats.bls.gov/newsrels.htm, and unpublished data from the Displaced Worker Survey.
Note: For workers over age of twenty with job tenure of at least three years.

able and persistent.[48] There is no debate about whether unemployed workers should receive government assistance. The question here is whether trade-displaced workers should benefit from a special government program beyond that given to other displaced workers. Special adjustment assistance for workers laid off as a result of imports has been justified on efficiency, equity, and political grounds, but unfortunately all three rationales are open to question. Such programs are also difficult to implement.

The efficiency rationale is that government assistance can speed up the process of adjusting to trade and thereby make it more efficient. This is doubtful on both theoretical and empirical grounds. In theory, the government should intervene to accelerate adjustment only if some market failure is associated with that process. The simple fact that the adjustment process sometimes operates slowly and with friction is insufficient grounds for intervention.[49] In addition, the empirical studies of displaced workers alluded to earlier generally suggest that the labor market experiences of those displaced from trade-sensitive industries are not much different from workers with similar characteristics who have been displaced from industries not sensitive to trade. Therefore, efficiency considerations do not seem to justify singling out trade-affected workers for more generous treatment than that extended to other displaced workers.

The equity rationale—fairness dictates that workers displaced by imports should be given special treatment—is also questionable. Workers may lose their jobs for any number of reasons: increasing domestic competition, fluctuations in the weather, changes in technology, shifts in consumer tastes, and so on. Even if it were possible to single out workers who have been dislocated for trade-related reasons, there is no

---

[48] Kletzer 1998a. Jacobson, LaLonde, and Sullivan (1993) dramatize the individual cost of displacement by focusing on long-tenure displaced workers in Pennsylvania in the early 1980s. Workers who had a long job tenure with previous employers, and therefore had accumulated substantial on-the-job experience, suffered earnings losses of about 25 percent for as long as five years after being laid off. This may be an extreme case for several reasons: the sample covers the worst recession in the United States since the Great Depression and covered only Pennsylvania, where workers in the iron and steel industry earned a substantial wage premium over other industries; and most displaced workers are not long-tenure but short-tenure workers. Nevertheless, the unmistakable point is that job losses can be costly for the individuals involved.

[49] See Mussa 1982.

compelling case for treating them differently from those who have lost their job for other reasons. In fact, it seems grossly unfair to provide a comfortable cushion for the workers displaced because of imports and not to those laid off because, say, higher interest rates cut into the demand for housing or automobiles. What is the reason for providing more generous compensation to the apparel worker in Georgia who loses a job to imports than to the typewriter assembler at Smith-Corona displaced because of computers or the Kellogg's worker laid off because General Mills begins producing tastier cereals?

The political argument for trade adjustment assistance is that it can mitigate the opposition to trade legislation by reducing the concentrated losses from liberalization. Ever since the Trade Expansion Act of 1962, Congress has ensured that trade adjustment assistance (TAA) has been a component of trade legislation. The original purpose of TAA was to compensate workers for loss of income, but since then, the goal has shifted toward other assistance, such as training and reemployment services.[50] TAA may have played a role in facilitating the passage of trade bills in 1962 and 1974, when Congress presumably included it in exchange for labor's support for (or muted opposition to) the trade legislation.[51] But there is little direct evidence since then that TAA has proven important in obtaining negotiating authority, in securing the passage of legislation, or in maintaining support for the system of open trade. The ability of TAA to buy the political support of labor groups has weakened due to the well-known shortcomings of the program.

TAA currently works in the following way. Unemployed workers can typically receive up to twenty-six weeks of unemployment insurance. If they exhaust this benefit and are declared eligible for TAA by the Department of Labor, they can then receive financial support under the trade readjustment allowance (TRA) for an additional fifty-two weeks, bringing total support to seventy-eight weeks (about a year and a half).[52] In the past, when the financial benefits of unemployment insurance

---

[50] The original 1962 legislation had little effect because workers were required to show that they were displaced as a result of a specific change in tariff. In 1974, this strict eligibility requirement was relaxed, and any worker displaced when imports were a contributing factor would be eligible for assistance.

[51] Destler 1998.

[52] This section draws on Schoepfle (2000). See Magee (2001) for an analysis of the factors behind the Labor Department's certification decisions.

were more generous, workers receiving TRA were apparently quite happy to take the benefits and wait for their old jobs to reappear, rather than seek retraining in an effort to adjust to the import competition. In 1988, therefore, Congress shifted the program's focus away from financial compensation and toward adjustment assistance by making enrollment in a government-certified training course a requirement for receiving TRA allowances.

A special NAFTA assistance program was also set up in 1994, relating only to those affected by trade with Canada and Mexico. Under this program, workers can receive benefits even as a result of trade diversion. In other words, if NAFTA diverts trade to Mexico in such as way that higher imports from Mexico substitute for lower imports from another country, workers may be eligible for assistance. As long as Mexican imports have increased, no causal link from NAFTA to the job loss is required. For example, when a sawmill in the state of Washington shut down because federal forest lands were declared off limits to save the spotted owl, the 135 workers affected were declared eligible for NAFTA-TAA because of timber imports from Canada subsequently increased.[53] A unique feature of the NAFTA program is that assistance is available not just to workers who lose their jobs as a result of imports, but also for those who lose their jobs if their employer shifts production to Canada or Mexico. Once again, participation in a government-approved training program is required for those receiving benefits.

In fiscal year 1997, the Labor Department spent about $90 million in TAA benefits (mainly training) and about $190 million in TRA assistance (extended unemployment insurance payments). These expenditures are a fraction of total spending on unemployment insurance. The program is inexpensive because few workers are actually involved in it; workers declared eligible for TRA do not necessarily collect benefits. In fact, only about 20 percent of workers who are declared eligible for some form of trade adjustment assistance actually take advantage of it.[54] This is because workers either get rehired or reemployed in the interim, receive union compensation, or do not wish to enroll in a training program.

While the budgetary outlays are not enormous, the TAA pro-

[53] Richards 1997.
[54] Schoepfle 2000, 109, 114.

gram is poorly designed. Workers provided with benefits over a longer period of time do not have an incentive to find a new job quickly. Unfortunately, prolonging the period of unemployment—as the TAA does—does not usually result in better labor market matches for those workers. The mandatory training programs have not addressed this problem because they do not work. As one study found, although TAA was well targeted in serving workers who were permanently displaced from their jobs and who experienced significant earnings losses, there was no evidence that training had a substantial positive impact on the earnings of the trainees. Those who went through the training program did not find better-paying jobs than those who did not attend the program.[55] This bleak assessment is not unique to TAA: there is little evidence that any government training program works well. After studying many such training programs, the OECD reached the sober conclusion that "broad training programs aimed at large groups of the unemployed have seldom proved a good investment, whether for society or for the program participants."[56]

Thus, as currently designed, TAA is clearly flawed. The program merely provides an incentive for trade-displaced workers to remain unemployed for a longer period of time than other displaced workers. This helps neither the workers nor economic efficiency. So how should the system be changed? The training requirement should clearly be dumped: workers do not like it anyway, and it provides no economic value. The benefits should not be too generous or tied to time out of work because doing so only prolongs the unemployment. Since it is not the case that a longer search leads to a better job match for workers, assistance programs should encourage quick reemployment.

One proposal is to provide time-limited wage insurance. Noting that the current TAA discourages work and fails to compensate for income losses, since payments cease when a worker takes a lower-paying

---

[55] Decker and Corson 1995.

[56] Organization for Economic Cooperation and Development 1994, 37. Heckman (1999, 106) is more blunt about government-sponsored job-training programs: "the evidence strongly suggests that investing in low-skilled, disadvantaged adult workers makes no economic sense." There is some evidence that programs targeted at specific groups, such as youths and women, may work better than others, but even here those who enter such programs seldom experience labor market outcomes that are much different from those who do not enter such programs.

job, time-limited earnings insurance provides compensation while preserving the incentive to find work.[57] Under this scheme, workers would receive compensation only when they became reemployed. If they took a job that paid a lower wage than before, they would receive some percentage of the gap between their previous wage and their new wage. If the compensation ratio of the insurance were 50 percent, for example, a worker displaced from a job paying two thousand dollars a month and accepting a new job paying one thousand dollars a month would receive government support of five hundred dollars a month. This support could be capped in terms of total payout and could be phased out gradually over a period of perhaps two years.[58] The support could also be targeted to older workers, who generally find it more difficult to find new jobs at their old wage.

Any proposal that seeks to provide compensation while preserving the incentive of workers to find employment is worth exploring. Such a scheme, however, would force a reexamination of the entire concept of unemployment insurance. A potential problem with earnings insurance is its high cost, although it could replace existing programs rather than be added to them. One researcher estimates that a two-year earnings insurance program would cost $1 billion. This is only about 5 percent of the cost of unemployment insurance during a recession and is just a fraction of the gains from trade. But a more expansive program could cost as much as $9 billion.[59]

Another potential problem with trade-related assistance is the inefficiency of any government program that attempts to redistribute income to a targeted group. The costs of administering a compensation program might well be much higher than the losses incurred by displaced workers.[60] Aside from the high costs of such a program, basing a

---

[57] Lawrence and Litan 1986.

[58] There is relatively little theoretical work on these questions. Brander and Spencer (1994) find it difficult to rank various compensation schemes in terms of their welfare effects, but suggest that a case can be made for providing time-limited compensation regardless of whether the displaced worker finds reemployment.

[59] Jacobson 1998, 515–16. Kletzer and Litan (2001) propose a program that would cost about $5 billion a year.

[60] Jacobson (1998, 476) argues that the "transaction costs associated with [compensation] are likely to be many times larger than the costs imposed on those adversely affected by change."

compensation program on past earnings runs the risk of trying to create a riskless society. Should the government insure against all losses that individuals incur in the labor market, particularly when the individuals themselves do not seem interested in purchasing such insurance?[61]

The lamentable conclusion is that there is no easy solution and no obvious government policy that can address all of the concerns. Trade adjustment assistance has not worked as promised, and may even be an impediment to economic efficiency. A broader government program to help displaced workers should be examined and might be a small price to pay to reduce anxieties about international trade and maintain political support for open markets. But even if such a program is affordable and gets the incentives right, there is absolutely no guarantee that demands for import barriers by labor groups in import-competing sectors (such as the steelworkers union) will diminish. Even if fully compensated for losing their job, these workers simply may not want to move to a different job in a different location when there is a chance they could stay where they are by stopping imports.

While there are many popular rationales for restricting trade, we have seen that none of the proposed solutions comes without a cost. An import tariff could increase the number of jobs in industries that compete against imports, but could also destroy jobs in export industries as well as downstream industries that rely on competitively priced intermediate goods. A trade deficit implies that the value of imports exceeds the value of exports, but also that the country is experiencing a net inflow of capital from abroad, which can have beneficial effects on domestic investment. Any analysis of trade policy must appreciate these oft-ignored indirect effects. And yet, as the next two chapters point out, trade policy is inherently political and rarely determined by purely economic considerations.

[61] As Jacobson (1998, 475) notes, "Neither society at large nor members of the risk pool potentially affected by costly job loss appear willing to pay for such [earnings] insurance. . . . Individuals adversely threatened by trade and other factors appear to lack the willingness to pay for actuarially fair insurance," although this may be due in part to the existence of government compensation programs.

4

Relief from Foreign Competition: Antidumping and the Escape Clause

We have seen how trade policies aimed at reducing imports also reduce exports and employment elsewhere in the economy. Yet import restrictions are often justified as a way of providing relief to industries suffering from "unfair" foreign competition. Antidumping laws, which provide for tariffs on unfairly low-priced imports, have become the primary instrument for addressing such concerns. This chapter examines the U.S. antidumping laws and asks whether they provide a remedy for unfair trade, or are merely a mechanism for protecting an industry from imports. We will also look at the escape clause procedure, which can provide industries with temporary relief for imports even if they do not face the threat of unfair trade.

Unfair Trade: Subsidies and Dumping

We are all familiar with the claim that imports cost jobs. But many people are equally afraid that American industries are being harmed by unfair foreign trade practices. These include export subsidies and the dumping of goods at low prices that undermine the sales of U.S. firms. To counter such practices, the United States enforces several "fair trade" laws that allow import tariffs to be imposed. For example, when a foreign government subsidizes its exports to the United States, the subsidy is considered to be an actionable unfair trade practice if it injures domestic producers. Of course, from a strictly economic point of view, an importing country might well benefit from receiving subsidized goods. Even if the subsidy harms domestic producers, the subsidy allows the importing country to purchase imports at a lower price, thanks to the generosity of foreign taxpayers. By improving the terms of trade, the foreign subsidy adds to the domestic gains from trade. For example, domestic oil producers would be understandably angry if the OPEC decided to subsidize oil exports to the United States, but the country as a whole would probably welcome the lower gas prices that would follow.

But such subsidies are not desirable from the standpoint of the world economy. For one thing, such subsidies cut into the exports of countries that have a natural comparative advantage in those products, and so distort the world's allocation of resources. Subsidies also generate political friction among trading partners, each viewing the other's government as putting its finger on the scales of international competition to tip the outcome toward its own favored producers.[1]

For these reasons, the United States led the effort to draw up an Agreement on Subsidies and Countervailing Measures in the Uruguay Round of multilateral trade negotiations in 1994. The subsidies agreement establishes rules on permissible types of subsidies and tries to ensure that such subsidies will not distort trade. Under the agreement, export subsidies and subsidies to industries that compete against imports are prohibited in principle, but subsides related to research and development, regional development, and environmental compliance purposes are permissible.

In the United States, domestic firms have legal recourse against subsidized imports. The remedy takes the form of tariffs known as countervailing duties (CVDs). Domestic firms initiate the legal process by filing a petition with the Department of Commerce and the U.S. International Trade Commission (ITC) alleging that imports have been subsidized by a foreign government. If Commerce determines that the imports have been subsidized and if the ITC rules that the domestic industry has been injured as a result of the imports, tariffs of the magnitude of the subsidy margin (as determined by Commerce) will be imposed.

In recent years the CVD process has been rarely invoked by domestic firms. Are foreign countries subsidizing fewer of their exports to the United States? As a result of the multilateral subsidy agreement,

[1] The United States, it should be noted, provides such export subsidies through the Export-Import Bank, which extends concessional loan guarantees and export credit insurance to U.S. exporters. Boeing and General Electric receive the bulk of the funding support.

perhaps so. But the more likely explanation is that domestic firms have found other ways to prevent such exports from entering the U.S. market. And in fact domestic firms find it much easier to obtain protection by accusing foreign firms of "dumping" in the U.S. market than by proving the existence of foreign subsidies.

Dumping has been deemed an unfair trade practice by country authorities and world trade agreements, and the antidumping law is intended to combat it. Yet the gap between the rhetoric and the reality of antidumping trade policy is simply enormous. Dumping sounds awful, as though foreign goods are being unloaded on America's docks and priced below cost to force domestic firms out of the market. But under the law, dumping simply means that a foreign exporter charges a lower price in the U.S. market than it does in its home market. This is nothing more than price discrimination. If the foreign exporter is found guilty, the United States can impose import duties to offset the difference.

Figure 4.1 shows the annual number of antidumping investigations since 1974. During the 1990s, five antidumping cases were initiated for every CVD case. The growth in antidumping dates from around 1980, when authority over the law was transferred from the Treasury Department (which was indifferent to such cases) to the Commerce Department (which took them up with great enthusiasm). The number of investigations fluctuates depending upon such factors as the business cycle, the foreign exchange value of the dollar, and the number of petitions filed by the steel industry, the most active user of the law. But from the standpoint of domestic firms seeking protection from imports, antidumping is where the action is.

While the details of antidumping (AD) are quite complex, it is important to understand why these laws have become such a nuisance.[2] The AD process is activated when a domestic industry, represented by an industry association or in some cases just a single firm, files a petition with the Commerce Department and the ITC. The legal fees associated with filing a simple AD case typically cost the petitioners about $250,000, although a more complex case can run about $1 million or more.[3]

---

[2] There is now a voluminous literature that finds fault with the antidumping laws. See, for example, Boltuck and Litan 1991 and Finger 1993.

[3] This is according to a U.S. International Trade Commission (1995, 4–3) survey

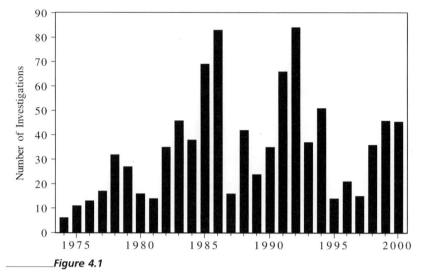

_____Figure 4.1_
Annual number of antidumping investigations, 1974–2000. (Data from Import
Administration, U.S. Department of Commerce, http://www.ita.doc.gov.)

The role of the Commerce Department is to determine if dumping has occurred and, if so, to calculate the dumping margin. Specifically, Commerce ascertains whether a foreign exporter made sales in the
United States at prices that are at "less than fair value." Sales are less than
fair value if the export price, the price charged in the U.S. market, is less
than the so-called normal value. The normal value is determined one of
three ways: the price charged by the foreign exporter in home market
sales, the price it charged in third country sales, or by constructed value,
which is an estimate of what the price should have been based on the
costs of production plus administrative expenses and a profit margin.
The dumping margin is simply the difference between the export price
and this determined normal value.

After receiving a petition, Commerce almost always rules that
dumping has occurred. From 1980 to 1992, Commerce ruled that dump-

---

of petitioners. The petitioners must have legal standing to file a petition. In 1999, for example, Commerce rejected an antidumping petition by a group of Texas oil producers against
Saudi Arabia, Mexico, Venezuela, and Iraq on the grounds that the petitioners did not
represent the entire industry.

_____*Table 4.1*
Antidumping Margins by Calculation Method, 1995–1998

Calculation Method	Determinations (Affirmative Only)	Average Dumping Margin (Affirmative Only)
U.S. prices to home market prices	4	4.00%
	(2)	(7.36%)
Constructed value	20	25.07%
	(14)	(35.70%)
Nonmarket economy	47	40.03%
	(28)	(67.05%)
"Facts available"	36	95.58%
	(36)	(95.58%)
Total	141	44.68%
	(107)	(58.79%)

Source: Lindsey 2000, 12.
Note: Not all methods are shown.

ing had occurred in 93 percent of all cases. And the dumping margins were large: the average AD duty imposed from 1991 to 1995 was a whopping 56.8 percent.[4] However, the average dumping margin varies widely depending upon the method used to calculate the normal value. As table 4.1 shows, during the 1995 to 1998 period, the average margin on (affirmative) cases that compared the U.S. price to the exporter's home market price was just 7.36 percent. When Commerce compared the U.S. price to its constructed value, the average margin was 35.70 percent. In cases involving nonmarket economies, such as China and the former Soviet Union, the average margin was about 67 percent. In cases using "facts available," in which Commerce essentially accepted the data presented by the petitioner, the average margin was nearly 96 percent. Because of a greater reliance on the constructed value method over the price comparison method, the average dumping margin has steadily increased over time.[5]

When U.S. prices are compared to actual foreign market prices, rather than to some constructed value, the dumping margins appear to

[4] Congressional Budget Office 1994, 50; 1998, 82.

[5] The average antidumping duty imposed during the 1981–83 period was 22 percent, while that in the 1993–95 period was 60.6 percent (Congressional Budget Office 1998, 25).

be quite low. Yet even when a foreign firm charges exactly the same price in the U.S. market as in its home market, dumping can be found to exist. This is because Commerce compares the average of the foreign firm's home price to the prices charged on individual sales in the United States. If any *individual* U.S. price is below the *average* home market price, which must be the case if there is any movement in the prices over time, then dumping is found to occur. Instances in which the U.S. price exceeds the foreign price are ignored. This not only guarantees a finding of dumping, but artificially inflates the dumping margin.[6]

In contrast, something is clearly amiss when a method other than the price comparison approach is employed. When Commerce is unable to collect enough data on the exporter's home market prices, it may resort to the constructed value method. When Commerce undertakes a constructed value calculation, it attempts to estimate the foreign exporter's costs of production plus an allowance for administrative, selling, and general expenses and profits. Prior to 1995, U.S. antidumping practice was to augment the estimated costs of production by at least 10 percent for administrative expenses and at least 8 percent for profits.[7] Since the Uruguay Round agreement, Commerce cannot tack on these arbitrary amounts to the estimated costs, but must use the actual administrative expenses and the actual profit, when available. However, there is still room for Commerce to use questionable numbers and thereby raise the dumping margin.

When dealing with nonmarket economies, such as China and the states of the former Soviet Union, where prices may not be market determined, Commerce estimates production costs using wage rates and other factor costs from a surrogate country of similar level of economic development. For example, in estimating China's costs of farming crawfish in 1997, Commerce used the cost of fish caught at sea in "comparable" economies with freer markets, such as India, Pakistan, Sri Lanka, and Indonesia, and took transport costs within China from a 1994 newspaper report on trucking costs in India. It is no surprise that this method leads to unusually large dumping margins. In this case, Commerce an-

---

[6] The Trade and Tariff Act of 1984 includes a provision that allows the method of averaging to be applied to the U.S. price as well, but Commerce has evidently chosen not to exercise this option. See Baldwin and Moore 1991, 260.

[7] Congressional Budget Office 1994, 31.

nounced dumping margins ranging from 85 to 201 percent, implying that Chinese crawfish farmers sold their product for just one-third to two-thirds of production costs.[8] In another case using the constructed value method, Commerce once determined (with apparent precision) that natural bristle paintbrushes from China were sold at 351.9 percent less than their fair value and imposed tariffs of the same amount.

The International Trade Commission's role in an antidumping case is to determine if the domestic industry has suffered or is threatened with "material injury" as a result of the less-than-fair-value imports. The definition of material injury,' according to the law, is "harm which is not inconsequential, immaterial, or unimportant."[9] Only the harm to the competing industry is considered, not the harm or injury to consumers or other domestic industries that result from the imposition of import duties. Yet the injury determination is a more difficult hurdle for the domestic petitioner to clear because of the injury standard itself and because the ITC is a quasi-independent agency (as opposed to Commerce, which is typically an advocate of the domestic industry in the process). Still, the ITC ruled affirmatively in 66 percent of final determinations during the period 1980 to 1992.[10] Economic factors, such as changes in the industry's output, employment, and capacity utilization, are the main determinants of a favorable injury finding. But political factors, such as whether the industry is a constituent of the chairman of the ITC's congressional oversight committee, also appear to matter.[11]

If dumping is found to exist and the domestic industry is deemed to have suffered material injury, then antidumping duties are imposed. As of June 30, 2000, the United States had 300 AD duty orders in effect, 41 percent of them on iron and steel products.[12] AD orders existed on such narrowly defined goods as frozen concentrated orange juice from Brazil, cotton shop towels from Bangladesh and China, oil

[8] Passell 1997.

[9] U.S. House of Representatives 1997, 454.

[10] Congressional Budget Office 1994, 50.

[11] See the research by Moore (1992), Baldwin and Steagall (1994), and Hansen and Prusa (1997).

[12] By contrast, there were only 46 U.S. countervailing duty orders in effect. In terms of antidumping measures, the European Union had 190 in place, and South Africa had 104, India had 91, Canada had 88, and Mexico had 80. World Trade Organization 2001, 65.

_____**Table 4.2**
Trade Effects of Antidumping Duties

AD Duties	Import Volume	Import Price (Unit Value)
Over 50 percent	−73%	33%
Between 20% and 50%	−22%	2%
Under 20%	−16%	−10%
Nonaffirmative decision	−3%	3%

Source: U.S. International Trade Commission 1995, 3–9.

Note: Figures are the year following the intiation of AD investigation as a percentage of year prior to initiation. Import price effect does not include the AD duties.

country tubular goods from Canada, fresh salmon from Chile and Norway, paper clips from China, large newspaper printing presses from Germany, stainless steel wire rod from France and elsewhere, fresh kiwi fruit from New Zealand, pasta from Italy and Turkey, aspirin from Turkey, and a host of other products.[13]

What happens when AD duties are imposed? Not surprisingly, imports fall sharply. Looking at table 4.2, we can see that imports subject to AD duties of over 50 percent fell 73 percent in volume and rose 33 percent in price, on average, from the year before the petition to the year after the petition. Imports subject to AD duties in the 25 to 50 percent range fell 22 percent in volume and rose 2 percent in price. The ITC study also found that developing countries were disproportionally harmed by AD duties: the quantity of their imports tended to fall over twice as much as imports from developed countries.

To a large extent, however, imports from countries not subject to the AD duties fill the void left by those smacked with the AD duties. This is because AD duties are only imposed on imports from countries named in the petition, leaving the market open to others who can produce similar products. Table 4.3 indicates that while imports from countries affected by the AD duties fell by 32 percent, imports of the same product from countries not subject to the duties rose 24 percent. Because of this effect, antidumping petitions are often filed sequentially to squash the imports that arise from other sources as a result of the initial antidumping action.[14]

[13] For updated statistics and information on the U.S. antidumping administration, see http://www.ita.doc.gov/.

[14] Prusa 1997.

_____Table 4.3
Evidence of Trade Diversion in Antidumping Actions

	Import Volume	Import Price (Unit Value)
Affirmative, subject country	−32%	5%
Affirmative, nonsubject country	24%	−5%
Nonaffirmative, subject country	−24%	4%
Nonaffirmative, nonsubject country	19%	−3%

Source: U.S. International Trade Commission 1995, 3–15.

Note: Affirmative denotes cases in which AD duties were imposed; *subject* denotes imports subject to the duties, and *nonsubject* denotes imports from other countries or firms not subject to the duties.

For example, Micron Technology, a producer of dynamic random access memory (DRAM) computer chips in Boise, Idaho, filed an AD petition against DRAM imports from Japan in 1985. After the imposition of restrictions on Japanese exports, foreign DRAM production shifted to South Korea, so Micron filed an AD petition against Korean producers in 1991. After Korean exports were similarly restricted, Taiwanese producers entered the market, so Micron filed an AD petition against DRAM exports from that country in 1998. The story is similar in the case of salmon. Antidumping duties were imposed against imports of fresh salmon from Norway in 1991. After Chile began to develop its fishing industry and filled the void left by the Norwegians, they too were hit with AD duties in 1998.

The simplest way for domestic petitioners to avoid this problem is to file multiple petitions against several sources. When the Coalition for Fair Preserved Mushroom Trade filed an AD petition concerning imports of preserved mushrooms in 1998, for example, they targeted imports from Chile, China, India, and Indonesia all at the same time. In 1992, the steel industry filed petitions against virtually all flat-rolled steel products imported from twenty-one countries.

Congress facilitated the move toward multiple filings by changing the law in 1984. Prior to that time, the injury determination was conducted on a country-by-country basis, even if multiple petitions were filed. After the 1984 change, the ITC had to consider the combined impact of imports from all named countries on the domestic industry. The cumulation provision is estimated to have raised the probability of an affirmative decision by 20 to 30 percent, thereby changing the ITC's determination from negative to positive in one-third of such cases.[15] This, in turn, has given petitioners an additional incentive to file petitions against multiple countries.

Sometimes petitioners exclude certain countries from petitions as a matter of corporate strategy. For example, in 1994, the Maui Pineapple Company in Hawaii filed an AD petition against imports of canned pineapples from Thailand, resulting in the imposition of AD duties up to 51 percent, depending on the company. Thailand's canned pineapple exports to the United States fell from $101 million in 1993 to $51 million in 1997. Over the same period, imports of canned pineapple from Indonesia jumped from $9 million to $51 million because that country's exports were not subject to AD duties. But Maui did not file an AD petition against Indonesian imports because at that time it was forming a joint venture with one of the country's largest pineapple producers. Similarly, in 1994 Bic filed a petition alleging that disposable lighters from China and Thailand were being dumped in the U.S. market, but did not include Mexico in the petition because Bic had a factory there.[16]

It is important to note that trade diversion occurs even in cases where the final ITC injury decision is negative and no duties are imposed. Even when the domestic industry was found not to have suffered injury, imports from countries that had been the target of the case fell 24 percent on average, while imports from countries not targeted rose 19 percent. Thus, simply filing an antidumping petition can reduce imports from targeted sources even if duties are not imposed. According to one study, when a petition is ultimately rejected, imports from the sources named in the petition fall by about 15 to 20 percent, whereas if the petition is accepted, imports fall about 50 to 70 percent. A reason for this "chilling effect" on imports is the uncertainty surrounding the AD process: if dumping is found, domestic importers will be liable for the payment of dumping duties after Commerce issues its preliminary determination. To minimize their potential financial exposure, importers quickly stop purchasing from the foreign suppliers named in the petition. There is also an "investigation effect" on imports when an antidumping petition is filed: before Commerce has even made a prelimi-

---

[15] Hansen and Prusa 1996.
[16] *Rushford Report*, September 1999, 3.

nary determination about dumping, import volumes fall and prices rise by about one-half of the full effect of imposing duties.[17]

_The Costs of Antidumping

Despite the apparent ease with which domestic firms can obtain some form of protection under the antidumping laws, only a tiny fraction of total U.S. imports are covered by AD duties. AD and CVD orders covered just 1.8 percent of all imports in 1991.[18] Given this relatively small figure, does the antidumping process really matter?

There are several reasons why antidumping continues to merit close scrutiny. First, these tariffs quickly add up. The net welfare cost of AD and CVD actions in the United States was a whopping $4 billion in 1993.[19] This puts them second only to the Multifiber Arrangement as the most costly of all U.S. import restrictions.

These costs are only going to mount over time as more cases are filed. This is because AD duties are hard to remove once they are imposed. The mean duration of AD measures terminated in the period from 1980 to 1994 was over nine years in the case the United States, as opposed to five years in the European Union.[20] One of the few reforms of AD actions in the Uruguay Round was to introduce a sunset rule starting in 1995. This required that all AD duties be terminated after five years unless a review finds that this would lead to a recurrence of dumping and injury. Yet Commerce is unlikely to revoke an antidumping order over the objections of the domestic industry. In 180 sunset cases considered between July 1998 and December 1999, the ITC revoked AD or CVD duties only 31 percent of the time.[21]

Second, the coverage figures understate the harm in antidumping actions. In the past, relatively few petitions actually resulted in the imposition of AD duties, but the very threat of their existence has an

---

[17] See Prusa 2001; and Staiger and Wolak 1994.

[18] U.S. International Trade Commission 1995, 4-1.

[19] Gallaway, Blonigen, and Flynn 1999. In an earlier study for 1991, prior to the filing of many petitions by the steel industry and excluding some cases, the ITC itself found that the economy-wide cost of antidumping actions was about $1.6 billion (U.S. International Trade Commission 1995).

[20] Congressional Budget Office 1998, 85.

[21] Moore 1999. See http://www.ia.ita.doc.gov/sunset.

effect on the market. For example, when an exporter is confronted with the prospect of potentially severe duties that exporters from other countries will not have to endure, targeted exporters have a powerful incentive to negotiate some sort of export restraint agreement that will allow them to avoid the imposition of duties. In many cases, the foreign exporter reaches either a suspension agreement with Commerce (and approved by the petitioner) that terminates the petition or concludes a side deal directly with the petitioner who then withdraws the petition. As the Congressional Budget Office noted, "Almost 70 percent of these cases filed from 1980 through 1988 led to restrictive outcomes, but since 45 percent were superceded by quotas or suspension agreements, less than 25 percent of cases led to antidumping or countervailing duties."[22] Thus, even when no duties are imposed, antidumping can result in trade restrictions. The quantity of imports falls by the same margin in cases that are settled as those in which duties are imposed, although the import price does not rise as much in settled cases.[23]

Prior to 1995, a voluntary export restraint could be negotiated in lieu of antidumping duties. Since the Uruguay Round agreement, however, such "gray area" trade restrictions are forbidden, and now suspension agreements are less frequent. However, the Uruguay Round does allow "price undertakings," in which the exporters agree to minimum export prices in order to avoid the imposition of duties. This can also promote a collusive outcome.[24]

Finally, the antidumping process is so heavily biased against foreign firms that it is prone to abuse and manipulation by domestic firms. The problem is not that the process is overtly political and subject to political influence, although that problem can arise in some high-profile cases. Rather, AD rules are intentionally stacked in favor of the domestic petitioner, both in reaching a conclusion that dumping has occurred and in the size of the dumping margin. Even the Congressional Budget Office notes that the Commerce Department "effectively serves as investigator, prosecutor, judge, and jury in dumping and subsidy determinations."

---

[22] Congressional Budget Office 1994, 59.

[23] See Prusa 2001. Prusa (1992) analyzes this phenomenon and concludes that antidumping measures are a mechanism for promoting tacit collusion between the domestic industry and its import competitors.

[24] See Moore 2000.

And although it should be neutral in these roles, Commerce is "actually an advocate of one of the parties to the case."[25]

The antidumping process is riddled with subtle tricks and arbitrary biases that invariably favor the domestic petition, making it ironic that they are a part of the "fair trade" laws. The application of AD measures often hinges on a narrow technicality, such as the definition of the relevant industry. In the case of cut flowers from Columbia, the ITC initially ruled that the domestic industry was not materially injured. After Commerce later accepted petitions maintaining that each individual flower species was a different "industry" (the rose "industry," the chrysanthemum "industry," etc.), the ITC then made an affirmative injury ruling. In the case of frozen concentrated orange juice, Commerce ruled that fresh oranges and industrial concentrate orange juice are "like products" even though the markets and pricing for the two products are quite different.[26]

Even the Commerce Department's Office of Inspector General was critical of the way that the Department's Office of Import Administration handled the eighty-four antidumping and countervailing duty petitions filed by the steel industry in June 1992. The Inspector General said that the agency "adopted several controversial and confusing policies that undermined the principles of transparency and consistency . . . [and were] not only inconsistent with past practice, but were also applied inconsistently from one case to the next." The report added that Import Administration "applied policies that made reporting more onerous for respondents, caused confusion among analysts, and made IA's decisions appear arbitrary, even to its own staff."[27]

And if there was not already sufficient incentive for firms to file antidumping petitions, Senator Robert Byrd (D-W.Va.) opened the door to more mischief in late 2000. Senator Byrd slipped into an agricultural appropriations bill a provision that hands over all the revenue from antidumping duties to the petitioning industry. This was done at the behest of the steel industry, and, although the Clinton Administration opposed the measure, the president signed the bill for its other provisions. Thus, petitioning firms will not only be able to charge domestic consumers

[25] Congressional Budget 1994, 41.
[26] Finger 1993.
[27] U.S. Department of Commerce 1993, 20.

higher prices for their products, but will receive a check from the government for a share of the tariff revenues. The Byrd provision encourages domestic firms to become bounty hunters and start filing AD petitions to receive tariff revenue payments from the government. This provision will cost taxpayers about $200 million a year in addition to costs that antidumping actions already inflict on consumers. Furthermore, this provision almost surely constitutes an illegal subsidy under world trade rules and also undercuts America's standing to persuade other countries to open their markets.

In other countries, antidumping is a widely criticized feature of U.S. trade policy. Yet the United States has adamantly refused to put antidumping reform on the agenda for future trade negotiations until the WTO ministerial conference in Doha, Qatar, in November 2001. This change is partly because the antidumping genie is out of the bottle: the United States is increasingly becoming a target as well as a user of these actions. Whereas antidumping actions were once instituted mainly by the United States, European Union, Australia, and Canada, now developing countries (such as Mexico, Argentina, South Africa, and others in Asia) have copied them and have become aggressive users of these measures against exports from developed countries.[28]

While the Congressional Budget Office did not find systematic evidence prior to 1995 that other countries were singling out American firms for antidumping enforcement in retaliation for AD actions, evidence did "lend some credence to fears that U.S. policy may be starting to come back to haunt U.S. exporters as other countries follow its lead."[29] Growing anecdotal evidence points to this conclusion. For example, Micron Technology, previously mentioned as the DRAM producer who filed a series of petitions, was itself accused of dumping memory chips in Taiwan shortly after it succeeded in getting AD duties imposed on Taiwanese exports. And even though the ITC rejected a petition accusing Mexico of dumping emulsion styrenebutadine rubber, the U.S. petitioner soon faced charges by its Mexican competitor of dumping the same product in that country. If antidumping actions remains unchecked, such retaliatory cases can only be expected to multiply in coming years.[30]

---

[28] Prusa 2001.

[29] Congressional Budget Office 1998, xiv.

[30] *Rushford Report,* April 1999, 7.

_____*Is Antidumping Defensible?*

The antidumping process involves many arbitrary judgments and is subject to abuse. Can any intellectual defense be mustered in favor of the AD laws? The problem is that price discrimination, charging different prices in different markets, is a normal business practice and an accepted feature of domestic competition. Exporters often find that competition is more intense in the international market than in their home market, where they have a more secure position with domestic consumers. Therefore, exporters have to offer price discounts in foreign markets. On economic grounds, the fact that a firm might charge two different prices in two different markets should not be considered unfair or a problem unless it somehow harms competition (such as through anticompetitive actions or predatory practices) or reflects a market-distorting policy. If geared toward preventing these actions, then antidumping policy could have some merit as a means of preserving competition or correcting alleged market distortions.

Unfortunately, the antidumping laws are not written to identify and respond to such situations, giving the impression that the laws exist only to protect domestic firms if they can jump through a few bureaucratic hoops. For example, the antidumping laws might be worthwhile if they prevented predatory pricing by foreign exporters. Predatory pricing would occur when an exporter prices its goods below cost in an effort to eliminate American producers and achieve a monopoly position. Firms engaging in predatory pricing must be prepared to incur substantial losses initially and then more than recoup those losses through the future exercise of monopoly position. But this makes sense only if the firm can effectively knock out most of its competitors in the United States and in other countries. Were the Bangladesh shop towel producers trying to eliminate their foreign rivals and achieve a monopoly position? Were the flower growers from Colombia trying to do the same? Most foreign exporters want to receive as high a price as possible from their sales rather than wipe out their competition, which must strike most firms as an impossible objective.

In fact, in the overwhelming majority of AD cases, such predatory motives can be ruled out as utterly implausible. One researcher examined the structural characteristics of every one of the 282 industries involved in every dumping case in the 1980s in which duties were imposed or in which the case was suspended or terminated. To isolate the cases in which predatory pricing might be considered plausible, she first eliminated all cases in which the industry in the United States and in the challenged country was relatively unconcentrated. These were excluded on the grounds that barriers to entry in such industries are probably not substantial. And without barriers to entry, anticompetitive practices are unlikely to exist because even if the firm drives rivals out of business, it cannot raise prices to finance the losses sustained in the price war if other firms can simply reenter the market once prices go up.

The researcher also eliminated cases in which there were multiple exporters from a single country or from several countries, reasoning that successful collusion by such firms would be unlikely and that there are enough firms to preserve competition. Finally, she eliminated all cases in which the import penetration level was not significant, or in which import growth was not rapid, since the imports would be unlikely to create market power if they did not comprise a large share of the U.S. market. In the end, only thirty-nine cases were left, just 14 percent of all those considered, in which the industries were characterized by substantial domestic or foreign concentration. Of the remaining thirty-nine cases in which the preconditions for predation did exist, we cannot say for sure that predation was in fact a motive, only that it could not be ruled out.

The antidumping statue is not employed to prevent predatory conduct or preserve competition, but simply to protect the domestic industry from foreign competition—at the expense of domestic consumers, of course. One legal scholar concludes that while the antidumping laws were "originally marketed as anti-predation measures, they are now written in a way that compels the administering authorities to impose antidumping measures in a vastly broader class of cases—all instances in which dumping causes material harm to competing domestic firms."[31] A ITC commissioner once tried to shift the interpretation toward an antipredation remedy. But petitioners appealed to the U.S. Court of International Trade, which ruled that focusing on competition effects "seems to assume that the purpose of the antidumping statute is merely

[31] Sykes 1998, 29–30.

to prevent a particular type of 'injury to competition' rather than merely 'material injury' to industry."

Some antidumping advocates claim that foreign firms have a protected home market in which they can earn high profits, from which they can subsidize export sales. In their view, this counts as a market-distorting practice that antidumping should attempt to remedy. But as one antidumping critic aptly notes, "the [antidumping] law lacks any mechanism for determining whether the prices practices it condemns as unfair have any connection to market-distorting policies abroad."[32] The law does not distinguish cases in which there may be a sanctuary market effect, or ask if dumping is at all related to market distortions. If anti-dumping advocates are sincere in their desire for an antipredation remedy that is not simply protectionism, they should be willing to scrap the current law and include an explicit test for the protected sanctuary home market that is often alleged to exist.

The fundamental problem with antidumping, however, is not simply the way the law is administered. The problem is that antidumping laws are written with the presumption that price discrimination is a problem. But there is nothing inherently harmful or anticompetitive about price discrimination. Price discrimination is an accepted feature of domestic competition. It would be surprising if domestic prices were *exactly* the same as an exporter's home price.[33] In addition, the government rarely undertakes direct price comparisons when making a dumping determination, but more frequently makes some arbitrary calculations about production costs. The result is that "dumping is whatever you can get the government to act against under the dumping law."[34] The antidumping laws are simply a popular means by which domestic firms can stifle foreign competition under the pretense of "fair trade."

---

[32] Lindey 2000, 1.

[33] "In the typical antidumping investigation, the Commerce Department compares home-market and US prices of physically different goods, in different kinds of packaging, sold at different times, in different and fluctuating currencies, to different customers at different levels of trade, in different quantities, with different freight and other movement costs, different credit terms, and other differences in directly associated selling expenses (e.g. commissions, warranties, royalties and advertising). Is it any wonder that the prices aren't identical?" (Lindsey 2000, 8).

[34] Finger 1993, viii.

Antidumping is essentially used by firms to insulate themselves from falling import prices. Certain industries will always be faced with import surges, such as the domestic steel industry in the aftermath of the Asian financial crisis of 1997–98, when a collapse in foreign demand sent world steel prices tumbling. After the domestic computer production outstripped demand in 1985, world prices of semiconductors fell through the floor, triggering a round of dumping petitions.

In such cases, the problem facing the petitioning industry is not that there is a price differential between markets, that foreign firms charge a higher price in their domestic market than in the United States. The afflicted industry would find no consolation if the U.S. price were slightly higher than the foreign price even as both were falling sharply. Rather, the basic problem for the industry is that prices everywhere are falling due to unforeseen circumstances. It may be reasonable to provide an industry facing such difficulties with temporary protection without any claim that trade is "unfair." And that is precisely what the escape clause is designed to do.

_____*The Escape Clause*

If a domestic industry is suffering as a result of import competition and yet does not allege that the imports are unfairly dumped or subsidized, the industry can still receive temporary protection. Ever since the passage of the Reciprocal Trade Agreements Act in 1934, when the United States embarked on its policy of negotiating tariff reductions with other countries, Congress recognized that trade liberalization might force difficult economic adjustments on particular sectors of the economy. Because of this, Congress insisted that if lower tariffs brought about serious injury to certain domestic industries, they should be provided with temporary relief that would help them adjust to the new conditions of trade. To this end, the "escape clause" provides a mechanism for domestic industries to get a temporary exception to any negotiated tariff reduction.

Section 201 of the Trade Act of 1974 provides the current statutory basis for the escape clause.[35] It allows representatives of an industry (a trade association, firm, union, or group of workers) to file a petition

---

[35] The escape clause is also contained in Article 19 of the GATT and in the Agreement on Safeguards as part of the Uruguay Round negotiations.

with the International Trade Commission for temporary relief from import competition. The petition must include a specific plan that details how protection will be used to help the industry adjust. The ITC must then determine if the imports are or threaten to be "a substantial cause of serious injury," where "substantial cause" is defined as "a cause which is important and not less than any other cause."[36] Cutting through the legal verbiage, this simply means that imports must be the most important cause of injury. This legalistic language is nontrivial: The ITC rejected a Section 201 petition from the automobile industry in 1980 on the grounds that the most important source of the industry's difficulty was not imports, but the recession of that year.

If the ITC reaches an affirmative finding of injury, it must then recommend an appropriate remedy to the president. This remedy can include action on trade, such as higher tariffs, or other policies that would help facilitate the adjustment efforts of the domestic industry. The president then has wide discretion as to what action is taken. The import relief can take place over a period of four to eight years and must apply to imports from all sources (unlike antidumping, which, as we have seen, is selective).

Section 201 was invoked frequently in the 1970s, but has been used only sporadically in recent decades. Just nineteen cases were filed in the 1980s and only ten cases in the 1990s. This is partly because it has proven too difficult to get protection: of the nineteen cases considered in the 1980s, for example, the ITC ruled affirmatively in only seven. Even then, there is no guarantee that the president will provide any relief to the industry, and in practice presidents are often reluctant to grant it.[37] As a result, the escape clause has been completely overshadowed by antidumping, where the injury standard is not as strict and presidential action is not required. In view of the ease with which antidumping actions can be initiated and affect trade, it comes as no surprise that firms have avoided Section 201.

Section 201 has been criticized as being merely a protectionist loophole that allows firms to obtain protection, with no allegation of unfair trade, and therefore permits a country to backslide away from

---

[36] U.S. House of Representatives 1997, 100.

[37] This is why Senator Ernest Hollings (D-SC) once made the dismissive quip that "Section 201 is for suckers" (quoted in Low 1993, 57).

open markets.[38] But such provisions function as essential safeguards that make trade liberalizing agreements possible. As other economists have noted, "Safeguard provisions are often critical to the existence and operation of trade-liberalizing agreements, as they function as both insurance mechanisms and safety-valves. They provide governments with the means to renege on specific liberalization commitments—subject to certain conditions—should the need for this arise (safety valve). Without them governments may refrain from signing an agreement that reduces protection substantially (insurance motive)."[39] The presence of the escape clause, it can be argued, has encouraged cautious governments to liberalize trade more than might otherwise be the case.

With the increasing abuse of antidumping measures, escape clause actions have come to be viewed in a more benign light. Section 201 is now seen as a potential solution to the problem of antidumping. Escape clause actions have several advantages over antidumping measures: there are no bogus claims of unfair trade, they provide greater flexibility in the scope and duration of nondiscriminatory protection, and the president is allowed to take into account the overall economic, security, and political interests of the United States in tailoring a relief package. Relaxing the high standards of the escape clause would make it a more attractive method of obtaining import relief and provide an opportunity to rein in the use of antidumping. The danger, of course, is that Congress might simply expand the use of the escape clause without constraining the use of antidumping.

Clearly, the challenge for policymakers operating in an era of greater economic integration is one of balance—making the escape clause available without compromising open markets: "if the standards for obtaining import-related remedies are too restrictive, the escape clause mechanism cannot serve as an effective shock absorber for protectionist pressures. On the other hand, if the eligibility criteria are too

---

[38] Expressing skepticism about the "safety valve" explanation for the escape clause, Sykes (1991, 273–74) argues that the "likelihood of direct protectionist legislation also decreases if such legislation violates international obligations and results in international sanction." Therefore, "the ability of Congress to resist special interest pressures for protection . . . would likely be greater in the absence of Article XIX." Finger (1996) is equally skeptical about safeguards, dubbing it "legalized backsliding."

[39] Hoekman and Kostecki 1995, 161.

weak, any domestic industry that faces import competition may become eligible for temporary protection."[40] This trade-off is one of the most difficult challenges in trade policy.

Does Temporary Relief from Imports Work?

Some form of safeguards seems to be a political necessity. And we have seen that the escape clause can be a desirable alternative to antidumping actions. But does temporary relief from imports actually provide a remedy for the ills afflicting the domestic industry? Although protection has been justified as a way of revitalizing certain industries, it may not be able to accomplish this objective.[41]

Ideally, such relief would offer temporary protection to industries that compete against imports, in exchange for assurances that the industry will undertake measures to adjust to the new competition. But in providing temporary relief, the government encounters a problem with time consistency. The industry would like to reap the benefits of protection without undertaking the costs of adjustment. When the government cannot credibly commit to eliminating protection in the future, an industry may find itself able to perpetuate the protection by not investing sufficiently in cost reductions.[42] If the government bases its decision to renew protection on whether the industry has adjusted to the foreign competition, then the industry might have an incentive not to adjust in order to trigger a renewal of protection. Even making trade relief contingent on such investment does not eliminate the time consistency problem. Temporary, contingent protection may still end up becoming permanent protection.

This pattern of repeated renewals of protection is sometimes seen in practice. Some industries have used temporary protection to adjust to competition from imports. Such industries as automobiles, consumer electronics, and semiconductors have received temporary protection at one time or another, but adjusted to the new conditions of

[40] Lawrence and Litan 1986, 79.

[41] In addition to the discussion of certain industries below, Krueger (1996) presents a series of recent case studies on protection that examine whether import limits actually helped the domestic industry. See also Baldwin 1988 for a discussion of the inefficacy of protectionist measures.

[42] Tornell 1991.

competition. This does not mean that protection helped promote that adjustment, just that protection was temporary. Indeed, blocking imports failed to solve the fundamental problem these industries faced, either because foreign competition was located in the United States through direct investments or because the industry depended heavily upon foreign export sales and the importation of components. Given the inability of trade policy to solve the underlying problems confronting these industries, domestic firms adjusted by adopting new technology, moving to new market niches, and forming global alliances.[43]

Other industries have essentially received permanent protection over the past few decades by seeking and repeatedly receiving "temporary" protection. Two that stand out are the steel industry and the textile and apparel industry. Both face long-term structural adjustments to domestic and foreign competition and have stubbornly resisted pressures to adapt. The steel industry suffers from excess capacity worldwide, a strong union that has helped price domestic producers out of the world market, and growing domestic competition from smaller mills. The textiles and apparel industry, on the other hand, is struggling against the loss of comparative advantage in labor-intensive manufactures by becoming more capital-intensive, upgrading technology, and outsourcing.

The steel industry has received nearly continuous protection for over thirty years and is still seeking limits on imports. From 1969 to 1974, the large, integrated producers were protected from imports by a series of voluntary restraint agreements (VRAs). From 1978 to 1982, a Trigger Price Mechanism, consisting of minimum import prices, was in place. From 1982 to 1992, a new round of VRAs were in place. Most recently, in both 1992–93 and 1998–99, the industry filed a massive number of AD and CVD complaints. Still, the management and unions of Big Steel continue to blame their problems on imports. The industry has applied intense political pressure in Washington in an effort to stop foreign competition: in March 1999, the House of Representatives passed by a lopsided two-to-one margin a measure to restrict monthly steel imports

---

[43] Another way to adjust to import competition is simply to fade away, as has been the fate of the domestic footwear industry. Import penetration in the domestic footwear market rose from 13 percent in 1966 to 90 percent in 1996, while employment fell from 233,400 in 1966 to 46,100 in 1996. See Freeman and Kleiner 1998 on how the remaining firms in the domestic industry have adjusted their labor practices in order to survive.

for three years, although the Senate rejected it. Undeterred, the United Steel Workers union called in early 2001 for another "five-year period of import restraints to allow the industry to revitalize itself."

Yet protection has not led to revitalization. Rather, under protection, the big steel companies have reduced the share of profits they devoted to reinvestment, distributing the profits as dividends or investing in other sectors.[44] And the industry's labor union has helped price the domestic firms out of the market: even as productivity lagged, the wage premium steelworkers earned above the average worker in manufacturing increased from 24 percent in 1970 to nearly 60 percent in the early 1980s, then fell back to 36 percent by the end of the 1980s. As a result, the nonunionized, nonintegrated domestic producers—the minimills—have grabbed U.S. market share away from the big integrated producers. The minimills accounted for about 10 percent of U.S. production in the late 1960s, but about 50 percent today. Unlike imports, this domestic competition cannot be stopped at the border and is slowly forcing the integrated producers to adjust. But the process has been prolonged in part due to import restraints and the recalcitrant steelworkers union.

The textiles and apparel industry has also used its political influence to maintain an array of barriers designed to stop foreign competition. The United States negotiated export restrictions on cotton textile products with Japan in the 1950s. Although these trade restrictions were designed as a temporary measure to give the industry some breathing space to become more efficient, the industry always complained that the protection was inadequate. Rather than being eliminated, the temporary restraints slowly spread to include other countries and products, gradually filling in the gaps from which imports were seeping in. The Short Term Arrangement on Cotton Textiles trade was signed in 1961, followed by the Long Term Arrangement on Cotton Textiles in 1962. Set to last for five years, the long-term arrangement was renewed for three years in 1967 and again in 1970. These trade restrictions were extended to wool and man-made textiles products in the first Multifiber Arrangement in 1974. This was followed by the second MFA in 1978, the third MFA in 1982, and the fourth MFA in 1986, each of which continued to

---

[44] Tornell 1997. For an expose of steel's lobbying tactics and corporate welfare, see Barringer and Pierce 2000.

tighten the restrictions by expanding the country and product coverage. Under the Uruguay Round agreement in 1994, the MFA is to be phased out over ten years, but there could be enormous political pressures to postpone or delay its planned abolition in 2005.

Unlike the large integrated steel producers, the textile and apparel industry has made some adjustments to compete against foreign imports. The textile industry has become less dependent upon unskilled labor-intensive production techniques by adopting advanced technology and more capital-intensive production methods (often using imported machinery). The consequent increase in productivity has sharply reduced industry employment. The apparel sector, which is less able to substitute capital for labor, has been harder hit and has turned instead to foreign outsourcing to remain competitive. Despite the plant closings and employment losses at the aggregate level, new firms have entered the industry, and within-plant productivity has increased in both textiles and apparel.[45]

Despite the inefficacy of import protection in solving an industry's problems, many industries still identify imports as the problem and protection as the cure. Some have even claimed that temporary protection "played a major role in revitalizing key American industries" in the 1980s. For example, the steel and auto industries faced many difficulties in the early 1980s, but received import relief and by the late 1980s had significantly improved their output, employment, and productivity.[46]

This view of protection completely misrepresents the experience of the 1980s. Revitalization was in fact the result of the economic recovery after the recession of 1981–82, which had been the worst economic downturn since the Great Depression. In addition, the appreciation of the dollar in the early 1980s squeezed import-competing and export industries, with relief coming when the dollar began to depreciation after 1985. To conclude from the 1980s that temporary protection is a proven method of boosting industrial competitiveness not only overlooks the more important macroeconomic context of that period, but ignores the fact that foreign competition is precisely what motivated

---

[45] Levinsohn and Petropoulos 2001.

[46] Tonelson 1994. His article is entitled "Beating Back Predatory Trade," but it is absurd to think that the woes of the steel, automobile, and textile industries were due to foreign predatory practices.

American manufacturers to cut costs and improve their productivity. Diminishing competition through import restraints takes the pressure off domestic industries and dulls their incentive to improve efficiency.

As a final example, let us consider the celebrated Harley-Davidson motorcycle case. Even today, this is frequently heralded as a great success of "breathing space" protection. The story, as conventionally told, is that in the early 1980s Harley-Davidson was pushed to the wall by Japanese competition. After receiving temporary import relief in 1983 under the Section 201 escape clause, the company got its act together and came back stronger than ever.[47] In fact, Harley recovered so swiftly that it even requested that the final year of tariff protection be canceled.

The real story is different: import relief had nothing to do with Harley-Davidson's turnaround. At the time, Harley-Davidson produced only "heavyweight" motorcycles with piston displacements of over 1000cc, while Japanese producers mainly exported medium-weight bikes (700cc to 850cc of piston displacement) to the United States. But in 1975 Kawasaki opened a production plant in Nebraska, and in 1979 Honda opened a plant in Ohio, both of which produced heavyweight motorcycles to compete directly with Harley-Davidson. They did not produce them in Japan because there was virtually no market for such large motorcycles in Asia.

The deep recession of 1981–82 particularly affected blue-collar workers, the main consumer base for Harley's products, and put the company under severe financial pressure. So they filed for import relief under Section 201 in September 1982, making no allegation of unfair dumping or subsidies. The ITC had problems determining that imports were the substantial cause of Harley's injury because imports were plummeting from the recession too. They finally decided that Harley had been injured because unsold inventories of imported medium-weight bikes (700–850cc) were accumulating.[48] The ITC also ruled that Honda's

---

[47] The company's management fully conceded that Harley's production process was far behind the cutting-edge Japanese manufacturing practices at the time the Section 201 petition was filed; see Reid 1990.

[48] The inventory of medium bikes accounted for 80 percent of all unsold motorcycles, and the inventory buildup was much less for models larger than 1000cc because of production cutbacks.

Ohio plant and Kawasaki's Nebraska plant were part of the domestic industry that deserved protection.

The Reagan administration accepted the ITC's recommendation and adopted a tariff-rate quota on imports of motorcycles over 700cc. A tariff-rate quota allows a certain quantity of imports to enter paying the usual tariff, but imports above that quantity have to pay the higher protective tariffs. These were initially set at 45 percent and then declined over five years. The protection had almost no impact on Harley-Davidson because Honda and Kawasaki were already producing heavyweight motorcycles in the United States, production that was not constrained. In fact, Honda and Kawasaki favored the Section 201 case because it could protect them from their Japan-based rivals Suzuki and Yamaha. But even Suzuki and Yamaha were able to evade the tariff-rate quota on imports of motorcycles over 700cc: they simply produced a 699cc version that was not subject to the quota.[49] Then Suzuki and Yamaha had room under the quota to export more larger (1000cc) bikes before they had to pay the extra 45 percent duty.

Harley was deeply disappointed with the import relief. Because the final year of tariffs would have been very low and had virtually no effect on the motorcycle market, the company gave up the Section 201 relief a year before it was set to expire. Doing so gained Harley some favorably publicity and helped them convince President Reagan to visit a Harley plant in Pennsylvania, where he declared, amid a sea of red, white, and blue, that his administration was glad to lend Harley a helping hand.

Harley saved itself from bankruptcy and turned itself around because a new management team, appalled at the lax inventory control system and antiquated production methods, dramatically improved the efficiency of the production process. Close attention to production detail, as well as the rebounding economy, helped rejuvenate Harley's economic prospects. Blocking imports contributed virtually nothing to Harley's recovery. As the chief economist of the ITC during this period later recalled, "if the case of heavyweight motorcycles is to be considered the

---

[49] Harley engineers purchased two imported motorcycles because they suspected that only the label on the engine had changed, but incredibly the engines were exactly 699cc! See Reid 1990, 89.

only successful escape-clause case, it is because it caused little harm and it helped Harley-Davidson get a bank loan so it could diversify."[50]

Thus, one should not be overly optimistic about the ability of trade protection to help sectors with adjustment problems more severe than coping with a temporary surge of imports. Whether import restraints actually assist the domestic industry in its adjustment efforts is a debatable proposition. But even if protection contributes little to adjustment, the escape clause has been a political necessity and has helped maintain domestic support for the open world trading system.

[50] Suomela 1993, 135. In 1986, the company bought a mobile home producer, Holiday Rambler Corp.

5

U.S. Trade Policy and the World Trading System

Over the last three chapters we have seen the strength of the case for free trade and the weakness of most rationales for protection. Taken together, the two sets of evidence make a potent argument for reducing trade barriers. But a country's commercial policy is rarely decided on economic merits alone. Rather, it is determined in the political arena, where many factors enter into the decision-making process. This chapter opens by discussing how politics shapes trade policy in general, and then uses this analysis to explain how the United States broke with its protectionist past during World War II and began moving toward freer trade. As a result of this policy shift, the United States helped establish the multilateral trading system in 1947, centered on the General Agreement on Tariffs and Trade (GATT). Studying the historical evolution of U.S. trade policy helps us understand its current framework and provides a context in which we can examine the ongoing controversy surrounding the World Trade Organization, the GATT's successor, in chapter 6.

_____The Politics of Protection

As we saw in chapter 3, the essential economic reason for the conflict between supporters and opponents of free trade lies in the fact that any change in the relative prices of goods in an economy also alters the returns to various factors of production, such as the wages of skilled or unskilled workers. When a country adopts a more open trade policy, for example, domestic prices converge to those on the world market. Despite the overall benefits of this trade, the resulting change in prices benefits some groups and harms others, and those injured naturally seek to resist it. In this regard, free trade is no different from any other public policy that affects relative prices and hence the distribution of income.

Thus, the demand for protectionist policies arises principally from those who are harmed directly or indirectly by imports. Because of the conflicting interests of specific groups, there is no reason to believe that free trade will necessarily be adopted as a country's trade policy.[1] The actual policy depends upon the relative political strength of those supporting and opposing trade restrictions, based on underlying economic interests or any other motivation. The policy also depends upon how the conflict between these competing groups is mediated by policymaking institutions in the government. These institutions may be biased in favor of one group over another, either because certain groups have better access to decision makers or because those decision makers are more sensitive to the interests of some groups. This can obviously affect the direction that trade policy takes.

An interesting benchmark to consider is the trade policy that would emerge in a democratic vote under majority rule. While trade policy is rarely determined in this way, this is a useful starting point for thinking about the policy that would arise in a competitive, representative political system. In a direct democracy, trade policy would be determined by the preferences of the median voter.[2] So even if free trade raises aggregate income, the median voter would not support such a policy unless that voter saw some personal benefit. For this reason, free trade might not emerge as the outcome if trade policy were determined by majority voting in a referendum.

As an example, suppose workers who have no more educational attainment than a high school diploma lose one dollar as a result of free trade, while those with a college degree gain two dollars. If workers with a college degree constitute at least one-third of all voters, free trade would raise overall income. But if the less-educated workers comprise more than half of the electorate, the median voter would oppose the policy, unless guaranteed a compensatory income transfer.

This example points to the distribution of workers' skills as a

---

[1] Rodrik (1995) and Deardorff and Stern (1998) provide recent surveys of the academic literature on the political economy of trade policy.

[2] See the classic analysis of Mayer (1984). The median voter is the decisive marginal voter whose views determine which side will win under majority rule.

potentially important determinant of the median voter's interests. As noted in chapter 1, educational attainment appears to be a leading factor in shaping the American public's views of trade policy. Several studies have shown that the more education persons receive, the more likely they are to support open trade policies. This is consistent with the view that economic interests are at stake: the United States exports goods and services that require a highly educated workforce, whereas it imports more labor-intensive goods where, in the competing domestic industry, many years of formal education are not a requirement of employment. As the fraction of the population receiving advanced education has risen in recent decades, support for freer trade might be expected to grow over time.[3]

There is also evidence that home ownership is a factor that shapes an individual's preferences on trade policy. Even highly educated individuals tend to express support for protectionist policies if they own a home in a region that is adversely affected by imports.[4] Other factors also affecting the median voter's views on trade include the manner in which voters perceive their economic interests to be related to trade policy, such as their potential mobility between different sectors of the economy. For example, a worker who over time has built up sector-specific skills (such as steelworkers) may view trade policy differently from someone with a similar educational background but whose skills are useful in several different industries.

There are several notable instances in which voters have directly shaped their country's trade policy. The Canadian general election of 1988 was called by the government to determine whether the electorate supported the U.S.-Canada Free Trade Agreement. The government was returned to office and the agreement was enacted, unlike the situation in 1911 when Canadian voters rejected a similar agreement. Switzerland has also conducted popular referendums on trade policy issues.

The American presidential election of 1888 also hinged on trade policy. In December 1887, President Grover Cleveland, a Democrat, de-

---

[3] In 1999, for example, 36 percent of persons aged sixty-five to seventy-four had received some college education or had earned a higher degree, while 57 percent of persons aged twenty-five to thirty-four had reached this level of educational attainment (U.S. Bureau of the Census 2001, 158).

[4] Scheve and Slaughter 2001b.

voted his entire State of the Union message to making the case for lower tariffs. This sparked a nationwide debate over whether tariffs should be used only to raise revenue, as Cleveland wanted, or to protect domestic industries as well. Cleveland's Republican rival, Benjamin Harrison, campaigned in favor of maintaining high protective tariffs for domestic manufacturers. Thus, the electorate faced a clear choice about the future of tariff policy depending upon whom was elected to office. Cleveland won the popular vote with 48.6 percent to Harrison's 47.8 percent of the vote, but Harrison easily won the electoral college by 233 votes to 168. As president, Harrison raised tariffs considerably by signing the McKinley tariff of 1890.

This example illustrates that the nature of the electoral system is also important. If the election had been determined by whichever candidate received the greatest number of votes, Cleveland would have won. Because Harrison's support was concentrated in the heavily populated, industrial states of the north, he won the states with the largest electoral votes and hence the election. Thus, the distribution of economic interests across electoral districts can interact with the rules of the political system (a winner-take-all versus a proportionate representative system) and shape the outcome. For example, if a sizable minority of the electorate is opposed to free trade but is uniformly distributed across districts, then a winner-take-all system might result in the election of few opponents to free trade, whereas their political strength might be greater in a proportional system.

So far, this analysis has assumed that voters cast their ballots based on their economic interests. But those interests may be attenuated by several factors. Even if the entire electorate recognized that a clear majority would benefit from free trade, uncertainty about which individuals would benefit could bias the political system in favor of maintaining trade restrictions. Because of this, a reform in which most voters would benefit might not pass in a popular vote if the majority thinks that it is unlikely to gain from the reform. This uncertainty means that the expected value of reform could be negative for a majority of voters, in which case they would block it. This logic gives the political system a status quo bias.[5]

---

[5] Fernandez and Rodrik 1991.

The status quo bias is simply reinforced if voters are risk averse (wherein they prefer a lower but certain return over a higher but less certain return) or loss averse (wherein they are more sensitive to losses than to equivalent-sized gains, and thus prefer to avoid any loss). These factors might help explain why countries with trade restrictions find it politically difficult to eliminate them. In such cases, tariffs may be viewed as a social welfare mechanism to prevent substantial reduction of real incomes in broad sections of the community.[6] This function might explain why so many tariffs in the past seem to have had income mainte- nance as their goal and why they have continued, even when designed to be only temporary. For example, if the goal is to keep real incomes of certain farmers, steelworkers, or textile manufacturers higher than they would be otherwise, there is less of a motivation to reduce trade barriers, even though other income transfer policies would be more efficient than restricting trade.

In most developed countries, trade policy is determined by elec- ted representatives in the legislature. There are additional reasons to ex- pect that the political system will be biased in favor of restricting trade in a legislative forum. Particularly when policy is considered at the level of a specific commodity, political influence may be skewed in favor of those seeking government assistance because those who stand to gain have more at stake than those who stand to lose. As Vilfredo Pareto pointed out long ago, "a protectionist measure provides large benefits to a small number of people, and causes a very great number of consumers a slight loss."[7] This circumstance makes it easier to enact such measures. Pareto's idea that the benefits of trade protection are highly concen- trated, while the costs are widely diffused, has been a central point of departure for explaining the existence and persistence of import restrictions.

The U.S. sugar program, discussed briefly in chapter 2, illustrates this imbalance in costs and benefits. Import restrictions have kept do- mestic sugar prices at roughly twice the world price. The General Ac-

---

[6] Corden (1974, 107) first posited this "conservative social welfare function." Sim- ilarly, Rotemberg (2000) has shown that if voters are altruistic and care about the income of other groups in society, then direct democracy can lead to commercial policies that are biased against trade.

[7] Pareto [1909] 1971, 379.

counting Office estimated that in 1998 domestic sugar producers reaped about $1 billion as a result of this policy. However, 42 percent of the total benefits to sugarcane and sugar beet growers went to just 1 percent of all producers; indeed, just seventeen sugarcane farms collected over half of all the cane growers' benefits. Clearly, the owners of these few farms have a powerful incentive to maintain the import restrictions. Although the sugar policy imposes far larger costs on consumers of sweeteners ($1.9 billion according to the GAO) than are distributed to growers, consumers are far more numerous and these costs are spread widely among them.[8]

This combination of concentrated benefits and dispersed costs leads to an enormous imbalance in the relative size of the political forces opposing and favoring any change in the sugar policy. The incentive for household consumers to oppose the policy is virtually nonexistent: even though the total cost across all consumers is large, the cost to each individual consumer is small: only about seven dollars per person per year. On the other hand, the policy creates large, tangible benefits for a few producers, who are willing to devote substantial resources to defend the policy. As of early October 2000 in the 1999–2000 election cycle, sugar and sugar beet political action committees had spent more than $1.2 million in campaign contributions.[9] As a result, such special interests have an influence on policy that is disproportionate to their size.

Yet such imbalances are not the whole story. Many small groups could benefit from special government policies, but few actually succeed in organizing and obtaining it. Why are some special interests are able to form a political organization or interest group while others are not? And why do only some of those that organize succeed in influencing policy? The formation of interest groups is a critical element of the politics of trade policy.[10] Unfortunately, economists and political scientists have not

---

[8] U.S. General Accounting Office 2000a; 1993, 32–33.

[9] Data from http://www.tray.com/fecinfo.

[10] For example, taking the number of organized industries as given, Grossman and Helpman (1994) find that a government that is increasingly swayed by political contributions will respond by imposing more trade interventions. However, Mitra (1999) shows that this relationship breaks down when an industry is allowed to organize, if there is an incentive to do so. In this case, the increased sensitivity to contributions may induce other groups to enter the political market and thereby cancel out some of the demands of other

been overwhelmingly successful in revealing much about the organization of economic interests. However, several interesting hypotheses are worth exploring.

One difficulty in forming a successful political interest group is the *free-rider* problem. If a tariff benefits all firms in an industry regardless of whether they contributed to the political effort to get the tariff imposed, then some firms may choose not to contribute. They would prefer that others undertake the burden because, if protection is secured, the shirking firms cannot be excluded from the benefits of higher prices as imports are squeezed out of the market. But at the same time, the fewer firms who participate in seeking protection, the lower the probability of obtaining protection.[11]

One implication is that industries that are relatively concentrated, either economically (a small number of firms) or geographically (the same regional location), are better positioned to overcome the costs of collective action by monitoring the political contributions of others and punishing or excluding free riders.[12] The free-rider problem also explains the difficulty of mobilizing the dispersed opponents of programs. The numerous but widely dispersed consumers who pay higher prices for sugar have a collective interest in changing current policy, but there is a strong incentive to shirk from any organized effort to do so.

For other economic interests, however, political organization is not even necessary. For example, farmers in Kansas and Nebraska scarcely need a political action committee to ensure that their elected representatives take their interests to heart. Legislators represent the

---

protection-seeking industries. He shows that free trade is still a possible equilibrium even when government is highly sensitive to political contributions.

[11] This was stressed by Olson (1965) and Stigler (1971, 1974).

[12] Empirical evidence does not decisively support these predictions. Gawande (1998) finds evidence from the pattern of lobbying that supports the notion that geographically concentrated firms are more politically active than otherwise because they face lower organizational costs. But other studies, summarized in Potters and Sloof 1996, fail to find a strong relationship between concentration and political activity. In addition, Pecorino (1998) points out that the ability of an industry to cooperate does not, in theory, necessarily deteriorate with the number of firms. With an increase in the number of firms, the benefits to the industry from cooperation are higher, but the benefits of defecting and free riding also become larger. It is not clear which effect dominates.

preferences of important unorganized constituents in order to raise the probability that they will be reelected.[13] In addition, with the spread of antidumping and other legal mechanisms of obtaining protection, described in chapter 4, it is not even clear that political contributions by interest groups are the predominant means by which trade policy is affected. The free-rider problem is less of an obstacle in antidumping cases because the definition of an industry is often so narrow that even a single firm has the standing to file a petition.

Because of all these variables, generalizations are very difficult to make. So it should not be surprising that political economists have failed to answer basic questions about how firms achieve political influence. But one generalization seems fairly robust: once policies are in place, they are difficult to change, particularly if change involves taking benefits away from any industry.[14] Institutional biases that favor maintaining a policy contribute to this resistance to change. For example, the bureaucracies that administer programs often act as agents for the beneficiaries. Understandably, bureaucrats would prefer not to lose their jobs, as they might if a program ended.

Despite the biases that favor the imposition and maintenance of trade restrictions, political leaders in many countries have recognized the economy-wide benefits of free trade and have been able to overcome political inertia, throw off existing measures, and adopt more open trade policies. The United Kingdom eliminated virtually all protectionist policies in the mid–nineteenth century, the United States significantly reduced its tariffs in the mid–twentieth century, and many developing countries today have radically changed their economic policies in the direction of open markets. How have such reforms come about? By examining the dramatic shift in U.S. trade policy, we will understand the forces that brought about the creation of the current world trading sys-

---

[13] Denzau and Munger 1986.

[14] For example, Congress enacted subsidies for wool and mohair producers after the Korean War, when such products were considered strategic materials essential for military uniforms. Even though the subsidies were costing the government nearly $200 million a year, they were not terminated until 1993. However, "emergency" payments to these producers were reintroduced in the Agricultural Risk Protection Act of 2000.

tem and that continue to shape trade policy today. The place to start is with the Congress.

_____The Evolution of U.S. Trade Policy

Article 1, section 8 of the Constitution grants Congress the power to impose and collect import duties and "to regulate Commerce with foreign Nations." Recognition of this constitutional provision is critical to understanding U.S. trade policy past and present. In the past, Congress was solely responsible for trade policy, setting import duties on its own terms with little guidance from the president. Today, Congress closely controls the framework of trade policy in several ways. First, it delegates negotiating authority to the executive branch, and often puts conditions on the negotiations. Second, it retains the right to approve or reject trade agreements. Finally, it determines the criteria by which domestic industries can obtain relief from foreign competition through administrative procedures such as antidumping.

For much of its history, Congress has been biased in favor of domestic interests that compete against imports. Congress does not inherently favor these interests and does not deliberately neglect exporters and consumers. However, Congress responds to the major pressures and interests that confront it. The failure of exporters and consumers to organize (because of the difficulty of collective action, discussed above) has meant that their interests have been poorly represented in the Congress, an absence that has diminished their ability to affect policy. Congress has frequently had little reason to take these interests into account when formulating legislation. When Congress has been confronted with their views, however, the result has been more moderate tariffs.

Figure 5.1 depicts the average U.S. tariff on dutiable imports from 1821 (when the best statistics begin) to 1999. Vertical lines in the years 1861 and 1934 help identify three major periods of trade policy. The first period, from 1821 to 1860, saw tariffs slide from about 50 percent down to about 20 percent. In Congress during this period, manufacturers in Pennsylvania and elsewhere competed against imports and were well represented, but export interests also became forcefully represented by the southern states. About two-thirds of U.S. exports consisted of raw cotton, tobacco, and other crops that came almost exclusively

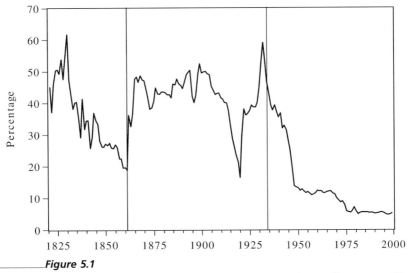

_____*Figure 5.1*

Average U.S. tariff rate on dutiable imports, 1821–1999. The tariff rate is tariff revenue) dutiable imports × 100. The vertical lines suggest dividing points between three major periods of trade policy. (Data from U.S. Bureau of the Census 1975 and U.S. International Trade Commission 2001.)

from the South. The growing importance of cotton exports, and the geographic concentration of the production of those exports, ensured that the members of Congress from the South stood solidly for free trade. They fought to reduce import tariffs because they recognized (as revealed in congressional debates) that an import tariff is effectively an export tax, and in this case one that directly harmed the South's interests.

In 1828, after a coalition of representatives from the North and the mid-Atlantic region passed a steep increase in import tariffs, known as the "Tariff of Abominations," southern states united in outrage. South Carolina vowed not to enforce the tariff but rather to open its ports without collecting customs duties. This action raised the political stakes by making it clear that high tariffs could be maintained only by deeply antagonizing the South. The "nullification" crisis was diffused when Congress agreed to accommodate southern concerns by setting tariffs on a declining path, which they did until the Civil War.

The second period, from 1861 to 1934, is one of consistently high tariffs (except around World War I). Ranging from 40 to 50 percent, these tariffs were originally introduced by the North after Southern members walked out of Congress to protest Lincoln's election. The tariffs were kept high to pay for the Civil War and persisted for many decades after the war because the domestic manufacturing interests that benefited from them resisted any reduction. The political strength of low-tariff forces was at a low point: the high-tariff Republicans dominated the federal government during this period, while the low-tariff Democrats (still drawing their main political support from the South) floundered.

Every few years during this period, Congress adjusted the rates of import duty on dozens of individual commodities. How were members of Congress from, for example, the few states containing sugar producers (such as Florida, Louisiana, and Utah) able to convince members from other states to vote for a sugar tariff that would only harm their own constituents? The answer, of course, is by vote trading. The legislative forum proved to be ideal for the logrolling that helped keep tariffs high. The constituents of Pennsylvania and Ohio may have been harmed by the sugar tariff, but their representatives were happy to vote for it in exchange for a vote to maintain or increase the tariff on iron and steel imports. After all, the iron and steel tariff would benefit Pennsylvania and Ohio producers much more than the sugar tariff would harm consumers in those states. In this way, the tariff became a pork barrel, and special interest politics was rampant.

While vote trading among import-competing interests ruled the day, exporters and consumers remained largely unorganized, and hence their interests were not effectively represented during Congress's deliberations. This led to many charges that the political process had become corrupt and beholden to big corporate interests. In the late nineteenth century, populist muckrakers such as Ida Tarbell argued strenuously that high tariffs protected big business from foreign competition and padded the profits of industrialists at the expense of consumers. The slogan "the tariff is the mother of the trust" became the rallying cry for the view that protection from competition enabled industries such as iron and steel, tobacco, and whiskey to form powerful cartels that exploited consumers and corrupted politics.

Republicans recognized the costs of protection, but the political forces influencing them were strong and one-sided. Cordell Hull, a Democratic congressman from Tennessee who later became secretary of state, once recalled, "Throughout my experience, I found many able Republicans in the House and Senate who, individually, were moderates rather than extremist in their tariff views. . . . But in practice, the chief tariff beneficiaries who had helped finance political campaigns would come to Washington and demand that the rates be increased rather than decreased, with the result that Republican leaders of moderate view were obliged to yield to ever rising rates as successive tariff revisions took place."[15] Their attitude was summed up by Joseph Fordney (R-Mich.), onetime chairman of the House Ways and Means Committee, who simply shrugged and stated that it was his duty to "give the boys what they wanted" when it came to setting the tariff.[16]

Yet as the twentieth century dawned, underlying shifts in economic structure brought about a realignment of these economic interests. Major manufacturing industries that faced import competition in the late nineteenth century had, by the early twentieth century, become exporters. These included the iron and steel and machinery industries, and newly emerging industries such as electrical equipment and automobiles.[17] As a result, these industries had less to gain from tariff protection than from the opening of foreign markets to U.S. exports. As these economic interests changed, they generated political pressures that could eventually succeed in changing policy. The evolution of William McKinley's trade policy views illustrates this switch. As chairman of the House Ways and Means Committee, he oversaw the passage of the protectionist McKinley tariff of 1890 to defend American manufacturers from foreign competition. Just eleven years later, as president, McKinley called for "reciprocity" agreements to expand the market for American exports. It is hard to image a change in policy taking place if export-oriented interests did not become larger and more politically active.

Yet the reciprocity agreements that McKinley proposed never came to fruition. Such agreements could always have been negotiated by the president as treaties with foreign countries, but treaties required the approval of two-thirds of the Senate and could be amended by that body. This effectively killed any U.S. participation in trade negotiations. The Dingley tariff of 1897, for example, authorized the president to reach trade agreements that would reduce tariffs up to 20 percent.

[15] Hull 1948, 358.
[16] Quoted in Irwin 1998a, 334.
[17] Irwin 2000.

Twelve treaties were negotiated, but not a single one was approved by the Senate. Since the United States apparently could not implement a negotiated agreement, foreign countries became reluctant even to open discussions about trade. Consequently, the executive branch lacked any negotiating credibility with other countries if potential agreements did not have Congress's prior approval.

Export interests remained inert in the Congress as well. In his classic book *Politics, Pressure, and the Tariff,* the political scientist E. E. Schattschneider reported his shock at the absence of virtually any pressure for lower tariffs in the tariff revision of 1929–30, later infamously known as the Smoot-Hawley tariff. As he put it, although "theoretically the interests supporting and opposed to tariff legislation . . . are approximately equal, the pressures upon Congress are extremely unbalanced" because "the pressures supporting the tariff are made overwhelming by the fact that the opposition is negligible."[18] Politically active business interests practiced "a policy of reciprocal non-interference" in which industries could seek import duties to benefit themselves but viewed opposition to duties that benefited others as "improper and unfair."[19] The result was "protection all around," or protection for everyone who asked for it, because Congress had no criteria for accepting some demands for tariffs and rejecting others. Since the prevailing attitude was that protection was good, Congress was not in a position to deny tariffs to any industry that desired them.

From the Morrill tariff of 1861 until 1930, this was the standard way of doing business. Yet the Smoot-Hawley tariff of 1930 was longer, more complex, more controversial, and more openly the product of political games than previous tariff legislation. Congress reopened the tariff issue in 1929 in order to help protect farmers from declining crop prices, but the process spun out of control as other industries got into the act and demanded higher tariffs as well. Warning of the adverse economic consequences of the high tariffs, 1,028 economists signed a petition urg-

[18] Schattschneider 1935, 285.

[19] Schattschneider also noted the concentrated benefits and diffusion of costs of the tariff and stated that this was "the logical basis for the generalization that producers usually desire protection for their own output more keenly than they object to duties on their materials and supplies" (1935, 128). Importers argued for lower tariffs, but, he notes, they were almost complete ignored in the deliberations.

ing President Hoover not to sign the final bill. This warning was not heeded, and the Smoot-Hawley tariff helped push up average duties to nearly 50 percent. As the economy slid into the Great Depression, the volume of exports and imports fell by nearly 50 percent between 1929 and 1933. While economic historians do not believe that the Smoot-Hawley tariff caused the depression, the high tariffs certainly contributed to the collapse of U.S. trade and exacerbated the overall economic decline.[20]

Schattschneider concluded his study of pressure politics and congressional tariff-making by arguing that there was "no significant concentration of forces able to reverse the policy and bring about a return to a system of low tariffs or free trade."[21] He was not alone in failing to anticipate that this is precisely what would happen. In 1933, the average tariff on dutiable imports was 54 percent, and the average duty on all imports was 20 percent. Twenty years later, the average tariff on dutiable imports was about 12 percent, and the average duty on all imports was about 5 percent. And by 1999, the average tariff on dutiable imports was 5 percent; the average tariff on all imports was 2 percent; and over 60 percent of imports were duty free. If Congress was inherently biased in favor of trade protection, how did the United States ever make the switch to more open trade policies?

_____The Reciprocal Trade Agreements Act

The opportunity to put trade policy on a new course came when the election of 1932 handed political power to the Democrats, the traditional supporters of moderate tariffs. In 1934, at the request of President Franklin Roosevelt, Congress enacted the Reciprocal Trade Agreements Act (RTAA), an important piece of legislation that set the stage for a new era in U.S. trade policy. With the RTAA, Congress abandoned the old system of making trade policy and established a new framework that eventually resulted in the General Agreement on Tariffs and Trade and the World Trade Organization. Even today, with some modifications, the RTAA serves as the basis of U.S. trade policy.

[20] For a discussion of the relationship between the Smoot-Hawley tariff and the Great Depression, see Irwin 1998a.

[21] Schattschneider 1935, 283.

The RTAA had the following provisions:

The president was authorized to enter into tariff agreements with foreign countries.

The president could proclaim an increase or a decrease in import duties by no more than 50 percent, but could not transfer any article between the dutiable and free lists, as a result of such agreements.

The proclaimed duties would apply to imports from all countries on an unconditional most-favored nation (MFN) basis.

The president's authority to enter into foreign trade agreements would expire in three years.

The United States could terminate any agreement after three years with six months' notice; otherwise it would stay in effect indefinitely.

The most important element of the RTAA was prior approval of any trade agreement reached by the executive, thereby overcoming the problems that had killed previous reciprocity treaties. The RTAA allowed the president to reduce U.S. tariffs in agreements negotiated with other countries, without the specific approval of Congress. Congress also endorsed the unconditional most-favored nation (MFN) clause, under which the lower U.S. tariffs negotiated with one country would be automatically extended to other countries.

The negotiating authority in the RTAA itself, however, did require periodic renewal. While President Roosevelt had proposed no time limit, the House of Representatives chose to limit the authority to three years, after which it would automatically terminate unless Congress renewed it. Had the House not added this provision, Congress would not have been able to stop the president from implementing trade agreements until a two-thirds majority of both houses voted to strip him of negotiating authority, because he surely would have vetoed any such measure. This renewal requirement ensured that the executive branch would remain sensitive to the legislature's concerns because the president would have to return periodically to seek renewal of his negotiating authority.

Why was the RTAA regarded as necessary in 1934? A unilateral

_____Table 5.1
Average Tariff Levels in Selected Countries

	1913	1925	1931	1952
Belgium	6	7	17	
France	14	9	38	19
Germany	12	15	40	16
Italy	17	16	48	24
United Kingdom	—	4	17	17
United States	32	26	35	9

Source: Irwin 1995, 138.

tariff reduction, such as a repeal of Smoot-Hawley, was not a serious option: political support for repeal was weak in the midst of the depression, and in any event such unilateral actions had been taken by Democrats in the past, only to be reversed when the Republicans took office.[22] Furthermore, a unilateral tariff reduction would have failed to counteract the significant worsening of the international economic environment in the early 1930s. As table 5.1 indicates, foreign tariffs increased sharply between 1925 and 1931. Protection also took the form of restrictive import quotas, foreign exchange controls, and preferential trading blocs. To some extent, the United States was at fault for these developments. In passing the Smoot-Hawley tariff of 1930, Congress did not take into account the international effects of its actions. After the imposition of Smoot-Hawley, many countries also raised their trade barriers, some in retaliation and others because economic contraction and high unemployment made demands for protection irresistible.[23]

In order to reduce foreign barriers against U.S. exports, stimulate export growth, and thus help recover from the depression, the Roosevelt administration sought better access to foreign markets by offering lower tariffs at home in exchange for lower tariffs abroad. The administration sold the RTAA as an emergency measure to spur economic recovery from the depression. As already noted, the volume of U.S. exports had

[22] The Democratic tariff reduction of 1894 was reversed by the Republican tariff of 1897, while the 1913 Democratic tariff was undone by the 1921 Republican tariff. Those were the only two opportunities that the Democrats had to enact a tariff in the seventy years after 1860.

[23] According to the League of Nations (1933, 193), the Smoot-Hawley tariff was "the signal for an outburst of tariff-making activity in other countries, partly at least by way of reprisals."

fallen nearly 50 percent between 1929 and 1933. Democrats supported the RTAA on the hope that the executive branch, now given more authority over trade policy, would reach trade agreements that would stimulate exports as well as moderate import duties. Politicians did not undergo an ideological conversion to free trade, and there was no apparent shift in underlying trade-related interest groups between the passage of Smoot-Hawley in 1930 and the RTAA in 1934.[24] Rather, the political shift in favor of the Democrats created an opportunity that was exploited by those who favored a more liberal trade policy and those who wanted to address the dismal developments in the world economy. And, in fact, one person—Cordell Hull, President Roosevelt's secretary of state—must receive the bulk of the credit for the RTAA. After World War I, Hull became a strong proponent of international cooperation on tariffs, believing it essential for economic and political reasons. Hull's dedication to this idea almost single-handedly ensured the success of the RTAA.[25]

As an economic policy, the RTAA failed to live up to its expectations. By 1940, the United States had signed bilateral trade agreements with twenty-one nations that accounted for over 60 percent of U.S. trade. But the reduction in U.S. and foreign tariffs was modest and thus had only a limited impact on trade. The RTAA could not reverse the outbreak of protectionism around the world during the 1930s. As figure 5.2 shows, world output resumed its growth after 1932, but trade failed to keep pace: if the depression led to the contraction of world trade, the protectionist policies of the 1930s constricted its recovery.

Instead, the original RTAA had a lasting impact as a political innovation, one of much greater significance than its proponents could ever have imagined. The RTAA fundamentally changed American trade

[24] Schnietz (2000) notes that members of Congress who supported Smoot-Hawley did not change their mind and vote for the RTAA. Economists also played no role in promoting the passage of the RTAA. As Pastor (1980, 91) writes, it is "not surprising that there are few interest group political analyses of the 1934 Trade Act," although changing economic interests were soon to play a critical role in perpetuating the RTAA.

[25] Butler (1998, ix) does not exaggerate in writing that "Cordell Hull's determination, persistence, and legislative experience were determining factors at every stage of the conception, passage, and implementation of the Trade Agreements Act." See also Allen 1953.

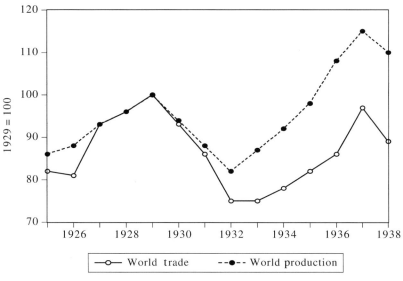

_____*Figure 5.2*

Volume of world trade and production, 1925–38. (Data from General Agreement on Tariffs and Trade 1953, 110.)

politics by tipping the political balance of power in favor of lower tariffs in several ways.[26]

First, when Congress delegated tariff negotiating power to the chief executive, it effectively gave up the ability to legislate duties on specific goods. Congressional votes on trade now came to be framed in terms of whether or not, and under what circumstances, the RTAA should be continued. Vote trading among interests that favored various tariffs was no longer feasible. Thus, the RTAA reduced access to legislative mechanisms that supported redistributive bargains and logrolling coalitions that had led to high tariffs.

Second, the RTAA delegated authority and agenda-setting power to the president, who represented a broad-based constituency and was therefore likely to favor more moderate tariffs than Congress. The na-

[26] See the analysis of Bailey, Goldstein, and Weingast (1997) and Irwin and Kroszner (1999).

tional electoral base of the president is often thought to make the executive more apt to favor policies that benefit the nation as a whole, whereas the narrower geographic representative structure of Congress leads its members to have more parochial interests. Furthermore, the president is more likely than Congress to take into account trade policy's ramifications for foreign policy.

Third, the RTAA reduced the threshold of political support needed for members of Congress to approve negotiated agreements reducing tariffs. Prior to the RTAA, a minority could block foreign trade agreements because treaties had to be approved by a two-thirds majority in the Senate. Now, renewal of the RTAA required a simple majority in Congress. This shifted the threshold of political support needed to approve trade agreements and made them easier to enact. Whereas protectionist forces in the past had to muster only 34 percent of all senators to block a reciprocity agreement, now they needed 51 percent senators to kill a renewal of the RTAA.

Finally, the RTAA helped to bolster the bargaining and lobbying position of exporters in the political process. Previously, the main trade-related special interest groups on Capitol Hill were domestic producers facing import competition since the benefits of high tariffs to these producers were relatively concentrated. Exporters were harmed by high tariffs on imports, but only indirectly. The cost to exporters of any particular import duty was relatively diffuse, and therefore exporters failed to organize an effective political opposition. The RTAA explicitly linked foreign tariff reductions that were beneficial to exporters to lower tariff protection for producers competing against imports. This fostered the development of exporters as an organized group opposing high domestic tariffs because they wanted to secure lower foreign tariffs on their products. In addition, the lower tariffs negotiated under the RTAA increased the size of export sectors and decreased the size of sectors that competed with imports, and thereby increased the political clout of interests supporting renewals of the RTAA.

These attributes of the RTAA reduced the costs and increased the benefits of organization and lobbying by free-trade interests. The RTAA did not make free trade inevitable, however, because at any point Congress could take back the president's negotiating authority or simply allow it to expire. Sustaining the RTAA required the ongoing support of a majority in Congress. In 1934, the RTAA passed easily because the Democrats had large majorities in both chambers. But the shift toward trade liberalization was not secure until a bipartisan consensus supported it. Traditionally protectionist Republicans, who rejected the RTAA throughout the 1930s, had to be persuaded to support it. By the mid-1940s, their position began to soften, and by the late 1940s the Republicans had joined the Democrats in supporting the RTAA, in principle. The switch ensured that changes in the partisan composition of Congress would not significantly alter trade policy and made the RTAA a durable feature of U.S. foreign economic policy.

How did the Republicans, who had enacted the Smoot-Hawley tariff in 1930 and vowed throughout the 1930s to repeal the RTAA, eventually come to support it? The change in relative strength of trade-related economic interests as a result of World War II was an important factor in breaking down the Republican opposition to freer trade. During and immediately after the war, the United States had a large export surplus in just about every category of manufactured goods, including machinery, motor vehicles, chemicals, and textiles. U.S. exports increased dramatically after World War II, while foreign competition was anemic. As figure 1.1 shows, during 1945–47 exports were an average of 5.4 percent of GDP, while imports were just 2.2 percent of GDP. Favorable export opportunities were expected to persist because the competitive position of American manufacturers was strong and European and Asian economies lay in ruins.

Powerful economic interests, including many manufacturers associations and labor unions, supported trade agreements to improve access to foreign markets, or at least to ensure that foreign governments did not raise barriers to U.S. exports. For example, in 1945, major labor organizations, such as the Congress of Industrial Organizations (representing over 6 million workers), the United Automobile and Aircraft Workers, the Textile Workers' Union of America, and the Amalgamated Clothing Workers of America, supported extension of the RTAA. Business groups did as well, including the Chamber of Commerce, the American Farm Bureau, and the American Bankers Association. The new configuration of constituent economic interests could also be seen in the broad support for the program of trade agreements in public opinion polls. Although the pro-protection share of oral and written testimony at

congressional hearings remained high, the many small industries opposed to lower tariffs (such as milk, mushroom, and wool producers)
belied the widespread support for lower tariffs among much larger organizations. Fears that lower tariffs would result in harm to domestic industries were secondary.

However, it is not just the increased size of export-oriented interests after World War II that explains the Republican conversion.
Rather, the RTAA also made those interests more politically active because they now had a specific mechanism by which to obtain lower
foreign tariffs on their products. A similar growth of exports, both absolutely and relative to imports, also occurred during and after World War I
but failed to generate bipartisan support for lower tariffs. Instead, it was
followed by the Republican enactment of the protectionist Fordney-
McCumber tariff of 1922. Without an institutional mechanism such as the
RTAA for harnessing and activating export interests, the simple growth in
the size of export interests did not bring about a basic change in policy.

Similarly, the RTAA alone was insufficient to cause the Republicans to change their position. The RTAA was passed in 1934 over the
objections of the Republicans, and by the 1940 renewal they were no
closer to supporting it than they had been six years earlier. Having a
mechanism in place to facilitate the organization and lobbying of exporters in favor of trade liberalization was itself insufficient to institu-
tionalize the RTAA until export interests grew larger. The combination of
the RTAA and the war-induced export expansion generated the forces
that prompted the Republicans to cross the aisle and support of the
cause of freer trade.

The congressional coalition favoring a more open trade policy
was also strengthened by the linkage of trade policy with foreign policy.[27]
As the Cold War with the Soviet Union intensified after World War II,
liberal trade policies were seen as a way of fighting Communism by
strengthening the economies of Western Europe and Asia. In light of the
experience of the 1930s, isolationism was on the defensive, and the reduction of barriers to world trade was viewed as a key part of the effort
to promote economic recovery and create a more peaceful world. Cordell Hull, Roosevelt's secretary of state and the father of the RTAA, em-

---

[27] Fordham 1998.

bodied this view. He originally supported lower tariffs simply because of their favorable impact on the domestic economy. But the interwar period forcefully demonstrated to him the political benefits of a liberal system of world trade. As he put it, "unhampered trade dovetailed with peace; high tariffs, trade barriers, and unfair economic competition, with war." Hull believed that freer trade might contribute to higher living standards and, by "eliminating the economic dissatisfaction that breeds war," might create "a reasonable chance for lasting peace."[28] By the mid-1940s, protectionism in the field of economic policy was likened to appeasement in the realm of diplomacy, a mistake that helped make the decade of the 1930s a political and economic disaster.[29]

The General Agreement on Tariffs and Trade

To officials at the time, the lesson from the 1930s was absolutely clear: after the war, cooperative actions must be taken to reduce barriers to international trade. Even as World War II raged, American and British officials began exploring possible postwar trade arrangements. The United States aimed to convert the piecemeal, bilateral RTAA approach into a broader, multilateral system based on nondiscrimination and the reduction of trade barriers. Unlike plans for the postwar international monetary system, which were completed at the Bretton Woods conference in 1944, the trade arrangements materialized more slowly. In December 1945, the State Department published its *Proposals for the Expansion of World Trade and Employment*, which envisioned an International Trade Organization (ITO) having wide-ranging rules and guidelines regarding trade policy, restrictive business practices, commodity agreements, employment policy, economic development, and international investment. This document became the basis for negotiations that dragged on for another two and a half years.

To expedite the more specific negotiations over trade policy, representatives from twenty-three countries gathered in Geneva from

[28] Hull 1948, 81.

[29] As Pastor (1983, 161) put it, the "Smoot-Hawley tariff of 1930 is to commerce what the Munich agreement of 1938 is to peace. . . . [T]hey remain indelibly imprinted on the consciousness of the world as historical errors of such magnitude that every generation of leaders has pledged to avoid repeating them."

April to October 1947. Representatives of these countries, which accounted for roughly 80 percent of world trade, agreed on tariff reductions and on the text of a General Agreement on Tariffs and Trade (GATT), setting out principles for the conduct of commercial policy. Accounts of the months of arduous negotiations indicate that the negotiations were almost derailed on multiple occasions.[30] As difficult as it is to conclude trade agreements today, the obstacles to reaching an agreement after the war were simply enormous, mainly because the negotiating positions were so far apart. Compromises on all sides were required to bring about this landmark agreement.

The main U.S. negotiating objectives were to reduce trade barriers and eliminate quantitative restrictions, export subsidies, and preferential trade arrangements, particularly tariff preferences within the British Commonwealth. The United States had mixed success in achieving these objectives. The United Kingdom resisted the elimination of tariff preferences within the British Empire and wanted to retain the option of using quantitative trade controls for the purpose of economic planning. Developing countries had a host of other objectives that they put ahead of trade liberalization. They wanted exceptions that would allow countries to intervene in trade to strengthen the balance of payments, to maintain full employment, and to promote economic development. In the end, the United States could not impose the terms of an agreement on other countries that did were reluctant to embrace all of its objectives. The final agreement therefore failed to eliminate existing preferences and allowed countries great latitude in maintaining trade restrictions.

Still, overall trade barriers fell significantly as a result of the Geneva conference. Tariff reductions were negotiated on a bilateral, product-by-product basis. Under the "reciprocal mutual advantage" principle, no country would be forced to make any unilateral concessions. If a bilateral agreement on specific commodity tariffs was reached, the lower negotiated rates would then be applied to all other members, through the most-favored nation clause, and considered bound at those rates. Precise estimates of the degree to which countries reduced their tariffs are unavailable, but table 5.1 shows that major European countries re-

---

[30] Zeiler (1999) provides a detailed account of the negotiations leading to the GATT.

duced their import tariffs significantly between the early 1930s and the early 1950s. Although average tariffs were in the 20 percent range in the 1950s, quantitative restrictions and exchange controls persisted until the mid-1950s in many of these countries.

The United States reduced its tariff about 20 percent in the first GATT round. These tariff reductions did not require congressional approval because of the authority granted the president in the 1945 renewal of the RTAA. But as figure 5.1 illustrates, average U.S. tariffs dropped sharply from about 45 percent in 1933 to just over 10 percent in the early 1950s. Most of this reduction was not actually the result of negotiated reductions in tariff rates, but the result of another less obvious, and less politically contentious, mechanism. About two-thirds of U.S. import duties during this period were a specific dollar amount per imported quantity rather than a percentage tax rate. Because the specific duties were unchanged in nominal terms, inflation during and after World War II dramatically eroded the ad valorem equivalent of these duties.[31] This erosion was simply permitted to run its course without congressional interference because foreign competition was not a significant problem facing domestic industries in the late 1940s and a bipartisan consensus had emerged in support of presidential authority to negotiate additional tariff reductions.

At the same time they were negotiating tariff reductions, the countries at the Geneva conference agreed upon a charter, a general agreement, regarding the broad principles that should govern trade policies. The main provisions of the General Agreement on Tariffs and Trade (GATT) are summarized in table 5.2.[32] First and foremost, Article 1 declared that all GATT signatories would extend unconditional most-favored nation treatment to all other contracting parties.[33] Governments would have discretion in choosing the terms on which they permitted foreign goods into their country, but as a matter of principle (if not al-

---

[31] See Irwin 1998b.

[32] See Jackson (1997) for an overview of GATT rules.

[33] The MFN clause in Article 1 simply reads: "With respect to customs duties and charges of any kind imposed on or in connection with importation or exportation . . . any advantage, favour, privilege or immunity granted by any contracting party to any product originating in or destined for any other country shall be accorded immediately and unconditionally to the like products . . . of all other contracting parties." The text of the 1947 GATT is available in World Trade Organization 1999a.

_____Table 5.2
Major Provisions of the General Agreement on Tariffs and Trade

Provision	Description
Article 1	General most-favored nation treatment
Article 2	Schedule of tariff concessions
Article 3	National treatment on internal taxes and regulation
Article 6	Antidumping and countervailing duties
Article 10	Transparency of trade regulations
Article 11	General elimination of quantitative restrictions
Article 12	Restrictions to safeguard the balance of payments
Article 14	Exceptions to rule of nondiscrimination
Article 16	Subsidies
Article 17	State trading enterprises
Article 19	Emergency action on imports of particular products (safeguards)
Article 20	General exceptions
Article 21	Security exceptions
Article 23	Nullification and impairment
Article 24	Customs unions and free-trade areas

ways practice) they would not be allowed to treat the goods from one signatory of the GATT differently from the same goods of another. The United States insisted on nondiscrimination in trade relations, a U.S. objective ever since the presidency of George Washington.

Similarly, Article 3 requires that countries imposing domestic taxes and regulations adhere to the standard of "national treatment." National treatment is another form of nondiscrimination by which domestic and imported goods should face the same regulatory standards. Under this provision, governments were prevented from setting one standard for domestic products and then imposing a more stringent standard for similar imported products.[34]

The other articles of the GATT deal with more specific trade policy issues. Article 6 condemns dumping if it causes or threatens material injury to an established industry and sets out very general standards for imposing antidumping and countervailing duties. Article 16 mandates that countries avoid the use of subsidies for primary products and proposes that countries limit subsidies. Article 11 is a sweeping prohibition

---

[34] The text reads that the products of one contracting partner "shall be accorded treatment no less favorable than that accorded to like products of national origin in respect to all laws" and regulations pertaining to their sale, distribution, or use.

on the use of quantitative restrictions, although Article 12 permits the imposition of import quotas during balance-of-payments difficulties. Article 18 is a general exemption for developing countries from GATT rules to give them flexibility to support infant industries and protect their balance of payments. Other articles of the GATT address such mundane details as the valuation of merchandise for customs purposes, marks of origin, and the transparency and publication of trade regulations.

The Geneva conference that founded the GATT was a tremendous success. In the interwar period, the major trading countries made virtually no attempt to stem the rising tide of trade barriers. Convinced that there must be international cooperation on trade policy after the war, the major trading countries sought to reduce barriers, establish a set of rules governing trade, and create a forum in which they could regularly discuss issues of policy with one another. These goals were all accomplished in Geneva under extremely difficult circumstances. This conference put international trade and trade relations on the right path for the postwar period.

Despite this early success, the years after Geneva were not easy ones for the GATT system. The GATT was supposed to be a component of a more comprehensive multilateral agreement that would create an International Trade Organization and cover such issues as commodities, investment, employment, and economic development. Although a final agreement on the ITO charter was reached in Havana in 1948, U.S. negotiators were forced to make so many compromises that they ultimately lost the support of the business community and key members of Congress. This effectively killed the ITO, and in 1950 the Truman administration announced that it would not be submitted for congressional approval.[35]

The downside of this failure to establish a formal trade organization was that the GATT lacked a strong institutional basis. The countries signing the GATT were "contracting parties" and not members because the GATT was simply an agreement between governments, and not formally an international organization. The GATT as an institution consisted

---

[35] As Zeiler (1999, 145–46) puts it, "the charter was so ridden with exceptions to free trade that much of its original meaning had been eroded in a morass of discriminatory measures. Government regulation and protectionism served as its foundation. This development owed much to the acceptance of big government during the Great Depression and the Second World War, as well as to the instability of the postwar economy."

_____Table 5.3
GATT Negotiating Rounds

Negotiating Round	Dates	Major Accomplishments
1. Geneva	1947	GATT established. Tariff reduction of about 20 percent negotiated
2. Annecy	1949	Accession of 11 new contracting parties. Minor tariff reduction (about 2 percent)
3. Torquay	1950–51	Accession of 7 new contracting parties. Minor tariff reduction (about 3 percent)
4. Geneva	1955–56	Minor tariff reduction (about 2.5 percent)
5. Dillon Round	1960–61	Negotiations involving external tariff of European Community. Minor tariff reduction (4 percent)
6. Kennedy Round	1964–67	Tariff reduction of about 35 percent.
7. Tokyo Round	1973–79	Tariffs reduction of about 33 percent. Six codes negotiated (subsidies, technical barriers, etc.)
8. Uruguay Round	1986–94	WTO established. Additional tariff reductions. New agreements on dispute settlement, agriculture, clothing, services, investment, and intellectual property
9. Doha Round	2001–	To be determined.

of an extremely small secretariat in Geneva, but its official standing was precarious.[36] The upside of this failure was that the GATT remained a small institution devoted to a single mission: promoting further attempts to liberalize trade and establishing broad rules for commercial policy. Having a narrow focus rather than a multifaceted agenda, in contrast to the World Bank and International Monetary Fund, proved to be an advantage.

The GATT lived on, but after Geneva there was a long period in which relatively little was accomplished. Subsequent negotiating rounds were held at Annecy (1949), Torquay (1950–51), and Geneva (1955–56) (table 5.3). These negotiations resulted in the accession of more countries to the GATT, but further tariff reductions were negligible, about 2 percent in each round, on average. The Dillon Round (1961–62) also produced little in terms of tangible results.

[36] Refusing to give it formal recognition, Congress inserted in trade legislation throughout the 1950s the statement that "this Act shall not be construed to determine or indicate the approval or disapproval by the Congress of the Executive Agreement known as the General Agreement on Tariffs and Trade." See Hudec 1990, 70.

Because of the passivity of the United States and other countries, the GATT did not achieve much for more than a decade after its establishment. However, Western European countries were actively dismantling various barriers on intra-European trade. In 1958, six European countries agreed to eliminate all tariffs on each others goods, thus forming the Common Market. U.S. exporters were concerned that their sales would suffer because American goods would still be subject to import duties in Europe. To reduce the margin of preference on intra-European trade, Congress took a serious interest in reducing trade barriers between the United States and Europe. They authorized the president to undertake new, substantive negotiations by passing the Trade Expansion Act of 1962. The Kennedy Round, begun in 1962 and concluded in 1967, resulted in a 35 percent reduction in tariffs, on average. These cuts were generally across the board, with each country receiving exemptions for sensitive sectors. The across-the-board approach proved to be more efficient and less cumbersome than the product-by-product negotiations used in previous rounds, although this was not obvious from the length of the negotiations.

The Tokyo Round negotiations (from 1973 to 1979) sliced tariffs by another third. By this time, tariffs on manufactured goods for the major industrialized countries had generally fallen to low levels. As a result, the Tokyo Round began the trend toward even more difficult negotiations about nontariff barriers. The Tokyo Round resulted in several codes dealing with nontariff issues such as subsidies, technical barriers, import licenses, government procurement, customs valuation, and antidumping procedures. These codes substantially broadened the scope of trade rules in certain areas, but also contained wide-ranging exceptions. In addition, countries could pick and choose which, if any, of the codes it wished to adopt, an approach that became known as "GATT à la carte." A majority of GATT members, including most developing countries, chose not to sign the codes.

_____What Explains the GATT's Success?

The reduction in trade barriers and the stability of trade policy in most countries produced an environment that was conducive to world trade expansion. As figure 5.3 indicates, world trade has grown much more rapidly than world output in the postwar period. The architects of the

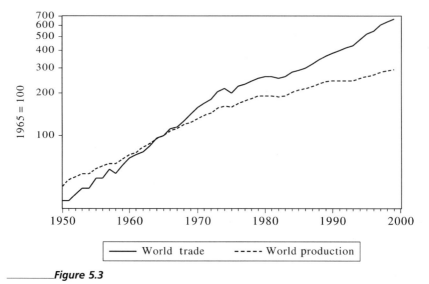

_____Figure 5.3
Volume of world trade and production, 1950–99. (Data from World Trade Organization 2000, table II.1.)

postwar world trading system desperately wanted to avoid a repeat of the interwar trade policies, and they succeeded in doing so. But why have multilateral trade agreements under the GATT system worked so well since 1947?

From a strictly economic point of view, the GATT's system of reciprocity in tariff reductions and rules for commercial policy is unnecessary because a country is better off pursuing a policy of free trade regardless of the trade policies pursued by other countries. As set out in chapter 2, the case for free trade is a unilateral one: as Joan Robinson famously put it, a country should not throw rocks into its harbors simply because other countries have rocks in theirs. The mercantilist language of international trade negotiations—that a reduction in one's own trade barriers is a "concession" to others—is wrong from an economic standpoint. But it turns out that reciprocity has worked fairly well since 1947.

The reason is that reciprocity, achieved through multilateral trade agreements, has both economic and political value for governments seeking to contain protectionist pressures. When countries choose their tariffs alone, outcomes can be inefficient economically because governments are pressured by import-competing producers into maintaining trade restrictions. Although unilateral free trade is beneficial, not all unilateral policies are free trade, as we have seen in the case of the United States. Multilateral tariff cooperation is a way to avoid an economically inefficient result. In addition, the gains from trade are magnified if other countries also reduce their trade barriers.[37] Multilateral trade agreements are beneficial politically because they enhance domestic support for open trade by making exporters more politically active, counterbalancing the power of interests opposed to imports and thus facilitating trade liberalization.[38]

The GATT's economic and political value can be seen in countries' adherence to its provisions even though it has no direct power to enforce them. Under Article 23, if any contracting party fails to carry out its obligation or undertakes an action that "nullifies or impairs" a benefit due to another party, other countries can ask the GATT to allow them to suspend their concessions or waive their obligations to the offending country. In other words, if one country fails to adhere to the rules, then other countries are not obligated to adhere to the rules with respect to it. They can retaliate by raising tariffs against the rule-breaker's goods. In the "chicken war" of 1962, the United States imposed tariffs on $26 million in European goods because Europe violated GATT rules by imposing a high variable levy on poultry imports.

Thus, the countries that have signed the GATT contract are responsible for enforcing the agreement; no independent power resides with the GATT itself, which essentially relies on the good will of the

[37] If tariff policies are interdependent, such that an increase in one country's tariff leads to an increase in another country's tariff, then a noncooperative equilibrium will include relatively high tariffs and be inefficient. The models of Mayer (1981) and Bagwell and Staiger (1999) help identify the economic and political advantages that arise from cooperation in trade policy, but fail to address why countries would ever remain mired in a noncooperative equilibrium if there were gains from cooperation. The models also have welfare-maximizing governments focus on the effects of tariffs on terms of trade, even though it is not clear that governments are motivated by this consideration. For example, Brown and Whalley (1980) point out that countries would have been better off by adopting the tariff-cutting formulas proposed by other countries rather than their own.

[38] Moser (1990), Hillman and Moser (1996), and Maggi and Rodríguez-Clare (1998) provide theoretical analysis of these points, rooted in domestic politics. In such models, free-trade agreements can be a commitment mechanism that allows the government to resist political contributions that could induce interventions harmful to economic efficiency.

signatories. Information and reputation are two critical factors that sustain trade agreements.[39] Information about adherence to them is more complete with multilateral than with bilateral monitoring. And reputation can be a powerful device for preventing their erosion because a country that fails to adhere to them forfeits the right to insist that other countries do so, and thus risks discrimination against its exports.[40]

Still, the postwar system has several notable defects. The GATT legal framework is written broadly, often with several exceptions for every rule. These exceptions give countries the flexibility to deal with unexpected contingencies and to maneuver through politically difficult decisions on policy. But they also provide loopholes and excuses for evading the basic principles of the agreement. For example, Article 1 contains the MFN clause, but Article 14 is entitled "Exceptions to the Rule of Nondiscrimination," and Article 24 permits countries to form customs unions and free-trade areas, which are inherently discriminatory. Article 11 generally forbids the use of import quotas and quantitative restrictions, but Article 13 states that when they are imposed, they should be administered in a nondiscriminatory way, a provision that would be unnecessary if Article 11 were fully effective.

Another problem has been gaps in the coverage of the rules. The agricultural sector and developing countries were exempt from many of the GATT disciplines. In 1935, Congress amended the Agricultural Adjustment Act of 1933 and authorized the president to impose quotas on foreign goods that interfered with farm programs and price supports. After 1952, the United States began imposing quotas on imports of such goods as oats, barley, butter, and milk and in 1955 received a broad waiver from the GATT—which was powerless prevent the quotas—to continue them. (The European Union similarly restricts agricultural trade with the Common Agricultural Policy.) Because policies affecting the agricultural sector are so politically sensitive, the Kennedy

---

[39] Maggi (1999) stresses these factors.

[40] In Hudec's (1998, 36) view, "other governments interested in maintaining the integrity of legal commitments are willing to go to considerable lengths to expose the defendant government to criticism for not keeping its word. . . . to be caught not performing one's own obligations is to lose the right to enforce the obligations on others, thereby losing specific trade opportunities as well as imperiling the entire liberal trading system. Rarely, if ever, does the gain from a violation of GATT obligations make it worth jeopardizing the benefits of the existing trade order."

Round and the Tokyo Round failed even to discuss the reduction of agricultural trade barriers.

Developing countries were given "special and differential treatment" under the GATT beginning in the mid-1960s. They were allowed greater flexibility in applying rules and were not bound by all of the GATT commitments. For example, reciprocity in tariff reductions was not expected of developing countries. (However, the degree of special and differential treatment was reduced, and agricultural trade measures were made subject to negotiation, in the Uruguay Round of negotiations; see chapter 6).

Despite these deficiencies, over the past half century the multilateral trading system has achieved many of its original goals. Countries that are party to the GATT have generally adhered to the rules. Nondiscrimination has been established as a benchmark for commercial policy, and tariff barriers have been significantly reduced in successive negotiating rounds. In addition, overall trade relations have been good: specific disputes have been contained and policies have been stable, providing an environment in which international commerce has flourished. To be sure, discriminatory policies remain, antidumping actions and some nontariff barriers have risen, and disputes still arise and sometimes fester. But on the whole, the postwar system must be judged a great success. This outcome is a formidable and enduring achievement of the architects of the postwar economic order.

Two other factors have made this outcome possible. First, the postwar economic expansion has been relatively smooth, punctuated only by a few recessions but free of major depressions. This experience has muted demands for protection and reduced the burdens of adhering to the rules. Economic growth mitigates the pain associated with structural shifts, due to international trade or other factors, by creating new opportunities for those displaced. In short, the economic shocks confronting the trading system have not been strong enough to bring about a systemic collapse, although the system was tested during the recession of the early 1980s.

Second, the bipartisan consensus forged in the United States during the 1940s in favor of reciprocal trade agreements has stayed largely intact. The tepid Republican support for trade liberalization faded as the postwar economic boom continued and as business interests continued to take an interest in opening up foreign markets for U.S. goods. By the early 1970s, on the other hand, several important Democratic constituencies had become less comfortable with liberalization efforts. Several labor unions, some of which had earlier supported reciprocal trade agreements, now began pressing for limits on trade as competition from imports intensified. The AFL-CIO's decision to support quotas in the Burke-Hartke bill in 1971 was the first clear signal that organized labor was now opposed to freer trade.[41] By the 1970s, union workers in the steel and automobile industries had joined others in taking a more aggressive stand against imports. Trade issues have become increasingly contentious, and the bipartisan consensus has frayed at the edges, and yet both Republican and Democratic administrations have continued to press for trade-liberalizing measures and have passed them through Republican and Democratic congresses.[42]

While a commitment to the multilateral system has been one central feature of U.S. trade policy, two other aspects of that policy have become increasingly important in recent decades. First, Congress has altered the administrative structure and legal framework in which trade policy is formed, reducing the president's discretionary powers and easing the requirements for industries seeking administered protection. Second, multilateral trade negotiations have been supplemented with regional and preferential trade arrangements, such as NAFTA, with uncertain effects for the GATT system.

_____The Administration of U.S. Trade Policy

On a regular basis Congress changes the domestic laws governing trade policy. The changes have created a set of rules governing a trade bureaucracy that is sensitive to specific import-competing and export-oriented domestic interests and empowered to act on their behalf.

The Trade Expansion Act of 1962 established the Office of the Special Trade Representative as the agency within the executive branch

---

[41] See Destler 1998.

[42] To those who believe that passing trade measures through Congress has become increasingly difficult, one should recall that such actions were not easy in the 1960s or 1970s either, as Dryden (1995) reminds us. See also Destler (1995) on the politics of American trade policy during this period.

having overall responsibility for trade policy and negotiations. (It was renamed the renamed the Office of the U.S. Trade Representative, or USTR, in 1979.) Congress feared that the State Department, which had handled previous trade negotiations, was too interested in maintaining good diplomatic relations with foreign countries and sacrificed business interests to that end. Congress created the Special Trade Representative as a strong negotiator for U.S. exporters and a guardian of the interests of industries that competed against imports.

In the Trade Act of 1974, Congress required that it approve trade agreements after their negotiation. Under the RTAA, as we have seen, Congress authorized the president to reduce import tariffs by executive order, without congressional approval. The Tokyo Round negotiations, however, aimed to reduce nontariff barriers to trade. Any agreement on nontariff barriers would require changes in domestic laws and could not, for constitutional reasons, be implemented simply by executive order. Congress would therefore have to pass legislation bringing U.S. law into conformity with the international agreement. To avoid the old problem of legislative undermining of trade negotiations, Congress agreed to a "fast track" procedure in which the president would submit the trade agreement and legislation making the necessary changes in domestic law, and Congress would vote expeditiously on the package without the possibility of amendment.

This mechanism was used to approve the Tokyo Round agreement in 1979, the U.S.-Canada Free Trade Agreement in 1988, and the North American Free Trade Agreement and the Uruguay Round agreement in 1993. The original motivation for the fast-track mechanism was simply to cope with the growing complexity of trade negotiations, which had moved beyond import tariffs to internal regulations affecting trade. The effect has been to give Congress greater influence over trade policy since now it must approve any agreement. Accordingly, the executive branch is now much more sensitive to congressional concerns about trade.[43]

The Trade Act of 1974 also made changes to the legal framework governing trade policy. The Tariff Commission was renamed the

---

[43] A commitment by Congress to fast-track consideration of any executive trade agreement lapsed in 1994, but in December 2001 the House of Representatives voted to grant the president "trade promotion authority" equivalent to fast track.

International Trade Commission with the task of making determinations of injury in trade cases. The criteria were relaxed for such a determination in cases that fell under the Section 201 escape clause. The injury-causing imports no longer had to be linked to a specific tariff reduction. Now, any imports that caused injury would be potential grounds for relief. In addition, imports no longer had to be a "major cause" of serious injury, but just a "substantial cause" of injury.[44]

Section 301 of the Trade Act of 1974 also established a mechanism for exporters to seek redress if any "act, policy or practice of a foreign country is unreasonable or discriminatory and burdens or restricts United States commerce." This provision is administered by USTR in response to petitions received from domestic exporters, although USTR can also initiate cases. If it accepts a petition, USTR is responsible for consulting with the foreign country. If negotiations fail to modify the objectionable policy, the president can impose retaliatory duties on goods from the offending country.

Likened to a "crowbar" used to pry open foreign markets, Section 301 has been controversial because the United States unilaterally judges the policies of other countries under the threat of retaliation.[45] A stronger version of the law, known as "Super 301," provides for the identification of "priority" countries and mandates retaliation if an adequate remedy is not forthcoming. Enacted in 1988 for three years, but later renewed by executive orders, Super 301 has drawn the ire of potential targets (such as Japan, India, and Brazil) as well as exporters in other countries, who fear being cut out of foreign markets if the United States uses it to reach special preferential deals for its own producers. Section 301 has also been blamed for waning interest among exporters in multilateral trade liberalization: exporters who can use Section 301 to reduce foreign trade barriers on their particular products no longer have as great a stake in multilateral negotiations.

Heavily used in the 1980s, Section 301 has faded in importance in recent years, perhaps because of the increased importance of the World Trade Organization's dispute settlement process, which will be

---

[44] All quotations from U.S. trade law come from U.S. Congress (1997).
[45] See Bhagwati and Patrick 1990.

discussed in chapter 6.[46] For example, when Eastman Kodak filed a Section 301 petition in 1995 alleging that Japan's market for photographic film and paper was closed, USTR deflected the petition and pushed the case to the WTO. (The WTO later ruled that there was insufficient evidence that government measures constituted a barrier to Kodak's sales.)

The Trade Act of 1979, which implemented the Tokyo Round agreements, brought additional changes to the administration of trade policy. Congress transferred from the Treasury Department to the Commerce Department investigatory power in cases involving dumping and countervailing duties. Firms facing competition from imports had criticized Treasury for lack of interest in such cases. The congressional steel caucus and other groups that wanted more liberal use of antidumping measures advocated this transfer with the (correct) view that Commerce, whose natural constituency is American businesses, would be much more enthusiastic about providing relief. The number of antidumping petitions filed increased sharply after Commerce took control.

The Trade and Tariff Act of 1984 broadened the definition of legal standing to bring an antidumping petition, instructed Commerce to provide assistance to small firms that could not afford to file a petition, and instituted the cumulation of imports in ITC's injury determination (see chapter 4). Concerned that presidents were too frequently rejecting relief in cases filed under the Section 201 escape clause, Congress allowed itself to overrule, with a joint resolution, any presidential escape clause determination. The Omnibus Trade and Competitiveness Act of 1988 made innumerable changes in the language of trade statutes, many apparently trivial, but all of which work in the same direction: to increase the number of cases alleging unfair trade, to increase the probability of finding injury, and to increase the likelihood and magnitude of protection once a case is concluded.[47]

---

[46] There were twenty-one Section 301 cases initiated from 1974 to 1979, fifty-eight cases from 1980 to 1989, and thirty-nine cases from 1990 to 1999, many self-initiated by USTR in the later period.

[47] The escape clause was also changed such that injury can be judged not only by lost sales, but by lost market share (of course, a firm can lose market share even as its sales increase in a growing market). The CVD law was changed so that any subsidy "in fact" is countervailable, whereas previously subsidies that were generally available to many

The combined impact of these small changes in legal language is substantial and biases the process in favor of more intervention and protection. They amount to "procedural protectionism," a reduction in presidential discretionary power and an easing of the legal requirements for industries seeking administered protection.[48] As a result, critics have charged that trade policy has been privatized: that any industry exporting to foreign markets or competing against imports in the United States can get the government to act on its behalf.

_____Preferential Trade Arrangements

In the early 1980s, at a time when the multilateral process had stalled, the United States began undertaking bilateral and regional trade agreements. Starting in 1983, the Caribbean Basin Initiative granted certain unilateral preferences to goods from countries in the region. The United States also started negotiations with Israel on a free-trade agreement, which was completed in 1985. Also in 1985 the United States and Canada began negotiating a free-trade agreement, which was signed in 1988 and implemented the next year. In 1990, negotiations opened to bring in Mexico, and the North American Free Trade Agreement was finalized in 1993. A free-trade agreement with Jordan was signed in 2000. And in April 1998, representatives of countries in North and South America agreed to undertake negotiations for a Free Trade Area in the Americas (FTAA) with the aim of eliminating tariffs in the Western Hemisphere by 2005.

The motivation for these agreements vary. In some cases, a diplomatic or foreign policy objective is at stake; in others cases, economic or sectoral interests are thought to be advanced. Whatever the case, economists have viewed these preferential agreements with skepticism, particularly in comparison to a multilateral approach to trade liberalization. The problem is that these so-called free-trade agreements are really preferential and discriminatory trade arrangements.[49] Although Article 23

---

industries could not be offset. And the "Super 301" provision reduced presidential discretion by requiring the administration to name priority countries that maintained unfair trade practices and by mandating the imposition of trade sanctions if negotiations were not successful.

[48] The phrase is due to Grinols (1989).

[49] Bhagwati and Panagariya (1996) stress this point.

of the GATT permits them, they are contrary to the most-favored-nation treatment (MFN) embodied in Article 1. And there is a risk that they could actually harm economic welfare.

The classic analysis of preferential trade arrangements distinguishes two effects: trade creation and trade diversion. When the United States and Mexico eliminate tariffs on each other's goods, prices to consumers fall and trade is created. However, U.S. and Mexican exporters are also given preference over other countries in the two partners' markets, possibly diverting existing trade away from nonmember countries. In other words, the tariff preferences may shift trade not on the basis of economic efficiency, but on the basis of preferential tax treatment. Countries may be induced to purchase their imports from less efficient producers, possibly harming economic welfare. Preferential agreements create a distortion because a tax incentive is given for trade with certain countries and not with others.

The precise magnitudes of trade creation and trade diversion are hard to determine. In the case of NAFTA, for example, it is extremely difficult to distinguish the effects of the slowly phased-in tariff preferences on United States–Mexico trade from those of the peso crisis in December 1994 and the ongoing rise of the maquiladoras.[50] The welfare effects of the preferences are even harder to gauge. Assessment hinges on whether (pretariff) import prices were actually higher than they would have been in the absence of the preferential treatment. There is precious little empirical evidence on this crucial point: some research suggests that preferences might harm the welfare of nonmembers by forcing them to reduce their export prices.[51]

Rules of origin are a potentially more serious distortion to trade that can arise in preferential agreements. In a preferential agreement, each member country retains its own tariff schedule that it applies to imports from nonmembers countries.[52] This gives rise to transshipment: the incentive to bring imports into the country with the lowest tariff and then ship them into the high-tariff country. To avoid transshipment,

---

[50] According to one assessment (Krueger 2000), there is not much empirical support for the concern that NAFTA would result in substantial trade diversion.

[51] Winters and Chang 2000.

[52] In a customs unions such as the European Union, all member countries have a common external tariff.

NAFTA mandates that duty-free treatment extends only to goods with sufficient "North American" content. About two hundred pages of the two-thousand-page NAFTA text is devoted to rules of origin, which are stricter than those in the U.S.-Canada Free Trade Agreement. In the Canadian agreement, automobiles must have 50 percent North American content to receive duty-free treatment, but this was raised to 62.5 percent in NAFTA. In the original agreement with Canada, textile and apparel goods must be made from North American fabric to be eligible, but under NAFTA the yarn from which the fabric is woven must also be of North American content. Thus, Mexican garments receive duty-free treatment in the United States only if the yarn is made, the cloth woven, and the cutting and sewing done primarily in North America.

Rules of origin can bring about trade distortions when exporters strive to achieve enough North American content. For example, Mexican producers may shift their imports from third-country suppliers to higher-cost U.S. sources.[53] This diversion raises the North American content so that the goods can qualify for duty-free treatment in United States.

Although preferential trade agreements have been subject to valid criticisms, such agreements may have countervailing benefits. The concerns about trade creation and trade diversion take a purely static view of trade, ignoring the beneficial effects on U.S. and Mexican productivity as a result of greater competition. Furthermore, trade diversion is not a serious concern from the standpoint of the United States because the margins of preferences are so low due to the low average tariffs. (The story may be different for high-tariff countries signing an agreement with the United States.) And sometimes regional trade agreements can provide templates that can be later adopted at the multilateral level, as was the case with the U.S.-Canada agreement on services trade.

One of the most important issues concerning regional trade arrangements is whether they are stepping-stones to multilateral liberalization of trade, or stumbling blocks that detract from the multilateral system and distort trade flows into artificial regional patterns.[54] It is difficult to know, a priori, whether regional and multilateral trade arrangements are complements or substitutes. This depends upon the intention of the

---

[53] Krueger 1999.
[54] This phraseology is due to Jagdish Bhagwati.

participants and upon reaction of other countries, whether they wish to join the agreement or respond by forming their own preferential arrangements. Fortunately, the preferential trade agreements are fundamentally different from the pernicious bilateralism of the 1930s: the momentum is entirely toward removing trade barriers, resulting in smaller preferential margins, rather than in creating even greater degrees of discrimination.

Bilateral and regional trade agreements have proliferated in recent years. The World Trade Organization reports that 114 regional trade agreements are in effect as of mid-2000. These agreements are complex and overlapping. There are sound reasons to be concerned about the effect of these agreements on the multilateral system. Many of the agreements, particularly among developing countries, liberalize trade only marginally and lack much substance. The political effort vested in these schemes could be better deployed at the multilateral level.[55] And because of their overlapping nature, to say nothing of their complexity, preferential trade arrangements detract from the simplicity that was part of the multilateral system's design. Regional trade arrangements are generally concluded no more quickly than multilateral initiatives, and thus the advantages of pursuing them are questionable.[56]

In many instances, these arrangements are pursued for their political importance more than for their economic effects. The formation of the European Economic Community, the precursor to the present-day European Union, was driven by a desire to solidify political and economic ties in a way not possible without some discrimination. When Mexico signaled that it was interested in pursuing a free-trade agreement with the United States as a way of promoting closer political ties and economic integration, it would have been nearly impossible for any administration to snub the request.

Despite these regional diversions, the United States continues to

[55] Levy (1997) examines a median voter model in which the choice of joining a preferential trade agreement affects the subsequent choice of whether to participate in a multilateral agreement. He finds that, in a model with differentiated products and variety gains from trade, PTAs can undermine political support for multilateral agreements.

[56] The Free Trade Area in the Americas initiative was first broached in 1994 (but dates from much earlier) and is now pledged to be completed by 2005. Liberalization under the guise of Asia Pacific Economic Cooperation (APEC) has languished for many years and appears to be going nowhere fast.

play a pivotal role in shaping the multilateral system and to have a great stake in the multilateral process. The best evidence of this is the most wide ranging and successful round of multilateral trade negotiations to date, the Uruguay Round, concluded in 1994. The Uruguay Round established the World Trade Organization and strengthened the world trading system's mechanism for settling disputes, but also made the WTO the target of hostile complaints, as the next chapter describes.

6

The World Trade Organization and New Battlegrounds

Over the past half century, the multilateral system of world trade rules has provided a stable environment in which international trade has flourished. The Uruguay Round of trade negotiations, concluded in 1994, proved to be the most sweeping to date, reaching agreements to liberalize trade in agriculture and textiles and apparel, and to extend trade rules to new areas such as services, investment, and intellectual property. In addition, the World Trade Organization was established as a formal multilateral institution with strong procedures for resolving disputes. The GATT had had a rather anonymous existence, but the WTO quickly came under the critical glare of nongovernmental organizations, including environmental groups and labor rights activists. These groups objected to WTO rulings on trade and environmental issues and demanded the inclusion of labor standards in trade agreements. This chapter assesses the WTO as an institution and examines the controversies surrounding trade, the environment, and labor standards.

The Uruguay Round

When the Uruguay Round of multilateral trade negotiations was launched in Punte del Este in 1986, the mood was one of guarded optimism. The previous decade had been a trying period for the world trading system. The Tokyo Round had been only a modest success. Slower economic growth, higher inflation, and persistent unemployment had diminished support for trade liberalization, and the painful recession of the early 1980s had fueled demands for new restrictions. Many observers believed that the GATT system was crumbling and blamed the proliferation of restrictions not covered by trade rules, such as voluntary export restraints. Moreover, countries were increasingly unwilling to adhere to existing rules.[1] The system appeared to be adrift, without leadership or direction.

And yet when the Uruguay Round negotiations were concluded in December 1993 and signed in April 1994, the resulting agreements turned out to be the most successful and comprehensive since the formation of the GATT. They not only liberalized trade in areas that had eluded previous negotiators, notably agriculture and clothing, but extended rules to new areas such as services, investment, and intellectual property. The Uruguay Round also brought about important institutional changes, both creating the World Trade Organization and strengthening the dispute settlement process.[2]

As in previous negotiations, participating countries agreed to reduce tariffs on merchandise goods. Developed countries reduced tariffs on industrial products (excluding petroleum) by about 40 percent on a trade-weighted average basis. This brought average tariff levels in these countries down from 6.3 percent to 3.8 percent. The remaining tariffs are highly uneven across sectors, relatively low on sophisticated manufactured goods but substantially higher on labor-intensive manufactured goods. Developing countries reduced their tariffs by 20 percent on average, bringing their average rates down from 15.3 percent to 12.3 percent.[3] Table 6.1 reports tariffs after the Uruguay Round on industrial, agricultural, and clothing products for selected countries.

More importantly, the Uruguay Round began to incorporate trade in agricultural goods and in textiles and apparel into the GATT system. Since the 1950s, the agricultural policies of many countries had been exempt from the GATT rules. The Multifiber Arrangement (MFA) in textiles and apparel set quantitative limits on trade, product by product, country by country, in a way that GATT rules did not generally permit.

---

[1] For example, the legal scholar John Jackson (1978) warned of the "crumbling institutions of the liberal trade system."

[2] Schott (1994) provides an overview of the accomplishments of the Uruguay Round, and Hoekman and Kostecki (1995) provide an overview of the WTO rules and world trading system. For histories of the Uruguay Round negotiations, see Croom (1995) and Preeg (1995). The texts of the GATT and Uruguay Round agreements were published by Cambridge University Press in World Trade Organization (1999a).

[3] Preeg 1995, 191.

_____Table 6.1
Average Applied Tariffs for Selected Countries after the Uruguay Round

	Industrial Tariffs	Agricultural Tariffs	Textiles and Clothing
Developed countries			
United States	3.1	2.2	14.8
European Union	2.9	3.7	8.7
Japan	1.4	10.5	7.2
Canada	2.6	1.5	14.2
Australia	9.7	3.3	21.6
Developing countries			
Argentina	10.6	4.9	12.1
India	29.0	60.1	42.4
Korea	7.6	11.6	13.0
Thailand	26.8	26.5	28.9

Source: Finger, Ingco, and Reincke 1996.

The Uruguay Round sought to normalize trade in these sectors, so that protection could only take the form of bound, nondiscriminatory tariffs and not be cloaked in special export restraint deals or country-specific quotas operating outside of GATT disciplines.

Reform of agricultural trade had also eluded negotiators ever since the GATT's formation because of the political sensitivity of domestic support for farmers. A key problem facing negotiators in the Uruguay Round was that countries protected agricultural producers through a complex host of measures, including tariffs, import quotas, domestic price supports, and export subsidies. The Uruguay Round agreement limits the use of export subsidies and internal price supports by capping and reducing these outlays from a given base period. The agreement also seeks to ensure greater market access by requiring countries to convert all nontariff barriers (variable import levies, import quotas and prohibitions, voluntary export restraints, etc.) into a single import tariff. After this "tariffication" of existing restrictions, the tariffs are to be reduced over ten years by an average one-third for developed countries and by one-quarter for developing countries.

The resulting tariffs, however, are incredibly high. Table 6.2 reveals just how imposing the remaining restrictions are. Many countries used the process of converting the complex trade barriers into tariffs as an opportunity to cheat, raising tariffs above the existing combina-

_____Table 6.2
Border Protection for Selected Agricultural Goods, 1986–1988, 1995, and 2000 (%)

	Wheat			Sugar		
	Actual Protection	As Bound in Uruguay Round		Actual Protection	As Bound in Uruguay Round	
Country/Region	1986–88	1995	2000	1986–88	1995	2000
European Union	106	170	82	234	297	152
United States	20	6	4	131	197	91
Japan	651	240	152	184	126	58
Brazil	98	45	45	—	55	35
Mexico	−1	74	67	−58	173	156
Other Latin America	−17	34	34	41	85	80
Sub-Saharan Africa	10		133	44		100

Source: Ingco 1996, 437.

tion of nontariff restrictions. This practice, known as "dirty tariffication," means that the actual liberalization in agriculture was slight. In addition, quantitative restrictions and export subsidies that are generally not permissible with manufactured goods persist in agricultural trade.

Still, the agreement on agriculture is a tremendous achievement because it constitutes a critical first step. Various impediments have been simplified into one single transparent metric: tariffs. Although these tariffs are high and severely distort production and trade, they are finally on the negotiating table. Reducing these tariffs and cutting export subsidies will be the task of the Doha Round negotiations, launched by WTO members in November 2001. The reform of agricultural trade will be an objective for many years to come.[4]

The Uruguay Round also abolishes the Multifiber Arrangement, the complex web of bilateral export restraints and import quotas that clogs trade in textiles and apparel. The MFA is scheduled to be phased out over ten years, and if all of these quantitative restrictions are eliminated by 2005 as planned, a major step will have been made toward freer trade in clothing. Yet because much of this liberalization occurs at the end of the transition period, many observers are skeptical that developed countries will have the political will to abolish the MFA without extending the phase-out period. Even if the MFA is abolished, the United States and other developed countries will continue to protect their textile

[4] See Josling (1998) on the tasks ahead in the agricultural trade negotiations.

Dairy			Meat		
Actual Protection	*As Bound in Uruguay Round*		*Actual Protection*	*As Bound in Uruguay Round*	
1986–88	*1995*	*2000*	*1986–88*	*1995*	*2000*
177	289	178	96	96	76
132	144	93	3	31	26
501	489	326	87	93	50
−21	53	46	−52	25	25
−3	66	54	42	50	45
	75	69		51	47
		100			100

and apparel producers with high tariffs, as table 6.1 shows. In addition, antidumping laws will surely remain a vehicle for blocking textile and apparel imports after the MFA is gone.[5]

The Uruguay Round made little progress in regulating the use of antidumping laws, but countries did pledge not to "see, take or maintain any voluntary export restraints, orderly marketing arrangements or any other similar measures on the export or the import side."[6] These so-called gray measures had been previously used by countries to restrict trade without explicitly violating GATT rules. They are now eliminated, at least in principle. When countries seek to protect domestic industries from foreign competition, they are obligated to follow existing procedures and rules regarding safeguards and escape clauses. If adhered to, this provision also constitutes a major improvement in discipline.

The Uruguay Round also produced a General Agreement on Trade in Services (GATS) and established rules regarding trade-related investment measures (TRIMS) and trade-related intellectual property (TRIPS). Although these agreements are weak by the standards of the GATT, they constitute the first attempt to extend the principle of non-discrimination to new areas of international commerce. The core obligations in the GATS are set around three principles: most-favored nation treatment, market access, and national treatment. The main sectors in-

[5] On the MFA, see Spinanger 1999 and Reinert 2000.
[6] Article 11:1(b) of the Agreement on Safeguards, in World Trade Organization 1999a, 280.

clude telecommunications, financial services, air and maritime transport, and construction. Although the agreement contains specific commitments to liberalization, coverage is incomplete because the important provisions of the GATS apply only to the sectors specified by the member countries. In general, trade in services was freed only slightly, but a framework was established in which liberalization could be pursued in the future.

The TRIMs agreement was even more modest in making national treatment the standard for regulating foreign investment. The agreement aims to eliminate quantitative restrictions on investment, including limits on the share of foreign ownership in certain industries. Because of opposition from developing countries, there was no attempt to consider such issues as the right of firms to establish enterprises in other countries, or the elimination of trade-related performance requirements on foreign investment.

The TRIPs agreement is one of the most controversial elements of the Uruguay Round. It consolidates previous international accords protecting copyrights, trademarks, patents, and industrial designs, and provides for the enforcement of these agreements within the WTO. But protection of intellectual property is not strictly speaking a trade issue that should be under the purview of the WTO, especially given the existence of the World Intellectual Property Organization. Many developing countries complain that, unlike mutually beneficial tariff reduction, the TRIPs agreement merely transfers income from developing to developed countries by strengthening the ability of multinational corporations to charge higher prices in poorer countries.[7] In addition, using instruments of trade policy to protect intellectual property makes it harder to reject demands to use them to enforce other non-trade-related objectives, such as environmental or labor standards. It opens the door to many interests who want to use the threat of trade sanctions to achieve their own non-trade objectives, and thus puts the WTO in the business of enforcing behavior in areas only tangentially related to trade. This would ultimately dilute the institution's focus on the reduction of trade barriers.

The Uruguay Round was a "single undertaking," meaning that all participants and future members of the WTO are bound to follow all

[7] Maskus (2000), for example, estimates that the full implementation of the TRIPS agreement would transfer $5.8 billion from developing countries to the United States, and another $2.5 billion to five other developed countries.

of the agreements reached. Unlike the "GATT à la carte" approach of the Tokyo Round, countries cannot pick which accords to adhere to, and "special and differential treatment" for developing countries is limited. Although the obligations are extensive, they are less than the costs of remaining outside the agreement and losing the benefits of MFN treatment by other countries. As a result, membership in the WTO has become increasingly attractive. At the start of the Uruguay Round in 1986, the GATT consisted of 91 contracting parties. The WTO was established in 1995 with nearly 130 members, and by early 2001 the membership had risen to 140 nations, accounting for over 90 percent of world trade. Another 30 countries are waiting to join the organization.

The Uruguay Round was the first round of multilateral trade negotiations in which developing countries played an active role, and their participation helped shape the outcome. Developed countries agreed to abolish the MFA's clothing quotas and to reform agricultural trade, increasing trade in sectors where developing countries have a comparative advantage. In return, developing countries accepted rules in the new areas of trade where developed countries have a comparative advantage. This exchange of market access came to be known as the "grand bargain." However, developing countries increasingly view the grand bargain as sour: they took on many new obligations in services, investment, and intellectual property, and yet developed countries have yet to grant significant access to markets in agriculture and clothing. The developing countries are now more suspicious about the benefits of multilateral negotiations, particularly if developed countries force them to consider labor standards in future negotiations, as will be discussed below. As developing countries become more assertive in the WTO, the developed countries will have to be more sensitive to their concerns, or the differences between the two could become a serious obstacle to completing the recently commenced Doha Round of trade negotiations.

_____The World Trade Organization

The WTO was established in 1995 as a result of the Uruguay Round. The WTO has been a much more visible and controversial organization than the GATT, so it is important to get a sense of what the organization is all about, particularly its dispute settlement mechanism.

The World Trade Organization is something more, but not much more, than the GATT. While the GATT was simply an intergovernmental agreement overseen by a small secretariat, the WTO is an international organization. But like the GATT, it has virtually no independent power. The power to make trade policy and to write the rules governing it resides with the member governments, not with the WTO. The director-general of the WTO, for example, has no policymaking authority and cannot comment directly on members' policies. The scope of the WTO is broader than that of the GATT because it oversees multilateral agreements relating not just to goods, but also to services, investment, and intellectual property. The WTO provides the forum for consultations and negotiations on these matters, assists with the interpretation of the legal texts, arranges for the arbitration of disputes, and conducts fact-finding surveillance reviews of members' policies, but ultimately the accords are intergovernmental agreements. The WTO has no power to force countries to obey the agreements or to comply with its rulings.

Because it is a forum for the discussion of trade policy more than anything else, the WTO as an institution is extremely small. The support staff and budget are limited in comparison to other international organizations. The WTO secretariat in Geneva consists of only five hundred employees, about three hundred of whom are translators. The WTO's budget in 2000 was about $77 million. These figures are paltry in comparison to other international economic organizations, and even some nongovernmental organizations.[8] Yet these small figures do not reflect the true importance of the organization as the cornerstone of the world trading system. Indeed, resources among the international economic organizations may be misallocated: the WTO's mission—to keep the international trading system functioning smoothly—is more clearly defined and perhaps even more important than the World Bank's more diffused mission of promoting economic development, but the WTO's

---

[8] For example, the World Bank employs about 6,000 people and has a budget of about $8 billion, the IMF employs 2,700 people and has a budget of $650 million, the International Labor Organization (ILO) employs 1,700 people and has a budget of $235 million, and the Food and Agriculture Organization (FAO) of the United Nations employs 4,000 with a budget of $325 million. Many nongovernmental organizations have larger budgets than the WTO, such as the World Wildlife Fund ($360 million) and Greenpeace (about $120 million).

budget is a tiny fraction of the bank's. Despite its heavy workload and the importance of its mission, the WTO makes do with relatively few resources. As more nations turn to the organization to resolve trade disputes and handle other commercial matters, those resources may be insufficient.[9]

What most distinguishes the WTO from the GATT, aside from the new agreements, is the dispute settlement process. The original GATT agreement made little provision for settling disputes between member countries. When conflicts arose in the early years, an informal and ad hoc process was developed to help resolve them through negotiation. As it evolved, the GATT would often convene a panel of experts to arbitrate the dispute and interpret GATT rules. The panel would issue a finding about whether the trade measure in question conformed to the rules, but would leave a solution to the parties themselves. Over time, these flexible procedures became more complicated and the growing body of case law was interpreted as having established legal precedent.

The Uruguay Round agreement established a dispute settlement mechanism that largely formalized existing practices. But it also strengthened the process by providing for specific time tables to expedite cases and, perhaps most importantly, by preventing countries from blocking the establishment of a panel or the adoption of a panel report. The GATT operated by consensus, meaning that unanimity was required for most decisions. As a result, a country accused of violations could block the establishment of a panel or, if a panel were set up, could object to the adoption of the panel's report.[10] Understandably, this procedure hampered the enforcement of the rules. Under the WTO, the default has changed. The creation of a panel and the adoption of its report now go forward automatically unless, according to a "negative consensus" rule, there is a consensus in opposition.[11]

---

[9] See Blackhurst (1998) for a discussion.

[10] In addition, the "nullification and impairment" provision of Article 23 allowed a country to raise tariffs against a violating country only if the GATT authorized that action. This authorization also could not occur without a consensus.

[11] As a U.S. Trade Representative (2000, 41) report noted, "Under the GATT, panel proceedings took years, the defending party could simply block any unfavorable judgment, and the GATT panel process did not cover some of the agreements. Under the WTO, there are strict timetables for panel proceedings, the defending party cannot block

How does the new dispute settlement mechanism work? Countries may file "violation" complaints, alleging that specific rules (such as nondiscrimination) have been violated, or "nonviolation" complaints, alleging that a government action "nullifies or impairs" a previous concession even if no specific rule has been broken. If initial consultations to resolve the dispute are not successful, a three-member panel is appointed to determine whether WTO rules have been violated. If it establishes a violation, the panel suggests that the disputed policy be brought into conformity with the rules, but generally leaves to the parties themselves the task of working out a solution. The panel decision can be appealed to an Appellate Body, which rules on matters of law and legal interpretation in the panel report.

As under the GATT, if the policy in question is found to violate the rules, the country can bring its policy into conformity with the rules, or keep the policy in place and offer compensation (lower tariffs) on other goods exported from the complaining country, which then has the option of accepting or rejecting the compensation offer. If neither alternative has been implemented, the complaining country can seek authorization to "suspend the application to the Member concerned of concessions or other obligations in the covered agreements." In other words, the complainant can retaliate by withdrawing previous tariff "concessions" to the country that has chosen not to comply with the finding. Such retaliations occur infrequently because most disputes are settled through negotiations. Two recent high-profile cases in which the United States was authorized to retaliate concern the European Union's ban on hormone-treated beef, which will be discussed shortly, and its discriminatory banana regime, which was settled in early 2001.

Why was the dispute settlement process strengthened in the Uruguay Round? Largely because Congress insisted. In Section 1101 of the Omnibus Trade and Competitiveness Act of 1988, which set out the objectives of the United States in the Uruguay Round, Congress instructed negotiators to seek the opening of foreign markets, the elimination of trade-distorting policies, and the establishment of "a more effec-

---

findings unfavorable to it, and there is one comprehensive dispute settlement process covering all of the Uruguay Round Agreements." Despite the weaknesses of the GATT approach, Hudec (1990) argues that the process actually worked reasonably well in practice because countries made serious efforts to resolve disputes.

tive system of international trading disciplines and procedures." Frustrated with the GATT system, Congress wanted to improve the speed and effectiveness of the dispute settlement mechanisms and procedures.[12]

How has the new dispute settlement process worked? In the first five years of the WTO (1995–99), the United States filed forty-nine complaints about foreign trade measures and was the subject of thirty-five complaints. Of the forty-nine complaints, twenty-five had been resolved by the end of 1999, thirteen through favorable rulings by WTO panels and ten through negotiated settlements.[13] Of the thirty-five complaints brought against the United States, only seven had been completed by the end of 1999, and in six of them some aspect of U.S. policy was found inconsistent with WTO rules. In a report to Congress, the independent General Accounting Office concluded that the dispute settlement process has worked well for the United States. Examining forty-two cases, the GAO found that most led to beneficial changes in foreign regulations and practices and that "none of the changes the United States has made in response to WTO disputes have had major policy or commercial impact to date, though the stakes in several were important."[14]

In Washington, D.C., there is a tendency to judge the dispute settlement mechanism only on the basis of whether the United States "wins" the cases it files and those brought against it. Clearly the mechanism is more important than that. It was established simply to ensure that the rules that countries agreed upon together and pledged to abide by are actually enforced. Sometimes the United States is on the wrong side. For example, in 1995 Costa Rica won a complaint against the United States concerning restrictions on imports of underwear. The fact that small countries can receive fair treatment under the rule of law is a

---

[12] U.S. House of Representatives 1997, 849. When members of Congress complain about the strong dispute settlement process as impinging upon U.S. sovereignty, it is helpful to remember that it was the Congress itself that demanded that the GATT approach be strengthened because of its inherent weaknesses.

[13] U.S. Trade Representative 2000, 41. The other two cases involve the United States and European Union: the beef hormone and banana regime cases, in which the United States had been authorized to retaliate against the European Union for noncompliance.

[14] U.S. General Accounting Office 2000b, 2–3. For a general assessment of the dispute settlement mechanism, see Jackson (2001).

strength of the world trading system. The alternative is that more powerful countries simply dictate outcomes to others.

But even when the United States loses a case, the WTO cannot
force change in U.S. laws, regulations, or policies. The WTO cannot
strike down any U.S. law, as an American court can. As the General
Accounting Office puts it: "The United States maintains that it has the
right not to comply with WTO rulings. However, the United States recognizes that it may bear a penalty for not complying with WTO rulings,
both in the form of retaliatory duties on U.S. exports and in terms of its
reputation as a key player in the world trading system."[15] WTO panels
merely determine whether disputed policies conflict with WTO rules
and, if they do, recommend that members bring those policies into conformity. The disputing countries must still resolve the matter themselves,
often through a negotiated settlement.

Some nonparticipants are disturbed by the closed proceedings
during disputes and ask whose interests get represented in the panels.
Many NGOs, particularly environmental groups, have complained that
the WTO is secretive and antidemocratic in its procedures. Although
they are now allowed to file amicus (friends of the court) briefs, NGOs
are generally barred from the dispute settlement process. This is because
the WTO agreements are strictly government-to-government agreements
that deal with governmental policy, and not the behavior of private
firms. The appropriate way for commercial and noncommercial domestic
interests to influence the WTO is through their member governments
because they are not parties to the negotiated agreements.[16] The GATT
and WTO have typically operated under a diplomatic veil rather than as
an open forum in the past because commercial negotiations involved
reducing tariffs in one sector to secure lower foreign tariffs for another
sector, thus trading off various domestic interests.

The United States wants the institution to become more open
and transparent, but other members have strongly resisted. Because the
WTO is a consensual body, the issue is not one to decide unilaterally
and against the wishes of the other members.[17]

---

[15] U.S. General Accounting Office 2000b, 16.
[16] Robertson (2000) provides an incisive examination of whether so-called civil
society should participate more directly in the WTO.
[17] As Sampson (2000, 42–43) notes, "the view of the significant majority of WTO
members is that it would be inappropriate to allow NGOs to participate directly even as

_____***Environmental Regulations and WTO Rules***

The dispute settlement process has become one of the most controversial aspects of the WTO. Several rulings have raised questions about whether WTO rules take precedent over domestic environmental, health, and safety regulations, thereby impinging on a country's sovereignty. Critics, such as Global Trade Watch, part of Ralph Nader's Public Citizen organization, charge that the WTO has undermined every environmental regulation it has reviewed. Unfortunately, the passionate opposition to certain rulings has given rise to much exaggeration and distortion. For example, Global Trade Watch charges that "in the WTO forum, global commerce takes precedence over everything—democracy, public health, equity, the environment, food safety and more."[18]

This accusation is clearly wrong. The General Accounting Office points out that "WTO rulings to date against U.S. environmental measures have not weakened U.S. environmental protections."[19] As of 1999, fewer than 10 of the more than 140 disputes brought before the WTO had dealt with environmental or health issues, and most trade dispute are quite banal. And these few environmental cases have mainly focused on whether the regulation in question has been implemented in a non-discriminatory way, not whether that regulation is justifiable. At the same time, however, some cases illustrate the difficult issues and potential conflicts that can arise when trade and environmental policy intersect.

What precisely are the trade rules that affect environmental measures? The most relevant provision of the GATT is Article 20, entitled "General Exceptions:"

> Subject to the requirement that such measures are not applied
> in a manner which would constitute a means of arbitrary or

---

observers in the proceedings of WTO meetings." If such groups were allowed, difficult questions would have to be answered: "Which groups of civil society should be represented at different meetings, and who would decide? . . . Should farmers' unions be present during negotiations on the reduction of agricultural subsidies that lead to environmental degradation, or should environmental NGOs? Should consumer groups be present during negotiations when trade liberalization leading to lower consumer prices was being discussed, or should it be the sectoral interests that would be adversely affected by a lowering of trade barriers? . . . Is it not preferable to have a democratically elected government represent the diverse interest groups in a given country?"

[18] Wallach and Sforza 1999, 7.
[19] U.S. General Accounting Office 2000b, 14.

unjustifiable discrimination between countries where the same conditions prevail, or a disguised restriction on international trade, nothing in this Agreement shall be construed to prevent the adoption or enforcement by any contracting party of measures . . .

(b) necessary to protect human, animal or plant life or health

. . .

[or]

(g) relating to the conservation of exhaustible natural resources if such measures are made effective in conjunction with restrictions on domestic production or consumption.[20]

The key element of Article 20 is the introductory paragraph. This provision allows countries to enact and enforce various measures that may restrict trade in order to achieve various objectives, provided that the measure is nondiscriminatory, does not constitute a disguised restriction on international trade, and is necessary to achieve the stated objective. The subsections of Article 20 specify objectives that would justify measures to constrain trade. The most important subsections, (b) and (g), permit regulatory measures to protect human and animal health and to conserve natural resources.[21]

Three of the WTO's environmental cases have become notorious, concerning imported gasoline, tunas and dolphins, and shrimps and turtles. They are worth considering in some detail because popular discussion of them is highly emotional but superficial, and therefore prone to distortion. Article 20 has been the focus of disputes not so much because of the exceptions specified in subsections (b) and (g), but because any environmental trade measure must be implemented in a

---

[20] World Trade Organization 1999a, 455. The remaining provisions relate to the protection of public morals, protection of national treasures of artistic, historic, or archaeological value, to trade in gold and silver, to products of prison labor, and include other measures such as intergovernmental commodity agreements and customs enforcement.

[21] Wallach and Sforza (1999, 15) complain that the Article 20 exceptions apply only "in certain narrowly defined circumstances" and that in many cases the "exceptions were so narrowly interpreted as to render them moot." But if this is really the problem, then the members of the WTO should simply amend the Article 20 exceptions to reflect a broader view. After all, those rules were not made up by the WTO as some independent entity, but were agreed upon by the member countries of WTO, among them the United States and the European Union.

nondiscriminatory fashion. As pointed out in chapter 5, the United States has long insisted that nondiscrimination be the basis of international trade relations, which is why the most-favored nation clause is instituted as Article 1, and national treatment is instituted as Article 3, of the GATT. The United States would be understandably upset if foreign regulations discriminated against American exports. If the United States insists upon receiving fair treatment abroad, it cannot be surprised that other countries demand nondiscriminatory treatment from the United States. This appears to be a noncontroversial proposition. Surprisingly, Public Citizen's most widely trumpeted example of the WTO's weakening of U.S. environmental regulations involves precisely this issue.

Reformulated Gasoline Case

The Global Trade Watch book *Whose Trade Organization?* opens by accusing the WTO of forcing the Environmental Protection Agency (EPA) to weaken its environmental standards on imported gasoline. This case "actualized environmentalists' gravest fears about the WTO," the authors argue, because it is "an example of how the WTO could be used to skirt a country's democratic policymaking and judicial systems . . . [and] was the first concrete evidence of the WTO's threat to environmental policy and to national sovereignty in setting and effectively enforcing important policies."[22]

Yet the case did not involve the stringency of the EPA's regulation, but simply the nondiscriminatory implementation of the regulation as required by the introductory paragraph of Article 20. Simply put, the U.S. regulation discriminated against imported gasoline to the benefit of domestically refined gasoline. The EPA was free to demand any standard of cleanliness it chose, but was obligated under Article 20 to apply the same standard to domestic and foreign producers.

In December 1993, the EPA issued a regulation to reduce the amount of contaminants in domestic and imported gasoline. Its purpose was to limit harmful emissions from automobile exhaust. Each domestic refiner was required to meet a new, more stringent standard based on its own 1990 benchmark quality level. This individual standard was permitted because a single industry-wide baseline would make compliance

[22] Wallach and Sforza 1999, 19.

very costly for certain domestic oil refiners, which vary in cleanliness. Imported gasoline, however, was subject to a uniform baseline, and foreign refiners were not offered the option of establishing an individual benchmark. And though this was partly for ease of administration, a less publicized reason was deliberate discrimination. As an EPA administrator later testified before Congress, the agency thought "that it was appropriate, if we had a choice, to lean in the direction of doing something that would favor their competitive position [i.e., that of domestic refiners] vis-à-vis the [foreign producers]."[23] In other words, the EPA built in discrimination to help domestic oil refiners compete against foreign refiners.

In 1995, Venezuela and Brazil brought a complaint to the WTO, charging that the United States was applying a more stringent standard on imported gasoline. A WTO panel ruled against the United States, which then appealed to the Appellate Body. The Appellate Body determined that while such regulations were permitted under Article 20, this regulation involved discrimination and therefore violated the introductory provision of the article. The Appellate Body recommended that the regulation be brought into conformity with WTO obligations, but left to the United States how it would comply.

At this point, the United States had three options: it could ignore the Appellate finding, let the regulation stand but offer compensation to Venezuela and Brazil in the form of lower tariffs on other products, or bring the regulation into conformity with the WTO obligation.[24] It is useful to consider the implications of each option.

If the United States chose to ignore the ruling, Venezuela and Brazil could legally withdraw previous tariff concessions extended to U.S. goods, equivalent in value to their lost gasoline exports. In signing the GATT, the United States agreed to abide by its rules. No authority can force compliance or negotiated settlement, but other countries can

---

[23] Quoted in Palmeter 1999, 83.

[24] Global Trade Watch makes the options appear more draconian, to "choose between repealing the EPA regulation and permitting imports of dirtier Venezuelan gasoline . . . or keeping the EPA regulation and facing the $150 million in trade sanctions each year in the form of higher Venezuelan tariffs on U.S. products that WTO would authorize for failure to comply" (Wallach and Sforza 1999, 21). The EPA regulation would not have to be "repealed," just modified to eliminate the discrimination. The regulation would not make imports "dirtier" as long as the domestic regulation was made as stringent as that on imports.

retaliate by withdrawing tariff concessions (i.e., raising tariffs) on their imports from the United States.[25] In practice, Venezuela and Brazil might choose not to retaliate against the United States, realizing that such actions would probably fail to accomplish anything. But they might choose this option, which would be permissible under WTO rules.

The second possible U.S. response would be to keep the existing regulation in place, but to compensate Venezuela and Brazil by lowering tariffs against other goods. If this compensation were acceptable to Venezuela and Brazil, the case would be over. But this response requires lowering tariffs on another industry, an unlikely outcome. As one trade lawyer explains, "imagine the U.S. Trade Representative explaining to an industry why the United States had agreed to lower tariffs on its products in order to keep in place a discriminatory rule that favored the oil industry."[26]

As a result, the United States chose to bring the regulation into conformity with the WTO nondiscrimination requirement. This could have been accomplished by requiring domestic refiners to meet the same statutory baseline that applied to imports, but the domestic industry did not want this option. Instead, in August 1997 the EPA allowed foreign refiners to use individual baselines, as domestic producers were allowed to do. To ensure that imports of "dirty" gas did not increase, the EPA established a benchmark for imported gasoline quality based on the volume-weighted average of individual benchmarks for domestic refiners. The EPA monitors imported gasoline closely and imposes remedies if imports do not meet that benchmark.[27]

Note that compliance with the WTO rules and resolution of this dispute had nothing to do with whether a more or less stringent standard was applied. It only required that the *same* standard be applied to domestic and foreign sources of gasoline. The EPA could have resolved the case by raising the domestic standard, rather than lowering the standard

---

[25] As Palmeter (1999, 90) puts it, "the sole remedy available to a WTO member that wins its case against the measure of another, if that measure is not changed and if adequate compensation is not forthcoming, is, effectively, cancellation of the bargain. . . . [In other words,] if some side backs out of its bargain, the other side may do the same."

[26] Palmeter 1999, 86.

[27] For a full description, see the EPA's notice in the August 28, 1997, issue of the Federal Register (45533–45568), available on-line at http://www.access.gpo.gov/.

applied to imports. Thus, the case is far from one in which the WTO "undermines" domestic environmental regulation, as Global Trade Watch and others have made it out to be. In fact, Public Citizen, which decries corporate influence on government policy, put itself in the position of defending a rule that worked to the advantage of the domestic petroleum industry, one of the nation's most politically powerful special interest groups. The United States may have lost this case, but the system worked exactly as the United States wanted it to. The United States can invoke the same rule against discriminatory regulations in other countries.

Finally, it is important to understand the small proportions of this case. Most of the gasoline consumed in the United States is refined in the United States from imported crude petroleum. The United States imports only a small amount of finished motor gasoline, just 3.7 percent of the total U.S. supply (domestic production plus imports) in 1998. By far the largest foreign supplier of gasoline in that year was the Virgin Islands, followed by Venezuela, with Canada a close third. Other countries such as Brazil supply just a tiny amount.[28]

_____The Tuna-Dolphin Case

The "tuna-dolphin" case is perhaps the most infamous recent trade dispute. In 1991, a GATT panel ruled that a U.S. ban on imported tuna that had been caught without using dolphin-safe methods was inconsistent with GATT rules. In some sense, this case is now completely moot: it was decided under the old GATT (rather than WTO) rules, did not force any change in U.S. policy, and was later resolved through negotiations. But the case is important because the panel's legal interpretation continues to cast a shadow over the debate about conflicts between environmental policies and world trade rules.

Many dolphins are accidentally killed by tuna fisherman who use purse seine fishing nets. Under the Marine Mammal Protection Act, the United States established dolphin protection standards for the American fishing fleet and for countries fishing for yellowfin tuna in parts of the Pacific Ocean. The Act required that the United States ban the importation of tuna from countries that failed to meet U.S. standards for dolphin-safe fishing methods.

[28] U.S. Department of Energy 1998, 1:17, 56.

unjustifiable discrimination between countries where the same conditions prevail, or a disguised restriction on international trade, nothing in this Agreement shall be construed to prevent the adoption or enforcement by any contracting party of measures . . .

> (b) necessary to protect human, animal or plant life or health
>
> . . .
>
> [or]
>
> (g) relating to the conservation of exhaustible natural resources if such measures are made effective in conjunction with restrictions on domestic production or consumption.[20]

The key element of Article 20 is the introductory paragraph. This provision allows countries to enact and enforce various measures that may restrict trade in order to achieve various objectives, provided that the measure is nondiscriminatory, does not constitute a disguised restriction on international trade, and is necessary to achieve the stated objective. The subsections of Article 20 specify objectives that would justify measures to constrain trade. The most important subsections, (b) and (g), permit regulatory measures to protect human and animal health and to conserve natural resources.[21]

Three of the WTO's environmental cases have become notorious, concerning imported gasoline, tunas and dolphins, and shrimps and turtles. They are worth considering in some detail because popular discussion of them is highly emotional but superficial, and therefore prone to distortion. Article 20 has been the focus of disputes not so much because of the exceptions specified in subsections (b) and (g), but because any environmental trade measure must be implemented in a

---

[20] World Trade Organization 1999a, 455. The remaining provisions relate to the protection of public morals, protection of national treasures of artistic, historic, or archaeological value, to trade in gold and silver, to products of prison labor, and include other measures such as intergovernmental commodity agreements and customs enforcement.

[21] Wallach and Sforza (1999, 15) complain that the Article 20 exceptions apply only "in certain narrowly defined circumstances" and that in many cases the "exceptions were so narrowly interpreted as to render them moot." But if this is really the problem, then the members of the WTO should simply amend the Article 20 exceptions to reflect a broader view. After all, those rules were not made up by the WTO as some independent entity, but were agreed upon by the member countries of WTO, among them the United States and the European Union.

Mexico objected to the embargo, and in 1991 requested that a panel review the case. Mexico argued that the ban violated Article 11 of the GATT, which prohibits quantitative restrictions or embargoes on the goods from other member countries. Mexico noted that dolphins were not an endangered species and there was no international agreement forbidding the use of purse seine nets. Eleven other countries made representations to the panel, all supporting the Mexican position. The United States was outnumbered in the GATT mainly because other countries objected to the unilateral nature of the ban. They believed that by imposing such standards, the United States was simply trying to force other countries to adhere to America's view of how non-American resources should be protected. They viewed this as bullying, and objected as a matter of principle.

The United States argued that the import restrictions were justified under GATT Article 3, allowing the enforcement of domestic regulations at the border, and Article 20, allowing trade measures to protect health and safety and promote conservation. The GATT panel rejected both defenses. The panel ruled that the trade restrictions justified by Article 3 apply only to products as such, and not to the process by which the product was produced. This distinction became known as the "product-process" doctrine. Because tuna caught by dolphin-safe methods was the same as tuna caught by dolphin-endangering methods, the panel saw no legal basis for differentiating between them.

The panel also rejected the Article 20 defense of the embargo. The United States could not invoke Article 20(b) because the "human, animal or plant life or health" was not within the jurisdiction of the United States, and GATT rules did not allow a country to take trade actions for the purpose of enforcing its own standards in another country (something known as extraterritoriality). Finally, the Article 20 defense failed because the measure was not shown to be "necessary" since other GATT-consistent options (such a multilateral negotiations) had not been explored. A later case brought by the European Community in 1994, known as Tuna-Dolphin II, resulted in a similar panel report regarding Article 3 but proposed a different interpretation of Article 20, allowing for the regulation of environmental resources that are not in the regulating country.

Under the old GATT dispute system, a panel report was not official until adopted by the GATT Council. Mexico did not pursue the panel decision any further, and the United States blocked the adoption of the Tuna-Dolphin II panel report. All during this time, the U.S. import ban remained in place. The tuna dispute was resolved in 1992 when the United States, Mexico, and eight other tuna-fishing nations signed an international agreement to regulate the conditions of tuna fishing. Since then, incidental dolphin deaths due to tuna fishing have dropped dramatically, according to the National Oceanic and Atmospheric Administration (NOAA). The American import embargo finally ended in 1997, thereby ending the seven-year dispute. Some implications of this case will be discussed shortly, although the ultimate outcome must be judged satisfactory: the import ban was replaced by an international treaty, which has been more effective at saving dolphins than any unilateral import ban.

_____The Shrimp-Turtle Case

Another high-profile case, this one involving the WTO, concerns U.S. regulations on imported shrimp. WTO critics charge that a ruling completely undermined U.S. efforts to require foreign shrimp trawlers to use "turtle excluder devices" (TEDs), which helped prevent the accidental drowning of endangered sea turtles. But as with the Venezuelan gasoline case, this WTO ruling did not concern the law itself but rather the way in which the United States implemented the law.[29] The ruling also opened the possibility that Article 20 exceptions could consider the "process" of production in designing trade-related environmental regulations.

In 1989, Congress prohibited imports of shrimp and shrimp-products harvested in a way that may harm endangered sea turtles. The prohibition was to be lifted only for countries that the State Department had certified as having a program to prevent accidental turtle deaths (or for countries whose fishermen trawl only in cold waters where there are no such turtles). For some reason, the State Department initially interpreted the law as applying only to countries in the Caribbean and Atlantic. As a result of a suit brought by environmental groups, however, in December 1995 the U.S. Court of International Trade determined that the law applied to imports worldwide. The court rejected a request by the State Department to delay the enforcement of the ruling to allow newly

[29] See Balton (1999) for details.

affected countries time to comply, and thus the worldwide embargo went into effect in May 1996, less than six months after the ruling.

In September 1996, India, Malaysia, Pakistan, and Thailand, all of which were newly affected by the ban, brought a case to the WTO. They argued that shrimp must be allowed in the U.S. market regardless of the "process" by which they are caught. The dispute settlement panel ruled against the United States on the grounds that the ban was inconsistent with Article 11 (limiting the use of import prohibitions) and could not be justified under Article 20. The United States appealed the verdict to the Appellate Body, which overruled most of the panel's decision. In October 1998, the Appellate Body held that the shrimp certification measure was justified under Article 20(g) relating to the conservation of exhaustible natural resources, but that its implementation was inconsistent with the nondiscrimination requirement. For example, in applying a countrywide standard, the State Department might not allow imports from a country even if some of the imported shrimp was caught by foreign trawlers using TEDs. In addition, the Appellate Body stated that the regulations were not transparent or predictable, and that the United States had negotiated a treaty to protect sea turtles in the Western Hemisphere but had not attempted to negotiate a treaty with governments in the Indian Ocean.

The WTO did not require the United States to lift its ban on shrimp imports, but only to implement the ban in a nondiscriminatory way. The import ban was not lifted at any point during the dispute process. Thailand and Pakistan have moved forward and adopted a TED program, and have since been certified. By mid-2002, the United States is expected to conclude an agreement on shrimp fishing with other Southeast Asian and Indian Ocean countries that would match the one in the Western Hemisphere.

There is little doubt, however, that the initial panel decision was not just legally questionable, but created immense political problems for the WTO. The initial decision left the impression that the GATT and environmental rules are necessarily in conflict and ruled against amicus briefs by NGOs, fueling their hostility to the WTO. The Appellate overruled most of the panel report, but the damage was already done. The fact that the Appellate Body report overturned so many of the legal aspects of the panel report made it seem as though the panel's findings were arbitrary and as though "law" could be made up by bad panels, or that the Appellate body was simply bowing to outside pressure and could therefore change legal interpretations on a whim.

Lessons from the Environmental Cases

These cases convey some sense of the issues involved in trade and environmental disputes. What are the lessons to be learned?

The first lesson is that, although there may be some tensions between trade policy and environmental objectives, world trade rules are not antienvironmental. Several less well publicized decisions reaffirm that Article 20 allows countries to maintain consistent and nondiscriminatory environmental regulations. For example, in 1994, a GATT panel affirmed that the corporate average fuel economy (CAFE) standards, regulating the fuel efficiency of automobiles sold in the United States, were a perfectly acceptable form of product regulation to protect public health and environment, as long as those standards did not explicitly discriminate on the basis of country of origin. Similarly, a WTO panel in 2000 upheld France's ban on asbestos imports, on the grounds that they were hazardous materials, after Canada had challenged the embargo.

Second, the "product-process" doctrine that prevents consideration of how tunas or shrimp are fished is a source of great difficulty. Never explicitly propounded or endorsed by WTO members, the doctrine emerged from a creative interpretation of a GATT panel and gradually took on a life of its own. The distinction is arbitrary and unsustainable because process-based regulation has already been introduced in the agreement on trade-related intellectual property. For example, original and copied software are similar products, but the process by which they were produced is quite different.

Many people in developed countries care about how products are made: tuna may be tuna, but tuna fished by dolphin-safe methods is not viewed as the same as tuna fished by dolphin-unsafe methods. Furthermore, as set out in the tuna-dolphin case, the product-process doctrine may not even be legally sound. One leading GATT legal scholar has written that "the underlying conceptual foundation based on 'product' focus of Article 3 tends to crumble on analysis" and that "the suggestion that Article 3 does not apply to ('cover') process-based regulation is just plain wrong."[30] Although the shrimp-turtle ruling weakened the product-process doctrine, it can still pose an obstacle to process-based regulation.

At the same time, there are sound reasons for not allowing any and all process regulations. Developing countries fear that process regulation will open the door to the imposition of standards that other countries cannot afford. They are concerned that if the method of production of a particular good becomes grounds for blocking trade, then labor and environmental conditions of production will be introduced as excuses for keeping out the products of developing countries.[31] The product-process distinction will be one of the most difficult and important issues that the WTO membership has to work out.

The third lesson is that unilateral trade sanctions are a poor instrument for achieving environmental objectives. Simply keeping foreign goods out of the U.S. market may be viscerally satisfying, but it does not solve the problem. The refusal of the United States to buy fish that have been caught in ways that harm other animals does nothing directly to help those other animals. Sanctions do not prevent a country from diverting tuna and shrimp caught with harmful methods away from the U.S. market toward other markets that would accept it. In the end, international agreements on standards are clearly preferable to trade embargoes, and a global approach must be taken in those negotiations because the lack of cooperation by a few key countries can undermine the goal.

While the threat of sanctions can sometimes provide the incentive for countries to join negotiations, it is also true that countries are apt to resent and resist the imposition of U.S. standards. When other nations are reluctant to negotiate about a problem, the carrot of subsidies rather

---

[30] Hudec 2000, 198.

[31] As Sampson (2000, pp 18–19) points out: "in the view of [developing] nations, permitting discrimination among imports on the basis of production methods would profoundly undermine a principle that lies at the heart of the WTO legal system. This concern manifests itself in a resistance to any attempts to provide for the extension of industrial country production standards to developing countries in order for their exports to be acceptable for import in industrial countries. The strength of feeling on this matter on the part of many developing countries cannot be overstated." See Bhagwati and Srinivasan (1996) for a spirited defense of the idea that diversity in production methods should not be grounds for trade intervention.

than the stick of sanctions can be used to promote the adoption of safer production methods. For example, a straightforward solution to the dolphin and turtle problem would have been to subsidize the purchase of dolphin-safe nets and turtle excluder devises for use around the world. These technologies are not expensive. Rather than spending millions of dollars on legal fees over many years in an effort to solve the problem through compulsion, a combination of foreign aid, World Bank assistance, and NGO financial resources should have been pooled to give these dolphin- and turtle-saving technologies to fishermen in developing countries.

Because trade controls are usually ineffective and sometimes counterproductive as environmental regulations, the whole issue of whether trade restrictions are a necessary part of the environmental effort should be considered. Although relatively few multilateral environmental agreements contain provisions calling for trade restrictions, those that do include the Convention on International Trade in Endangered Species (CITES), the Basle Convention on the Control of Transboundary Movements of Hazardous Waste and Their Disposal, and the Montreal Convention on Fluorocarbons.

CITES bans trade in ivory and other products to help save endangered animals. But an ivory trade ban is not the best policy to protect endangered African elephants because such a ban fails to deal with the underlying problem of domestic resource management. The convention hurts countries that manage their resources well, such as Zimbabwe, Botswana, and South Africa, where the number of elephants has risen. The sale of ivory from herd culls in these countries could generate valuable revenue that the cash-starved game reserves could use to improve the situation even more. Meanwhile, the decline in elephant populations in Kenya and Tanzania is not directly due to the ivory trade, but to poor national management that has failed to raise the costs of poaching to locals. Simply banning trade is no substitute for strong domestic measures, and a well-regulated and well-managed trade can prove better than import bans.[32]

---

[32] As Morris (2000, 279) puts it, "CITES imposes trade restrictions on trade in certain species. The ostensible ground for such restrictions is that demand for parts of those species outside the territory of the nations in which those species live is encouraging

The Basle convention bans illegal trade in toxic waste to prevent its dumping in developing countries. But illegal dumping was very infrequent in the past, and the ban did nothing to solve the underlying problem: that national laws that already regulated toxic waste dumping were not enforced. According to some analysts, the convention may even have impeded recycling efforts in developing countries.[33] The Montreal Protocol seeks to limit the production and use of chlorofluorocarbons (CFCs), but also imposes bans on the export or import of controlled substances and requires trade sanctions against nonsignatory countries. While the protocol has been effective in limiting CFC production, the question is how effective trade sanctions are against countries that choose not to comply with the agreement, since production and not trade is the main problem.

In the case of trade in ivory and trash, the problem is not that the WTO poses a barrier to effective environmental management, but that the multilateral agreements substitute trade restrictions for solutions that more effectively address the underlying problem. The Montreal Protocol is a more difficult issue. A global consensus could emerge that trade measures are an effective component of an international economic agreement. If provisions of an environmental agreement conflict with WTO rules on nondiscrimination, then the governments agreeing to the environmental accord could also form a consensus in the WTO that discrimination in certain products was acceptable for environmental reasons.[34] There should be enough common ground between the trade policy and the environmental community to work out these differences.

What has become clear is that it will not be acceptable for the world trade community to ignore or undermine environmental concerns when there appears to be a global consensus on those concerns. Effective environmental and safety regulations should not be blocked simply

---

people to poach those species, leading to dwindling stocks. However, this characterization of the problem misses what for most species is the most important factor in determining numbers, namely the opportunity cost of their continued existence to those people who live nearby. Indeed, by reducing the value of various species to the locals, CITES may in fact discourage conservation."

[33] See Montgomery 1995.

[34] As Sampson (2000, 97) argues, "If the agreed solution involves a loss of rights under the WTO (that is, being discriminated against), then providing all WTO members agree to forgo those rights, it is difficult to see where there could be a problem."

because they reduce international trade. The notion that all trade must be kept free at all costs is simply wrong. As Thomas Babington Macaulay put it in a parliamentary speech in 1845,

> I am, I believe, as strongly attached as any member of this House to the principle of free trade, rightly understood. Trade, considered merely as trade, considered merely with reference to the pecuniary interest of the contracting parties, can hardly be too free. But there is a great deal of trade which cannot be considered merely as trade, and which affects higher than pecuniary interests. And to say that government never ought to regulate such trade is a monstrous proposition, a proposition at which Adam Smith would have stood aghast.[35]

Public Health and the Beef Hormones Case

World trade rules do not stand in the way of government action to protect the public health. When the United States banned imports of livestock and meats from Europe in 2001 because of fears of mad cow and foot and mouth disease, the action was legal according to WTO rules. At the same time, public health is sometimes used as a justification for regulations intended only to protect special interests. International negotiators have attempted to allow health and safety regulations even if they restrict trade, while they have discouraged regulatory protectionism, that is, trade barriers designed to protect domestic producers but cloaked under a health or safety rationale. These two cases, however, can be extremely difficult to distinguish.

The use of public health as an excuse for protectionist regulations is not a new problem. In the late 1880s, for example, many European countries banned the sale of American pork after rumors spread that it was tainted with trichinosis. Even though there proved to be no evidence of such a problem, the ban was enormously beneficial to European pork farmers, who had well-known difficulties competing against low-priced American pork.[36] Today, the United States and other coun-

---

[35] Macaulay 1900, 102.

[36] According to one historian of the incident, "the general fear of trichinosis was a godsend for European protectionists." The American consulate in Le Havre reported that

tries maintain trade barriers that are ostensibly designed to protect the public health, but upon further examination are actually maintained for the benefit of producers. The Department of Agriculture estimates that questionable foreign regulations cost the United States about $5 billion in agricultural, forestry, and fishery exports in 1996.[37]

The U.S.-EU dispute over hormone-treated beef is a classic example of the extreme difficulty in drawing the line between regulations to protect consumers and regulations to protect producers. The long festering dispute remains unresolved despite countless attempts to negotiate a settlement. The conflict began in 1985, when Europe restricted the use of natural hormones for therapeutic purposes and banned the use of synthetic hormones for growth purposes in cattle and meat sold in the EU. At the same time, the EU prohibited the importation of animals or meat from animals that had been treated with such hormones. Thus, the regulation was seemed to be nondiscriminatory because the same standard was applied to domestic and imported meat. In such cases, the regulation cannot be held in violation of Article 1 or Article 20 of the GATT.

Implemented in 1989, the measure wiped out about $100 million in American beef exports to Europe. The United States strenuously objected, arguing that the EU ban was unjustifiable because the hormones had been found safe when used in accordance with good practices of animal husbandry. The safety of the hormones had been accepted not just by the U.S. Food and Drug Administration, but by numerous international scientific panels. Efforts to resolve the dispute under the Tokyo Round's Agreement on Technical Barriers failed because it dealt only with end-product characteristics, and naturally occurring hormones cannot be distinguished from cattle and beef treated with supplemental hormones. As a result, the United States retaliated in 1989 by imposing 100 percent tariffs on $100 million of agricultural imports from Europe.

The United States sought to clarify international rules on health

---

French inspectors were instructed to find trichinae in at least 25 percent of American pork that they examined. The Foreign Minister of Austria-Hungary publicly admitted that protection to domestic producers was a determining factor, but still justified the exclusion based on sanitary grounds. See Gignilliat 1961.

[37] Roberts and DeRemer 1997.

and safety regulations during the Uruguay Round, and the result was the Agreement on the Application of Sanitary and Phytosanitary Measures (SPS). The SPS agreement provides that trade-related sanitary measures should be based on scientific principles and maintained with sufficient scientific evidence (Article 2.2) or be based on international standards (if they exist). Sanitary measures should be nondiscriminatory and not be more trade-restrictive than required to achieve the appropriate level of sanitary protection. In addition, Article 5.5 of the SPS states that governments should strive to achieve consistency in the protection of health risks and "shall avoid arbitrary or unjustifiable distinctions in the levels it considers to be appropriate in different situations, if such distinctions result in discrimination or a disguised restriction on international trade."[38]

The United States (supported by Australia, Canada, and New Zealand) used the SPS to challenge the EU ban on beef imports, arguing that the ban failed to meet any of these requirements. The WTO panel convened experts, two chosen by the United States, two chosen by the European Union, and another by those four, to evaluate the scientific evidence regarding the hormones. The five scientists unanimously concluded that there was no public health risk. In 1995 the United Nations Codex Alimentarius Commission and a scientific panel convened by the EU declared that there is no human health risk from the hormones when used in accordance with proper animal husbandry, confirming what other international science bodies had stated.

The record also showed that high levels of several of the hormones occurred naturally in animal products, and yet these products were not regulated. For example, of the six hormones at issue, the one identified as most dangerous by the EU is found from ten times to hundreds of times more concentrated in such products as eggs, cabbage, broccoli, and soybean oil than in hormone-treated beef. If the objective was to protect the public from exposure to specific hormones, then why was the sale of eggs not banned, since there is seventy-five times more naturally occurring hormones in a single egg than in a kilogram of beef? In the view of the U.S. government, these facts made the ban arbitrary and inconsistent. According to the United States, the real motivation for

---

[38] World Trade Organization 1999a, 62. For an evaluation of the SPS Agreement, see Roberts 1998.

the measure was to protect domestic beef producers from foreign competition and to reduce surplus beef supplies in the EU. If consumer health were the true motivation, then the EU should not have continued to allow the use of growth additives by its competitive pork producers instead of disallowing it just in its less competitive beef industry.[39]

The EU countered by arguing that the ban was justified under Article 20(b) of the GATT and claimed that the United States was simply attacking the "level" of protection provided. The EU maintained that the WTO could not rule on the appropriate level of protection provided by any regulation, but merely whether the measure itself was in conformity with the SPS. The EU argued that the ban was based on the "precautionary" principle, which took the view that if scientific evidence did not establish beyond a doubt that the hormone residues were safe for humans, then a ban was appropriate.[40] The EU stressed that it did not ban all meat imports, and that hormone-free beef could be sold in Europe.

In 1997, the WTO panel ruled that the hormone ban was not based on scientific evidence or a risk assessment and therefore was inconsistent with the EU's obligations under the SPS agreement. The Appellate Body reaffirmed that decision in 1998. In 1999, after the EU failed to implement any changes in policy, the United States imposed 100 percent tariffs on European imports valued at nearly $120 million, the estimated annual amount of lost U.S. beef exports. Proposals to resolve the impasse by replacing the import ban with a labeling requirement, allowing consumers to make the choice about whether to purchase hormone-treated beef, ran into difficulties. As of late-2001, a negotiated settlement has yet to be reached.

[39] The United States noted that Europe introduced milk quotas in 1984 to reduce the oversupply of milk, and this resulted in an increase in cattle slaughter, which more than doubled the stock of surplus beef (World Trade Organization 1999c, 20). As Roberts (1998, 394) points out, "It was no coincidence, the United States argued, that EC officials were willing to allow the use of productivity-enhancing inputs in the internationally competitive pork sector, but substantially more conservative about allowing the use of such inputs in a sector which relied on costly domestic price support measures, import protection, and export subsidies to maintain producer profitability."

[40] Article 5.7 of the SPS states, "In cases where relevant scientific evidence is insufficient, a Member may provisionally adopt sanitary or phytosanitary measures on the basis of available pertinent information." The EU did not formally invoke this provision because its ban was permanent, and as the record made clear there was abundant scientific evidence that judicious use of hormones was not harmful.

As already noted, Article 20 allows trade restrictions with the proviso that they be imposed in a nondiscriminatory fashion, but also that they are not "a disguised restriction on international trade." Discrimination was never an issue in this case because the use of hormones was forbidden in domestic as well as imported meat. The question is whether the measure was a "disguised restriction" on trade. The problem is that this standard is virtually impossible to determine because it gets to the unobserved motives behind a trade action. If the intention was not disguised, it would be obvious. The head of the European Alliance for Safe Meat, and a member of the European parliament, admitted that "the decision to ban these substances was made for political and commercial reasons and not, as the public was led to believe, for consumer protection."[41] Such admissions only fuel the suspicion that there is no compelling health or safety reason for the ban, but that it was designed to help special interests, namely European beef producers.

The challenge confronting trade policymakers is to distinguish health and safety protection from regulatory protectionism enacted under the name of health and safety. As it turns out, there are tangible benefits to giving many of the existing regulations a hard look. As a result of the SPS agreement, the United States lifted a controversial eighty-three-year ban on Mexican avocados and allowed the importation of uncooked Argentine beef for the first time in eighty years (from regions of Argentina recognized as free of foot and mouth disease). In addition, Japan removed its forty-six-year ban on U.S. tomatoes, New Zealand citizens are now able to purchase Canadian salmon, and Australians are now able to buy cooked poultry meat. In each case, the restriction's public health rationale was questionable.

And yet merely writing rules (such as SPS) is not going to end such trade disputes. Negotiated rules are a useful way of finding common ground, but countries are bound to have different assessments of the risk trade-offs involved in any given regulation. For example, the United States and European Union have different assessments of the risks of genetically modified foods, such as corn and other agricultural crops.[42] In Europe, the food is under suspicion until proven safe,

---

[41] Quoted in Aaronson 2001, 153.
[42] See Perkidis, Kerr, and Hobbs 2001.

whereas in the United States, the food is acceptable until proven harmful. There is little scientific evidence that such foods are harmful, but Europe invokes the precautionary principle to justify restrictions on its use. These different principles cannot be easily bridged simply by writing down rules. The question is how far WTO members want to go in limiting the ability of governments to adopt trade restrictions when scientific evidence does not exist or is ambiguous about a particular rationale. One approach is to allow countries complete freedom in choosing their own product safety standards because they benefit the most from proper regulation and bear the cost of regulatory protectionism. Governments and the business community, however, appear to benefit from have some common ground, some rules that provide a transparent and stable system for distinguishing appropriate from inappropriate standards.

The WTO may have a limited role in such conflicts. Some trade disputes are not a matter for litigation and a legal solution, but negotiation and a diplomatic solution. As one astute observer of the WTO has put it: "Too much policy in the WTO is now formulated on the basis of finding legal 'solutions' to problems, often through legal interpretations of the GATT and WTO agreements, instead of through decisions taken by all members after a full-fledged policy debate. Today's WTO is moving toward being a 'House of Litigation,' lost in the intricacies of legal rulings, rather than an institution based on widely accepted principles that have produced time-tested policies."[43] This is a critical issue that the WTO membership will have to confront in coming years.

_____*The Economics of Labor Standards*

The world trading system has also come under attack for omitting labor standards from trade agreements and thus supposedly failing to protect

---

[43] Sampson 2000, 7. On this theme, see Barfield 2001. Sampson (2000, 111) has also noted that "perhaps [legal] rulings such as this have some short-term merit in finding immediate 'solutions' to politically sensitive matters, but in the long term, policy choices as important as the legitimacy of the unilateral application of trade measures to enforce domestic societal preferences extraterritorially should not be left to litigation of this nature, with confusing and uncertain outcomes."

the interests of workers. Demands for labor standards are not new but have recently come to the forefront of the debate over trade policy.[44]

There are many voices in the trade and labor debate. Student activists, human rights groups, and other NGOs have decried the poor working conditions and treatment of labor in developing countries, and are sharply critical of multinational corporations for their failure to pay a "living" wage to workers there. Labor unions in the developed countries have long maintained that countries with lower labor standards have an unfair competitive advantage in trade and that they attract jobs and investment at the expense of countries with higher standards. Most developing countries, by contrast, strenuously object to any linking of trade policy and labor standards. They fear that if countries are allowed to restrict import from others deemed not to have adequate labor standards, developed countries will have yet another excuse for denying low-wage countries access to their markets, thereby preventing them taking advantage of their comparative advantage in labor-intensive goods.

Before asking whether trade agreements should include provisions on labor standards, it is worth examining the claim that low wages give a country an unfair advantage in trade. The key lesson is that low wages reflect low labor productivity. Workers in developed countries enjoy high wages and benefits because of their high productivity. Figure 6.1 illustrates the strong relationship between labor costs per worker (a measure of wages and benefits that firms must pay) and value added per worker (a measure of productivity) in manufacturing for sixty-three countries during 1995–99. The correlation is striking: the higher a country's average productivity, the higher the country's average wages. Econometric evidence has regularly shown that labor productivity alone explains about 70 to 80 percent of the cross-country variation in average wages in manufacturing. After also accounting for differences in per capita GDP and in price levels across countries, over 90 percent of the variation in wages between countries can be explained.[45]

---

[44] Charnovitz (1987) traces concerns about trade and labor standards back to the early postwar trade negotiations and even well before then.

[45] Even though these purely economic variables explain almost all of the differences in wages rates across countries, Rodrik (1998) finds that indicators of political freedom contribute some additional explanatory power.

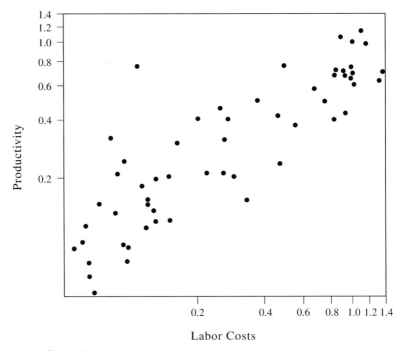

_____**Figure 6.1**
Labor costs and productivity in manufacturing for 63 countries, 1995–99. (Data from World Bank 2000, table 2.6.)

Since average wages reflect average productivity, the cost advantage of low wages is generally offset by the cost disadvantage of low productivity. This implies that unit labor costs are roughly comparable across countries. Figure 6.2 depicts this relationship. In India and the Philippines, for example, average wages are less than 10 percent of those in the United States. But the average productivity of workers is also less than 10 percent of that in the United States. Thus, the unit labor cost—the effective cost of hiring labor—is roughly comparable between the two countries. And, in fact, multinational corporations searching for cheap labor find that you get what you pay for: low wages imply a less productive workforce. Thus, multinationals generally find it profitable to turn to developing countries only for unskilled labor-intensive activities, particularly those in which the productivity of workers is comparable to

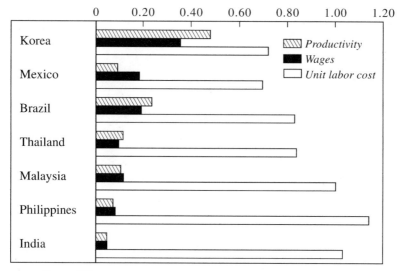

_____Figure 6.2
Labor productivity, wages, and unit labor costs in selected developing countries, 1990. (*Source:* Golub 1999, 23.)

that in developed countries but the average wage they have to pay is much less.[46]

As developing countries improve the productivity of their workers, through the acquisition of better technology or other mechanisms, competitive pressures bid up average wages. As a result, the growth in domestic wages tracks the growth in domestic productivity. (We saw this in the case of the United States in chapter 3.) Indeed, a country's average wage rate is determined almost exclusively by domestic productivity performance. As figure 6.3 shows, for example, the acceleration of productivity in South Korea in the 1980s was accompanied by a dramatic rise in labor compensation. By contrast, the Philippines has been much less successful at increasing productivity and therefore has not seen a comparable rise in wages. The evidence is clear: countries that successfully

_____

[46] It should be noted that productivity is not just a function of worker output, but the economy's infrastructure, the availability of technical and support personnel, and other factors. There are many stories of multinationals relocating back in the United States because, despite the availability of inexpensive labor in other countries, the general environment for business made it difficult to make full use of that labor.

A. South Korea

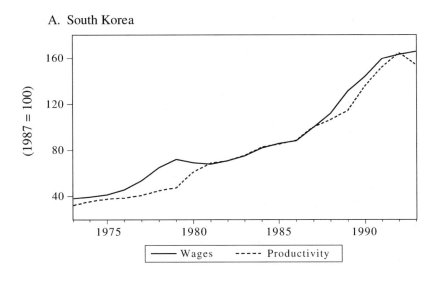

B. The Philippines

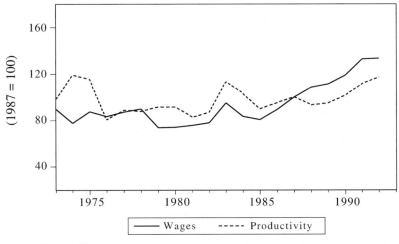

Figure 6.3
Real wages and labor productivity in manufacturing, South Korea and the Phi-
lippines, 1972–93 (1987 = 100). (Data from World Bank, World Tables.)

increase productivity experience a rise in wages, while countries whose productivity is stagnant see little change in wages.

Countries with low wages tend to specialize in unskilled labor-intensive goods. Beyond this, there is little empirical evidence that low labor standards, in themselves, exert an important influence on trade flows. Several studies have failed to find a strong relationship between measures of labor standards and international trade flows (such as export performance in labor-intensive goods) or direct investment flows (such as whether countries with low standards attract more foreign investment).[47] The OECD recently concluded that "empirical findings confirm the analytical result that core labor standards do not play a significant role in shaping trade performance. The view which argues that low-standard countries will enjoy gains in export market shares to the detriment of high-standard countries appears to lack solid empirical support."[48]

Low wages and poor working conditions in developing countries have sparked protests from concerned citizens in developed countries. The Worker Rights Consortium, established by students, unions, and human rights groups, has accused the athletic shoe manufacturer Nike and other multinationals of subjecting workers to sweatshop conditions and not paying a living wage.[49] Working conditions in many developing countries are indeed horrible by the standards of developed countries, and everyone wants to see those standards of living improve. These activists have changed working conditions for the better by putting companies in the spotlight of bad publicity if their contractors treat their workers poorly.

Still, the best and most direct way to raise wages and labor standards is to enhance the productivity of the workers through economic development. Trade and investment are important components of that development, and therefore efforts to limit international trade or to shut down the sweatshops are counterproductive. For example, most foreign-owned firms pay higher wages than comparable domestic firms.[50] The

[47] See, for example, Rodrik 1996.

[48] Organization for Economic Cooperation and Development 1996, 33. The OECD (2000b, 33) concluded that "this finding has not been challenged by literature appearing since the 1996 study was completed."

[49] Elliott and Freeman (2001) examine the motives and objectives of groups in developed countries that are pressing for a better treatment of labor in developing countries.

[50] See Aitken, Harrison, and Lipsey (1996) for a study of foreign firms in Mexico,

"sweatshops" in poorer countries also pay better than the local labor market, which may explain, for example, the low turnover (or quit) rate of workers at such firms.

Even if the wages and working conditions in developing countries are dismal by the standards of the present-day United States, these multinational firms are at least providing employment opportunities and incomes that might not otherwise exist, enabling the poor to support their families. Two reporters for the *New York Times* provide a vivid example. When they were first assigned to cover Asia, they, like most people, were outraged at the sweatshop conditions. They later changed their opinion: "In time, though, we came to accept the view supported by most Asians: that the campaign against sweatshops risks harming the very people it is intended to help. . . . Those sweatshops tended to generate the wealth to solve the problems they created. . . . it may sound silly to say that sweatshops offer a route to prosperity, when wages in the poorest countries are sometimes less than $1 per day. Still, for an impoverished Indonesian or Bangladeshi woman with a handful of kids who would otherwise drop out of school and risk dying of mundane diseases like diarrhea, $1 or $2 a day can be a life-transforming wage."[51]

The fundamental problem facing workers in developing countries is not the existence of sweatshops, but the lack of good alternative employment opportunities. Efforts to stop exports from low-wage countries, to prevent investment there by multinationals, or to impose high minimum wages or benefits beyond the productivity level of the domestic workforce will simply diminish the demand for labor in those countries and take away one of the few opportunities that workers have to better themselves and their families. Opponents of sweatshops have failed to consider what alternative opportunities for employment can be created.

_____*Should Trade Agreements Have Labor Standards?*

Can including labor standards in trade agreements help improve labor conditions in developing countries? Almost alone, the United States has pressed for considering such standards in trade negotiations. And yet

---

Venezuela, and the United States. Lipsey and Sjöholm (2001) show that foreign-owned firms in Indonesia pay higher wages than locally owned firms.

[51] Kristof and WuDunn 2000, 70–71.

there is a great deal of ambiguity about which standards should be included, their precise definition, and how they should be enforced. Two categories of labor standards are typically discussed. "Core" standards are related to fundamental human rights and can be universal in their application, such as a prohibition on forced labor. "Economic" labor standards, by contrast, are tied more closely to a country's level of economic development and include minimum wages and working conditions.

Core labor standards have been defined by the International Labor Organization (ILO), an international body created in 1919 and composed of member governments, employers, and workers. In 1996, the ILO issued a Declaration on Fundamental Principles and Rights at Work stating that all countries, regardless of their level of economic development, have an obligation to promote the following principles and rights: freedom of association and the effective recognition of the right to collective bargaining; elimination of all forms of forced or compulsory labor; effective abolition of child labor; and elimination of discrimination in respect of employment and occupation.

Although such core labor standards are generally recognized and attract wide support, there is (with the exception of slavery) remarkably little international consensus on the precise definition of these standards and the method of implementing them. The ILO oversees over 180 conventions on various aspects of labor rights and practices, but very few of them have been ratified by all of the ILO members. As of early 2001, for example, the United States had ratified just 14 and had agreed to only two of the core conventions (on the abolition of forced labor and the prohibition of the worst forms of child labor). The United States has ratified few conventions partly because domestic labor law is largely the prerogative of state governments and partly because the language of the conventions may conflict with national policy. For example, convention number 111 seeks to abolish employment discrimination on the basis of sex and race, but has not been ratified by the United States because it might conflict with affirmative action.

Other countries have also failed to adopt ILO conventions because they are perceived to be inflexible or irrelevant to local circumstances. For example, convention numbers 87 and 98 deal with the right to organize and collective bargaining. The United States has not ratified these conventions because many states allow the hiring of replacement workers, which under the ILO convention could be viewed as interfering with the right to strike. Many developing countries are simply indifferent to these conventions. As one economist has noted, "for an overwhelming majority of poor workers in developing countries whose dominant mode of employment is self-employment in rural agricultural activities or in the urban informal sector, unionization has little relevance. Even where relevant and where the freedom to form unions has been exercised to a significant extent, namely in the organized manufacturing and public sector in poor countries, labor unions have been promoting the interests of a small section of the labor force at the expense of many."[52]

Child labor has been a particularly controversial issue, and illustrates the limits of using ILO conventions and trade policy to reduce this practice. Convention number 182, signed by President Clinton at the WTO summit in Seattle in 1999, aims to eliminate the worst forms of child labor, such as slavery, the sale of children, forced labor, prostitution, and illicit activities. The United States prohibits imports of goods made with forced or indentured child labor, but does not have a generic ban on imported goods made with child labor. Indeed, dealing with nonexploitative child labor is a more difficult issue. The ILO charter establishing minimum ages of work has not been ratified by the United States, Canada, or other developed countries because of differing national views on the details. For example, Canada chooses not to prohibit work at night for children under thirteen.

Of course, child labor is a major issue in developing countries, and some activists have suggested that developed countries should refuse to import any goods made with child labor. But just as trade policy is an inefficient instrument for achieving environmental objectives, it is also an inefficient instrument for raising labor standards. A import ban on goods made with child labor might stop the use of children to produce goods for the U.S. market, but it would not put an end to child labor. Only about 5 percent of working children are employed in the export sector in developing countries. An import ban might simply shift them to other sectors of the domestic economy (about 80 percent are employed in the primary agricultural sector). At worst, an import ban

[52] Srinivasan 1998, 76.

could push them into less desirable or more hazardous work, or even leave them without work and thus condemn them to starvation.[53] Import bans fail to address the root cause of child labor or offer any resolution to the underlying conditions that create the need for it.

The most effective way of eliminating child labor is to attack the fundamental causes, which are poverty and the lack of affordable or adequate educational opportunities.[54] As figure 6.4 indicates, the incidence of child labor is strongly related to per capita GDP. In fact, about 80 percent of the international variation in child labor is explained by this variable alone. Child labor virtually disappears once a country's per capita income reaches five thousand dollars. Developing countries can help reduce child labor by raising rural incomes through agricultural price liberalization. Evidence from Vietnam suggests that when the domestic price of rice rose after the government permitted more rice exports, farmers responded by reducing the use of child labor.[55] Developed countries can help developing countries raise their income by allowing them to sell their products more easily in the markets of the richer economies. Instead, developed countries have maintained high trade barriers on agricultural goods and clothing, precisely the goods that developing countries have a comparative advantage in producing. Compulsory education laws that mandate school attendance have also proven effective in reducing child labor and are more easily monitored than direct bans. Rising income and compulsory education accounted for the decline in the employment of children in the United States, and will in developing countries as well.[56]

The WTO is not the proper forum for dealing with the issue of

[53] "Caroline Lequesne of Oxfam, a British charity, has just returned from Bangladesh, where she visited factories to determine the impact of American retailers' human-rights policies. She reckons that between 1993 and 1994 around 30,000 of the 50,000 children working in textile firms in Bangladesh were thrown out of factories because suppliers feared losing their business if they kept the children on. But the majority of these children have, because of penury, been forced to turn to prostitution or other industries like welding, where conditions pose far greater risks to them" (*Economist*, June 3, 1995, 59).

[54] See, for example, Basu 1999.

[55] Edmonds and Pavcnik 2001.

[56] The United States, it should be noted, did not ban child labor until the Fair Employment Act of 1938, a point when per capita income was well above that in many developing countries today.

Percentage of children working, 1995

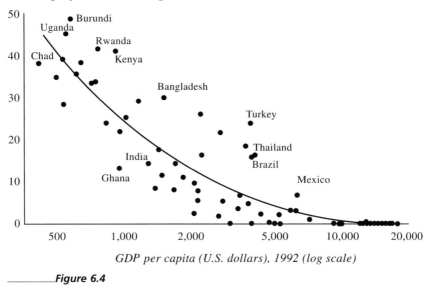

GDP per capita (U.S. dollars), 1992 (log scale)

_____**Figure 6.4**

Child labor and GDP per capita, 1995. (*Source:* Krueger 1996, 295.)

core labor standards because they are not directly related to international trade.[57] Even if a country did not engage in international trade but suppressed worker rights, labor standards should still be an issue because of the universality of core labor standards. Put differently, if a country had a problem with the treatment of child labor but did not use that labor in exported goods, that practice should still be a source of global concern. Furthermore, the WTO lacks the institutional expertise and resources to deal with labor issues. As the WTO membership itself declared at the 1996 ministerial meeting in Singapore, the ILO is the competent body to set and administer labor standards. The effort to push labor standards onto the WTO's lap would undermine the ILO as well as burden the WTO with something it is not well equipped to handle.

The WTO has been tagged with the issue of labor standards primarily because trade sanctions are believed to be the most effective way of enforcing such standards. As we have seen, however, the threat

[57] For a general analysis of using trade policy to improve labor standards, see Maskus 1997 and Brown 2000.

of trade sanctions to enforce labor standards in developing countries risks harming the very workers we are trying to help. As Paul Krugman puts it, "even if we could assure the workers in Third World export industries of higher wages and better working conditions, this would do nothing for the peasants, day laborers, scavengers, and so on who make up the bulk of these countries' populations. At best, forcing developing countries to adhere to our labor standards would create a privileged labor aristocracy, leaving the poor majority no better off."[58] At worst, those export industries would be shut down, throwing those workers out of their jobs. Furthermore, the threat of using trade sanctions to enforce labor standards is precisely why developing countries are so afraid of including them in the WTO. Developing countries adamantly oppose efforts to link trade and labor standards, which is why pressing this issue is asking for a stalemate in the WTO.

To the extent that international cooperation in the ILO is considered useful, how should ILO charters be enforced? The problem is that if countries lack the political will to adhere to international rules, then the enforcement of those rules is beside the point. "Bad" regimes unlikely to be moved by trade sanctions. Furthermore, under ILO rules, a government can only bring a complaint against another government if both have ratified the relevant convention. Through its failure to ratify many of the ILO conventions, the United States has effectively forfeited its right to use that organization to enforce labor rights abroad. For those countries that have ratified ILO charters or agree to accords on labor standards, enforcement is best carried out by embedding the ILO commitments in domestic law and enforcing them through civil actions and punitive judgments (such as fines) in the domestic legal system. The ILO is an international organization that is open to the participation of governments, business groups, and labor representatives, and so its charters have implications for private businesses (unlike the WTO, which is a

---

[58] Krugman 1998a, 84. Economic development is the only known way to increase wages. The alternatives—massive foreign aid, stronger demands for social justice—are unrealistic or ineffective. "[A]s long as you have no realistic alternative to industrialization based on low wages, to oppose [trade and industrialization] means that you are willing to deny desperately poor people the best chance they have of progress for the sake of what amounts to an aesthetic standard—that is, the fact that you don't like the idea of workers being paid a pittance to supply rich Westerners with fashion items" (Krugman 1998a, 85).

government-to-government agency that sets rules only on government trade policies, not the practices of private firms).

_____The Politics of Labor Standards

If dealing with "core" labor standards is difficult enough, there are political pressures in developed countries to go beyond core standards and into the realm of "economic" standards. Labor unions and other NGOs have pressed for standards that include minimum wages, employment hours, occupational health and safety regulations, minimum age of employment, and so on. Without these standards, it is argued, developing countries will attract investment and gain jobs at the expense of developed countries, which will then face pressures to reduce labor standards. Such economic standards, however, have no place in a trade agreement because they are a function of economic development.[59] To the extent that labor unions are behind this push is worrisome from the standpoint of developing countries because all too often those unions have simply sought to block trade.

As a result, while most advocates of higher labor standards are genuinely motivated by concerns about workers in developing countries, the politics of labor standards are such that attempts will be made to use them to limit the market access of low-wage developing countries. In January 1999, the United States signed an agreement with Cambodia that promised a 14 percent increase in Cambodia's annual quota for textile shipments if the country agreed to meet certain core labor standards. Although the Cambodian garment industry established high minimum wages and agreed to paid vacations, unionization rights, and a ban on child labor, the Union of Needletrades, Industrial and Textile Employees (UNITE) wrote to the U.S. Trade Representative opposing any increase in the quota. Following this, and without consulting other views, USTR ruled in December 1999 that Cambodia was not in "substantial compliance" with the agreement and denied the quota increase. The Cambodian gov-

---

[59] As Robert Reich (1994), secretary of labor in the Clinton administration, stated, "it is inappropriate to dictate uniform levels of working hours, minimum wages, benefits or health and safety standards. The developing countries' insistence that they must grow richer in order to afford American or European labor standards—and that they must trade if they are to grow richer—is essentially correct."

ernment and garment industry were shocked because they believed they had gone beyond the agreement in improving standards. Five months later, USTR agreed to a smaller 5 percent increase after Cambodia and the ILO established a program to monitor work conditions.[60]

Unions such as UNITE, the Teamsters, and the AFL-CIO also opposed legislation that would give to African countries the same tariff preferences that the United States currently extends to Caribbean and other poor developing countries. The African Growth and Opportunity Act of 2000 aimed to help the continent by giving duty-free access to the U.S.-market in selected goods. Instead of being viewed as a small way of helping African countries improve their economies, labor-backed opponents dubbed the legislation as "NAFTA for Africa." The proposal to allow African textile producers duty-free access to the U.S. market proved to be quite controversial even though Africa's share of U.S. apparel consumption was only 0.45 percent. The U.S. International Trade Commission concluded that the impact of removing the quota on the U.S. apparel industry would be negligible and that, at most, only 676 U.S. jobs would be affected.[61] Other analysts have suggested that the preferences might have an even smaller domestic impact because it would simply improve the position of Africa at the expense of China. The staunch opposition simply fuels suspicions that the labor unions are not really interested in helping poor African workers deeply mired in poverty, but just stand ready to oppose any measure that promises to increase trade.[62]

At the 1996 WTO ministerial meeting in Singapore, the United States pressed for the creation of a working group on labor standards.

[60] Cooper 2000.

[61] U.S. International Trade Commission 1997, 3–12.

[62] The experience of the Europe may be instructive. In 1989 the European Community adopted the Community Charter on the Fundamental Rights of Workers, known as the Social Charter, which set out social regulations for the health and safety of workers and equitable wage and labor conditions. As one political analyst points out, this "could never have gotten off the ground had it not been consistent with the purely protectionist impulses of the northern continent. The rich northerners [France, Germany] feared losing jobs and investment to the poorer Club Med states [Spain, Portugal, Greece] unless northern labor and social costs could be imposed on them." But the northern Europeans remain "happy to ignore even gross violations of social rights, so long as they do not lead to job and investment transfers. No one, for example, has cried 'social dumping' against Portugal, where child labor is endemic, simply because Portuguese children as yet pose no direct threat to northern jobs" (Steil 1994, 17).

After sharp opposition by developing countries, the WTO membership agreed that the ILO instead was the appropriate venue for considering labor standards. Despite this agreement, the United States again called for an examination of labor standards in the WTO at the 1999 Seattle ministerial meeting. Developing countries were completely hostile, and even Canada failed to support the United States, while the European Union was willing to consider greater cooperation between the WTO and the ILO only if any linkage between labor standards and market access was ruled out. When President Clinton let slip the idea that labor standards should be included in trade agreements and enforced with trade sanctions, developing countries accused the United States of bad faith (ignoring the Singapore declaration) and were galvanized to oppose any new trade round on this basis. The president's statement almost single-handedly ensured the failure of the Seattle meeting.

If the United States continues to press for including labor standards in trade agreements, it may succeed at the bilateral level; indeed, the U.S.-Jordan Free Trade Agreement of 2000 has such a provision.[63] But at the multilateral level, the press for labor standards is to ensure failure due to the staunch opposition of developing countries. Any continued emphasis of the United States on labor standards, therefore, amounts to an enormous and unprofitable diversion from the true task of helping developing countries improving their economic performance. Those countries and organizations that genuinely want to see an improvement in labor standards should encourage the allocation of additional resources from the World Bank to help finance schooling and foster a commitment among developed countries to keep their markets open to the exports of developing countries, while encouraging developing countries themselves to continue to reform their own antigrowth policies.

Experience has shown that it is all too easy to mask an antitrade agenda with labor and environmental concerns. This is evident in many

---

[63] Provisions regarding the protection of worker rights are included directly in the U.S.-Jordan FTA, rather than in a side agreement (as with NAFTA). Both countries agreed to support the 1998 ILO declaration on fundamental principles and rights at work, agreed that lowering standards to encourage trade is inappropriate, and agreed to enforce existing labor laws and settle disagreements on the enforcement of these laws through a dispute settlement mechanism.

positions of anticommercial NGOs and anti-import labor unions. This is regrettable because there are deep and legitimate questions about using trade measures to enforce labor and environmental standards, and therefore the possibility of common ground gets lost in extreme positions. Yet there are inherent flaws in giving the WTO a non-trade-related mission, such as enforcing environmental agreements or enforcing labor standards. The risk is that these poorly targeted and indirect instruments for improving the environment and labor standards will fail to achieve their objective while at the same time will expand the allowable rationales for trade barriers, thus undermining the liberal trading system without generating compensating benefits.

No nation was ever ruined by trade.
—*Benjamin Franklin (1774)*

_____Conclusion

In a recent speech at Dartmouth College, former senator George Mitchell said that he had drawn two conclusions from his role as mediator in the conflict in Northern Ireland: that economic opportunity is a prerequisite for peace, and that America's vision of that economic opportunity is the basis of its influence in the world.

These simple lessons have some connection to trade policy. For nearly three-quarters of a century, the United States has nurtured a rules-based world trading system centered on the principle of nondiscrimination and the goal of gradually reducing trade barriers. The United States is admired around the world as a place of economic opportunity, where individuals are given a chance to succeed regardless of their background. America's commitment to a system of open trade and willingness to accept products from around the world is one reason it is so highly regarded. The choices that the United States makes in its own trade policy have ramifications far beyond America's shores and have implications well beyond economics.

Today, the open world trading system supported by the United States faces challenges from two different sources. The first is the threat of protectionism. Protectionist pressures are always present because, as this book has noted many times, economic interests that are adversely affected by trade always seek to limit it. But given the rapid increase in trade integration over the past few decades, it is surprising that these pressures are so weak.[1]

---

[1] The threat of protectionism may have been exaggerated over the postwar period. Pastor (1983) says that there has been a repeated "cry and sigh" syndrome since the

Why have protectionist demands been so muted? Postwar economic growth and macroeconomic stability have tempered such demands by creating new opportunities for those displaced by imports. Transfer payments and social insurance have also mitigated the cost to those adversely affected by economic change. Businesses that depend upon imported intermediate goods have become a countervailing force against those that demand new trade restrictions. Finally, many industries facing foreign competition, such as televisions and automobiles and semiconductors, have found that international diversification or joint ventures with foreign partners are a more profitable way of coping with global competition than simply stopping goods at the border. Firms that have failed to adjust, diversify, or join with foreign partners, such as the integrated steel industry and the footwear industry, either continue to resist foreign competition or have shrunk to the point where they have lost their political impact.

These factors have sustained political support for an open trading system and have prevented a globalization backlash on the basis of economic interests. As a result, the political appeal of economic nationalism, with protectionism as a central part of its program, has not been strong. A century ago, protectionism was associated with industrial strength and independence. As the robust Theodore Roosevelt once quipped, "Thank God I am not a free-trader. In this country pernicious indulgence in the doctrine of free trade seems inevitably to produce fatty degeneration of the moral fibre."[2] But today, protectionism is taken as a sign of weakness. As Senator John McCain put it, building walls is for cowards.

While those supporting the liberal trading system should always remain vigilant with respect to protectionist demands, the second challenge facing the world trading system is perhaps a more difficult one. This new challenge comes from NGOs who do not represent sectional interests, but stand for particular causes. These "public interest" groups include "consumer associations, conservation and environmental groups, societies concerned with development in poor countries, human rights groups, movements for social justice, humanitarian societies, organiza-

---

late 1940s, i.e., a constant cry that protectionist pressures are on the rise and then a sigh that the pressures are defused, and trade liberalization resumes.

[2] Quoted in Viner 1991, 246.

tions representing indigenous people, and church groups from all denominations." Together, they are said to comprise "civil society."[3]

In most instances, these groups are opposed to the current system of world trade. "With some exceptions, they are hostile to, or highly critical of, capitalism, multinational corporations, freedom of cross-border trade and capital flows, and the idea of a market economy. They are a force on the side of interventionism."[4] The antagonism of these groups goes well beyond international trade to include most forms of market-based commerce. Despite differences of interest and emphasis among these groups, the more radical elements "share a vision of the world in which past history and present-day market-based economic systems are portrayed in terms of patterns of oppression and abuses of power. Free markets and capitalism are seen as embodying and furthering environmental destruction, male dominance, class oppression, racial intolerance, imperialist coercion and colonial exploitation."[5]

Although these groups have not been represented in the corridors of power, they cannot be dismissed as insignificant. The more radical groups have gained respectability by positioning themselves with mainstream organizations, such as moderate NGOs, UN agencies, labor unions, and some political leaders and other public figures. They have been able to achieve a broader appeal by focusing on human rights, corporate responsibility, and sustainable development, all of which are agreeable enough in principle but behind which are very different views of policy.[6] As a result, these groups have not only been politically active, but have become an increasingly influential part of the public debate.

[3] From Henderson (2001, 19), whose incisive analysis I have drawn upon here. See also Robertson 2000.

[4] Henderson 2001, 20.

[5] Henderson 2001, 30. Alan Greenspan (2000, 5) has also referred to this in stating that "even among liberal democracies, one can still find deep-seated antipathy toward free market competition and its partner, creative destruction . . . . While recognizing the efficacy of capitalism to produce wealth, there remains considerable unease among some segments about the way markets distribute that wealth and about the effects of raw competition on the civility of society."

[6] "All three appear, and are presented, as proof against doubt and objections: who could want to oppose, deny or restrict human rights, to prefer that corporations should act non-responsibly, or to advocate development that was unsustainable? Yet all these virtuous-seeming notions, as now interpreted, bear a collectivist message" (Henderson 2001, 31).

International agencies, national governments, and even corporations that in the past have had a stake in promoting markets have begun to acquiesce to their demands. Yet reconciling their interests with much of the NGO agenda will be difficult because there is often a fundamental incompatibility in outlook. For many of the more militant NGOs, the attack on trade is simply an attack on the most visible part of the market economy. They are just starting with the easiest target, but the objective is much bigger. As the *Economist* put it several years ago:

> It is no coincidence that the keenest economic reformers among the developing and ex-communist countries are the new champions of free trade. It is also no coincidence that those in the industrial countries who are most fearful about the future seek to lessen the rich world's reliance on the market economy, and have made it their first goal to smash the GATT and the other institutions of liberal trade. Both sides, in their different ways, are right. Each has recognized that the market economy is ultimately inseparable from a liberal order of international trade.[7]

Although the classical liberal conception of a market economy is not compromised by prudent government regulation or transfer payments to the less fortunate, it will become compromised if open markets are closed by governments. Dealing with this challenge may prove extremely difficult in the years to come.

Trade policy has always been one of the most contentious areas of economic policy and is therefore the subject of a never-ending debate. Though the postwar period has been marked by a concerted reduction in trade barriers, the matter is not settled because the pressures to weaken the commitment to open markets never abate. The world trading system is far from perfect, and many reforms and changes in rules should be under discussion. But to further the cause of trade liberalization, much remains to be done, including a defense of what has been accomplished.

[7] "Battle Lines," *Economist*, December 24, 1994, 14.

References

Aaronson, Susan A. *Taking Trade to the Streets: The Lost History of Public Efforts to Shape Globalization*. Ann Arbor: University of Michigan Press, 2001.

Ades, Alberto, and Rafael Di Tella. "Rents, Competition, and Corruption." *American Economic Review* 89 (September 1999): 982–993.

Addison, John T., Douglas A. Fox, and Christopher J. Ruhm. "Trade and Displacement in Manufacturing." *Monthly Labor Review* 118 (April 1995): 58–67.

Aitken, Brian, Ann Harrison, and Robert E. Lipsey. "Wages and Foreign Ownership: A Comparative Study of Mexico, Venezuela, and the United States." *Journal of International Economics* 40 (May 1996): 345–71.

Allen, William R. "The International Trade Philosophy of Cordell Hull, 1907–1933." *American Economic Review* 43 (March 1953): 101–116.

Anderson, Kym. "Effects on the Environment and Welfare of Liberalizing World Trade: The Cases of Coal and Food." In Kym Anderson and Richard Blackhurst (eds.), *The Greening of World Trade Issues*. Ann Arbor: University of Michigan Press, 1992.

Anderson, Kym. "Agricultural Trade Reforms, Research Initiatives, and the Environment." In E. Lutz (ed.), *Agriculture and the Environment: Perspectives on Sustainable Rural Development*. Washington D.C.: The World Bank, 1998.

Anderson, James, and Eric van Wincoop. "Gravity with Gravitas: A Solution to the Border Puzzle." NBER Working Paper No. 8079, January 2001.

Antweiler, Werner, Brian R. Copeland, and M. Scott Taylor. "Is Free Trade Good for the Environment?" *American Economic Review* 91 (September 2001): 877–908.

Audley, John J. *Green Politics and Global Trade: NAFTA and the Future of Environmental Politics*. Washington, D.C. : Georgetown University Press, 1997.

Bagwell, Kyle, and Robert W. Staiger. "An Economic Theory of GATT." *American Economic Review* 89 (March 1999): 215–248.

Baier, Scott L., and Jeffrey H. Bergstrand. "The Growth of World Trade: Tariffs, Transport Costs, and Income Similarity." *Journal of International Economics* 53 (February 2001): 1–27.

Bailey, Michael, Judith Goldstein, and Barry Weingast. "The Institutional Roots of American Trade Policy: Politics, Coalitions, and International Trade." *World Politics* 49 (April 1997): 309–338.

Baldwin, Robert E. "The Inefficacy of Trade Policy." In *Trade Policy in a Changing World Economy.* Chicago: University of Chicago Press, 1988.

Baldwin, Robert E. "The Changing Nature of U.S. Trade Policy since World War II." In Robert E. Baldwin and Anne O. Krueger (eds.), *The Structure and Evolution of Recent U.S. Trade Policy.* Chicago: University of Chicago Press for the NBER, 1984.

Baldwin, Robert E., and Michael O. Moore. "Political Aspects of the Administration of the Trade Remedy Laws." In Boltuck, Richard, and Robert E. Litan (eds.). *Down in the Dumps: The Administration of the Unfair Trade Laws.* Washington, D.C.: The Brookings Institution, 1991.

Baldwin, Robert E., and Jeffrey W. Steagall. "An Analysis of ITC Decisions in Antidumping, Countervailing Duty and Safeguard Cases." *Weltwirtschaftliches Archiv* 130 (no. 2, 1994): 290–308.

Balke, Norman, and Robert J. Gordon. "The Estimation of Prewar Gross National Product: Methodology and New Evidence." *Journal of Political Economy* 97 (February 1989): 38–92.

Balton, David. "Setting the Record Straight on Sea Turtles and Shrimp." Remarks to the Eleventh Annual Judicial Conference of the U.S. Court of International Trade on Social Justice Litigation: The CIT and WTO New York, New York, December 7, 1999. Available at http://www.state.gov/www/policy—remarks/1999/991207—balton—turtles.html

Barbier, Edward B., Nancy Bockstael, Joanne C. Burgess, and Ivar Strand. "The Linkage Between the Timber Trade and Tropical Deforestation—Indonesia." *The World Economy* (May 1995): 411–442.

Barbieri, Katherine. "Economic Interdependence: A Path to Peace or a Source of Interstate Conflict?" *Journal of Peace Research* 33 (February 1996): 29–49.

Barfield, Claude. *Free Trade, Sovereignty, Democracy: The Future of the World Trade Organization.* Washington, D.C.: AEI Press, 2001.

Barringer, William H., and Kenneth J. Pierce. *Paying the Price for Big Steel: $100 Billion in Trade Restraints and Corporate Welfare.* Washington, D.C.: American Institute for International Steel, 2000.

Basu, Kaushik. "Child Labor: Cause, Consequence, and Cure, with Remarks on International Labor Standards." *Journal of Economic Literature* 37 (September 1999): 1083–1119.

Berman, Eli, John Bound, and Zvi Griliches. "Changes in the Demand for Skilled Labor within U.S. Manufacturing: Evidence from the Annual

Survey of Manufacturers." *Quarterly Journal of Economics* 109 (May 1994): 367–397.

Bernard, Andrew B., and J. Bradford Jensen. "Exporters, Jobs, and Wages in U.S. Manufacturing: 1976–1987." *Brookings Papers on Economic Activity: Microeconomics.* 1995: 67–112.

Bernard, Andrew B., and J. Bradford Jensen. "Exceptional Exporter Performance: Cause, Effect, or Both?" *Journal of International Economics* 47 (February 1999): 1–26.

Bernard, Andrew B., Jonathan Eaton, J. Bradford Jenson, Samuel Kortum. "Plants and Productivity in International Trade." NBER Working Paper No. 7688, May 2000.

Bernhofen, Daniel M., and John C. Brown. "A Direct Test of the Theory of Comparative Advantage: The Case of Japan." Working Paper, Clark University, January 2000.

Bhagwati, Jagdish. "The Demands to Reduce Domestic Diversity among Trade Nations." In Jagdish Bhagwati and Robert Hudec (eds.), *Fair Trade and Harmonization: Prerequisites for Free Trade?* Cambridge: MIT Press, 1996.

Bhagwati, Jagdish, and Hugh Patrick (eds.). *Aggressive Unilateralism: America's 301 Trade Policy and the World Trading System.* Ann Arbor: University of Michigan Press, 1990.

Bhagwati, Jagdish, and Arvind Panagariya. "Preferential Trading Areas and Multilateralism: Strangers, Friends, or Foes?" In Jagdish Bhagwati and Arvind Panagariya (eds.), *The Economics of Preferential Trading Areas.* Washington, D.C.: AEI Press, 1996.

Bhagwati, Jagdish, and T. N. Srinivasan. "Trade and the Environment: Does Environmental Diversity Detract from the Case for Free Trade?" In Jagdish Bhagwati and Robert Hudec (eds.), *Fair Trade and Harmonization: Prerequisites for Free Trade?* Cambridge: MIT Press, 1996.

Blackhurst, Richard. "The Capacity of the WTO to Fulfill its Mandate." In Anne O. Krueger (ed.), *The WTO as an International Organization.* Chicago: University of Chicago Press, 1998.

Boltuck, Richard, and Robert E. Litan (eds.). *Down in the Dumps: The Administration of the Unfair Trade Laws.* Washington, D.C.: The Brookings Institution, 1991.

Bordo, Michael D., Barry Eichengreen, and Douglas A. Irwin. "Is Globalization Today Really Different From Globalization a Hundred Years Ago?" In Susan Collins and Robert Z. Lawrence (eds.), *Brookings Trade Forum, 1999.* Washington, D.C.: The Brookings Institution, 1999.

Borjas, George J., Richard B. Freeman, and Lawrence Katz. "How Much Do Immigration and Trade Affect Labor Market Outcomes?" *Brookings Papers on Economic Activity* 1 (1997): 1–67.

Bovard, James. *The Fair Trade Fraud*. New York: St. Martin's Press, 1991.

Brander, James A. "Strategic Trade Policy." In Gene M. Grossman and Kenneth Rogoff (eds.), *Handbook of International Economics*, Vol. III. New York: Elseivier, 1995.

Brander, James A., and Barbara J. Spencer. "Trade Adjustment Assistance: Welfare and Incentive Effects of Payments to Displaced Workers." *Journal of International Economics* 36 (May 1994): 239–61.

Branstetter, Lee G. "Are Knowledge Spillovers International or Intranational in Scope? Microeconometric Evidence from the U.S. and Japan." *Journal of International Economics* 53 (February 2001): 53–80.

Brown, Drusilla K. "International Trade and Core Labor Standards: A Survey of the Recent Literature." Discussion Paper No. 2000–05, Department of Economics, Tufts University, January 2000.

Brown, Drusilla K., Alan V. Deardorff, and Robert M. Stern. "Impacts on NAFTA Members of Multilateral and Regional Trade Arrangements and Initiatives and Harmonization of NAFTA's External Tariffs." Research Seminar in International Economics Discussion Paper No. 471. University of Michigan, June 2001.

Brown, Fred, and John Whalley. "General Equilibrium Evaluations of Tariff-Cutting Proposals in the Tokyo Round and Comparisons with More Extensive Liberalisation of World Trade." *Economic Journal* 90 (December 1980): 838–66.

Buchanan, Patrick. *The Great Betrayal: How American Sovereignty and Social Justice Are Being Sacrificed to the Gods of the Global Economy*. Boston: Little, Brown, & Co., 1998.

Burtless, Gary, and Robert Z. Lawrence, Robert E. Litan, Robert J. Shapiro. *Globaphobia: Confronting Fears about Open Trade*. Washington, D.C.: Brookings Institution, Progressive Policy Institute, & Twentieth Century Fund, 1998.

Butler, Michael A. *Cautious Visionary: Cordell Hull and the Trade Reform, 1933–1937*. Kent State, OH: Kent State University Press, 1998.

Casas, Francois R. "Lerner's Symmetry Theorem Revisited." *Keio Economic Studies* 28 (January 1991): 15–19.

Charnovitz, Steven. "The Influence of International about Standards on the World Trading Regime: A Historical Overview." *International Labour Review* 126 (September/October 1987): 167–190.

Clark, Gregory, and Robert C. Feenstra. "Technology in the Great Divergence." In Michael Bordo, Alan Taylor, and Jeffrey Williamson (eds.), *Globalization in Historical Perspective*. Chicago: University of Chicago Press, 2002.

Clerides, Sofronis K., Saul Lach, and James R. Tybout. "Is Learning by Exporting Important? Micro-dynamic Evidence from Colombia, Mexico, and Morocco." *Quarterly Journal of Economics* 113 (August 1998): 903–47.

Collins, Susan (ed.) *Imports, Exports, and the American Worker.* Washington, D.C.: The Brookings Institution, 1998.

Congressional Budget Office. *How the GATT Affects U.S. Antidumping and Countervailing Duty Policy.* Washington, D.C., September 1994.

Congressional Budget Office. *Antidumping Action in the United States and Around the World: An Analysis of International Data.* Washington, D.C., June 1998.

Cooper, Helene. "A Trade Deal Helps Cambodian Workers, But Payoff is Withheld." *Wall Street Journal,* February 28, 2000, p. A1.

Corden, W. Max. *Trade Policy and Economic Welfare.* Oxford: Clarendon Press, 1974.

Council of Economic Advisers. *Economic Report of the President, January 2001.* Washington, D.C.: GPO, 2001.

Croom, John. *Reshaping the World Trading System: A History of the Uruguay Round.* Geneva: WTO, 1995.

Dai, Xiudian, Alan Cawson, and Peter Holmes. "The Rise and Fall of High Definition Television: The Impact of European Technology Policy." *Journal of Common Market Studies* 34 (June 1996): 149–66.

Das, Gurcharan. *India Unbound.* New York: Knopf, 2001.

Davis, Steven J., John C. Haltiwanger, and Scott Schuh. *Job Creation and Destruction.* Cambridge: MIT Press, 1995.

de Melo, Jaime, and David Tarr. *A General Equilibrium Analysis of U.S. Foreign Trade Policy.* Cambridge: MIT Press, 1992.

de Melo, Jaime, and David Tarr. "Industrial Policy in the Presence of Wage Distortions: The Case of the U.S. Auto and Steel Industries." *International Economic Review* 34 (November 1993): 833–851.

De Long, J. Bradford, and Lawrence H. Summers. "Equipment Investment and Economic Growth." *Quarterly Journal of Economics* 106 (May 1991): 445–502.

Deardorff, Alan V., and Robert M. Stern. "An Overview of the Modeling of the Choices and Consequences of U.S. Trade Policy." In Alan Deardorff and Robert Stern (eds.), *Constituent Interests and U.S. Trade Policies.* Ann Arbor: University of Michigan Press, 1998.

Decker, Paul T., and Walter Corson. "International Trade and Worker Displacement: Evaluation of the Trade Adjustment Assistance Program." *Industrial and Labor Relations Review* 48 (July 1995): 758–774.

Denzau, Arthur T., and Michael Munger. "Legislators and Interest Groups: How Unorganized Interests Get Represented." *American Political Science Review* 80 (March 1986): 89–106.

Destler, I. M. *American Trade Policies.* 3rd Edition. Washington, D.C.: Institute for International Economics, 1995.

Destler, I. M. "Trade Politics and Labor Issues,1953–1995." In Susan Collins (ed.), *Imports, Exports, and the American Worker*. Washington, D.C.: Brookings Institution Press, 1998.

Dickens, William T. "Do Labor Rents Justify Strategic Trade and Industrial Policy?" NBER Working Paper No. 5137, May 1995.

Dryden, Steve. *Trade Warriors: USTR and the American Crusade for Free Trade*. New York: Oxford University Press, 1995.

Eaton, Jonathan, and Gene M. Grossman. "Optimal Trade and Industrial Policy under Oligopoly." *Quarterly Journal of Economics* 101 (May 1986): 383–406.

Eaton, Jonathan, and Samuel Kortum. "Trade in Capital Goods." NBER Working Paper No. 8070, January 2001.

Edwards, Sebastian. "Openness, Productivity and Growth: What Do We Really Know?" *Economic Journal* 108 (March 1998): pp. 383–98.

Edwards, Sebastian, and Daniel Lederman. "The Political Economy of Unilateral Trade Liberalization: The Case of Chile." NBER Working Paper No. 6510, April 1998.

Elliott, Kimberly Ann, and Richard B. Freeman. "White Hats or Don Quixotes? Human Rights Vigilantes in the Global Economy." NBER Working Paper No. 8102, January 2001.

Faini, Riccardo, Jaime De Melo, and Wendy Takacs. "A Primer on the MFA Maze." *The World Economy* 18 (January 1995): 113–135.

Feenstra, Robert C. "Integration of Trade and Disintegration of Production in the Global Economy," *Journal of Economic Perspectives* 12 (Fall 1998): 31–50.

Feenstra, Robert C. (ed.) *The Impact of International Trade on Wages*. Chicago: University of Chicago Press, 2000.

Feenstra, Robert C., and Gordon H. Hanson. "Global Production and Rising Inequality: A Survey of Trade and Wages." In James Harrigan (ed.), *Handbook of International Trade*. New York: Basil Blackwell, 2002.

Feenstra, Robert C., James R. Markusen, and William Zeile. "Accounting for Growth with New Inputs." *American Economic Review* 82 (May 1992): 415–421.

Fernandez, Raquel, and Dani Rodrik. "Resistance to Reform: Status Quo Bias in the Presence of Individual-Specific Uncertainty." *American Economic Review* 81 (December 1991): 1146–1155.

Field, Alfred J., and Edward M. Graham. "Is There a Special Case for Import Protection for the Textile and Apparel Sectors Base on Labour Adjustment?" *The World Economy* 20 (March 1997): 137–157.

Finger, J. Michael (ed.). *Antidumping: How it Works and Who Gets Hurt*. Ann Arbor: University of Michigan Press, 1993.

Finger, J. Michael. "Legalized Backsliding: Safeguard Provisions in GATT." In Will Martin and L. Alan Winters (eds.), *The Uruguay Round and Developing Countries*. New York: Cambridge University Press, 1996.

Finger, J. Michael, Merlinda D. Ingco, and Ulrich Reincke. *The Uruguay Round: Statistics on Tariff Concessions Given and Received.* Washington, D.C.: The World Bank, 1996.

Flam, Harry. "A Heckscher-Ohlin Analysis of the Law of Declining International Trade." *Canadian Journal of Economics* 18 (August 1985): 602–15.

Flamm, Kenneth. *Mismanaged Trade? Strategic Policy and the Semiconductor Industry.* Washington, D.C.: The Brookings Institution, 1996.

Food and Agriculture Organization. *FAO Annual Yearbook: Fertilizer 1997.* Rome: FAO, 1998.

Fordham, Benjamin O. "Economic Interests, Party, and Ideology in Early Cold War Era U.S. Foreign Policy." *International Organization* 52 (Spring 1998): 359–396

Francois, Joseph F., Hugh M. Arce, Kenneth A. Reinert, and Joseph E. Flynn. "Commercial Policy and the Domestic Carrying Trade." *Canadian Journal of Economics* 29 (February 1996): 181–98.

Francois, Joseph F., and Laura M. Baughman. "Cost to American Consuming Industries of Steel Quotas and Taxes." Washington, D.C.: The Trade Partnership, April 30, 2001.

Frank, Charles R., Jr., Kwang S. Kim, and Larry E. Westphal. *Foreign Trade Regimes and Economic Development: South Korea.* New York: National Bureau of Economic Research, 1975.

Frankel, Jeffrey. "Globalization of the Economy." In Joseph Nye and John Donahue (eds.), *Governance in a Globalizing World.* Washington, D.C.: The Brookings Institution, forthcoming. Available as NBER Working Paper No. 7858, February 2000.

Frankel, Jeffrey A., and David Romer. "Does Trade Cause Growth?" *American Economic Review* 89 (June 1999): 379–399.

Freeman, Richard B., and Morris M. Kleiner. "The Last American Shoe Manufacturers: Changing the Method of Pay to Survive Foreign Competition." NBER Working Paper No. 6750, October 1998.

Gallaway, Michael P., Bruce Blonigen, and Joseph E. Flynn. "Welfare Costs of the U.S. Anti-Dumping and Countervailing Duty Laws." *Journal of International Economics* 49 (December 1999): 211–244.

Gates, Scott, Torbjørn Knutsen, and Jonathon Moses. "Democracy and Peace: A More Skeptical View." *Journal of Peace Research* 33 (February 1996): 1–10.

Gawande, Kishore. "Stigler-Olson Lobbying Behavior in Protectionist Industries: Evidence from the Lobbying Power Function." *Journal of Economic Behavior and Organization* 35 (May 1998): 477–499.

General Agreement on Tariffs and Trade. *International Trade 1952.* Geneva: GATT, June 1953.

Gibbons, Robert, and Lawrence Katz. "Does Unmeasured Ability Explain Inter-

Industry Wage Differentials?" *Review of Economic Studies* 59 (July 1992): 515–535.

Gignilliat, John L. "Pigs, Politics, and Protection: The European Boycott of American Pork." *Agricultural History* 35 (January 1961): 3–24.

Golub, Stephen S. *Labor Costs and International Trade.* Washington, D.C.: The AEI Press, 1999.

Golub, Stephen S., and Chang-Tai Hsieh. "Classical Ricardian Theory of Comparative Advantage Revisited." *Review of International Economics* 8 (May 2000): 221–234.

Greenspan, Alan. "Opening Remarks." In *Global Economic Integration: Opportunities and Challenges.* Kansas City: Federal Reserve Bank of Kansas City, 2000.

Grinols, Earl L. "Procedural Protectionism: The American Trade Bill and the New Interventionist Mode." *Weltwirtschaftliches Archiv* 125 (1990): 501–520.

Grossman, Gene M., and Alan B. Krueger. "Environmental Impacts of a North American Free Trade Agreement." In Peter Garber (ed.), *The Mexico-U.S. Free Trade Agreement.* Cambridge: MIT Press, 1993.

Grossman, Gene M. and Elhanan Helpman. "Protection for Sale." *American Economic Review* 84 (September 1994): 833–850.

Grossman, Gene M. and Giovanni Maggi. "Free Trade vs. Strategic Trade: A Peak into Pandora's Box." In R. Sato, R. V. Ramachandran and K. Mino (eds.), *Global Competition and Integration.* Boston: Kluwer Academic Publishers, 1998.

Hansen, Wendy L., and Thomas J. Prusa. "Cumulation and ITC Decision-Making: The Sum of the Parts is Greater Than the Whole." *Economic Inquiry* 34 (October 1996): 746–69.

Hansen, Wendy L., and Thomas J. Prusa. "The Economics and Politics of Trade Policy: An Empirical Analysis of ITC Decision Making." *Review of International Economics* 5 (May 1997): 230–245.

Hanson, Kenneth A., and Kenneth A. Reinert. "The Distributional Effects of U.S. Textile and Apparel Protection." *International Economic Journal* 11 (Autumn 1997): 1–12.

Harrison, Ann E. "Productivity, Imperfect Competition and Trade Reform: Theory and Evidence." *Journal of International Economic* 36 (February 1994): 53–73.

Harrison, Glen W., Thomas F. Rutherford, and David G. Tarr. "Quantifying the Uruguay Round." In Will Martin and L. Alan Winters (eds.), *The Uruguay Round and the Developing Countries.* New York: Cambridge University Press, 1996.

Hart, Jeffrey A. "The Antidumping Petition of the Advanced Display Manufacturers of America: Origin and Consequences." *The World Economy* 16 (January 1993): 85–109.

Hart, Jeffrey A. "The Politics of HDTV in the United States." *Policy Studies Journal* 22 (Summer 1994): 213–228.

Hausman, Jerry A. "Valuation of New Goods under Perfect and Imperfect Competition." In Timothy F. Bresnahan and Robert J. Gordon (eds.), *The Economics of New Goods*. Chicago: University of Chicago Press, 1997.

Heckman, James. "Doing it Right: Job Training and Education." *Public Interest* 135 (Spring 1999): 86–107.

Helpman, Elhanan. "R&D and Productivity: The International Connection." NBER Working Paper No. 6106, July 1997.

Henderson, David. *Anti-Liberalism 2000: The Rise of New Millennium Collectivism*. London: Institute of Economic Affairs, 2001.

Hicks, John R. *A Theory of Economic History*. Oxford: Clarendon Press, 1969.

Hillman, Arye, and Peter Moser. "Trade Liberalization as Politically Optimal Exchange of Market Access." In Matthew Canzoneri, Wilfred Ethier, and Vittorio Grilli (eds.), *The New Transatlantic Economy*. New York: Cambridge University Press, 1996.

Hinojosa-Ojeda, Raul, David Runsten, Fernando De Paolis, and Nabil Kamel. "The U.S. Employment Impacts of North American Integration after NAFTA." Working Paper, University of California at Los Angeles, School of Public Policy and Social Research, January 2000.

Hoekman, Bernard, and Michel Kostecki. *The Political Economy of the World Trading System: From GATT to WTO*. New York: Oxford University Press, 1995.

Huber, J. Richard. "Effect on Prices of Japan's Entry into World Commerce after 1858." *Journal of Political Economy* 79 (May-June 1971): 614–628.

Hudec, Robert. *The GATT Legal System and World Trade Diplomacy*. 2nd ed. Salem, N.H.: Butterworth Legal Publishers, 1990.

Hudec, Robert. "The Product-Process Doctrine in GATT/WTO Jurisprudence." In Marco Bronckers and Reinhard Quick (eds.), *New Directions in International Economic Law: Essays in Honour of John H. Jackson*. Boston: Kluwer Law International, 2000.

Hudec, Robert. "Does the Agreement on Agriculture Work? Agricultural Disputes After the Uruguay Round." International Agricultural Trade Research Consortium Working Paper No. 98–2. April 1998. http://www.umn.edu/iatrc

Hufbauer, Gary C., and Kimberly A. Elliott. *Measuring the Costs of Protection in the United States*. Washington, D.C.: Institute for International Economics, 1994.

Hufbauer, Gary C., and Jeffrey J. Schott. *NAFTA: An Assessment*. Revised Edition. Washington, D.C.: Institute for International Economics, October 1993.

Hull, Cordell. *Memoirs*. 2 vols. New York: Macmillan, 1948.

Hummels, David. "Transportation Costs and International Integration in Recent History." Working Paper, University of Chicago, 1999.

Hummels, David. "Time as a Trade Barrier." Working Paper, Department of Economics, Purdue University, October 2000.

Hummels, David, Jun Ishii, and Kei Mu Yi. "The Nature and Growth of Vertical Specialization in World Trade." *Journal of International Economics* 54 (June 2001): 75–96.

Hummels, David, Dana Rapoport, and Kei-Mu Yi. "Vertical Specialization and the Changing Nature of World Trade." *Federal Reserve Bank of New York Economic Policy Review* (June 1998): 79–99.

Ingco, Merlinda D. "Tariffication in the Uruguay Round: How Much Liberalization?" *The World Economy* 19 (July 1996): 425–446.

International Monetary Fund. *International Financial Statistics Yearbook 2000.* Washington, D.C.: IMF, 2000.

Irwin, Douglas A. "The GATT's Contribution to Economic Recovery in Post-War Europe." In Barry Eichengreen (ed.), *Europe's Postwar Growth.* New York: Cambridge University Press, 1995.

Irwin, Douglas A. "The United States in a New Global Economy? A Century's Perspective." *American Economic Review* 86 (May 1996): 41–46. (A)

Irwin, Douglas A. *Against the Tide: An Intellectual History of Free Trade.* Princeton: Princeton University Press, 1996. (B)

Irwin, Douglas A. "Trade Politics and the Semiconductor Industry." In Anne O. Krueger (ed.), *The Political Economy of American Trade Policy.* Chicago: University of Chicago Press, 1996. (C)

Irwin, Douglas A. "From Smoot-Hawley to Reciprocal Trade Agreements: Changing the Course of U.S. Trade Policy in the 1930s." In Michael Bordo, Claudia Goldin, and Eugene White (eds.), *The Defining Moment: The Great Depression and the American Economy.* Chicago: University of Chicago Press, 1998. (A)

Irwin, Douglas A. "Changes in U.S. Tariffs: The Role of Import Prices and Commercial Policies." *American Economic Review* 88 (September 1998): 1015–1026. (B)

Irwin, Douglas A. "Explaining America's Surge in Manufactured Exports, 1880–1913." NBER Working Paper 7638, April 2000.

Irwin, Douglas A. "The Welfare Costs of Antarky: Evidence from the Jeffersonian Trade Embargo, 1807–1809." NBER Working Paper, January 2002.

Irwin, Douglas A., and Peter J. Klenow. "Learning-by-Doing Spillovers in the Semiconductor Industry." *Journal of Political Economy* 102 (December 1994): 1200–1227.

Irwin, Douglas A., and Randall S. Kroszner. "Interests, Institutions, and Ideology in Securing Policy Change: The Republican Conversion to Trade Liberalization after Smoot-Hawley." *Journal of Law and Economics* 42 (October 1999): 643–673.

Irwin, Douglas A., and Marko Terviö. "Does Trade Raise Income? Evidence from the Twentieth Century." *Journal of International Economics,* forthcoming 2002.

Jackson, John H. "The Crumbling Institutions of the Liberal Trade System." *Journal of World Trade Law* 12 (March/April 1978): 93–106.

Jackson, John H. *The World Trading System.* 2nd ed. Cambridge: MIT Press, 1997.

Jackson, John H. "The Role and Effectiveness of the WTO Dispute Settlement Mechanism." In Susan Collins and Dani Rodrik (eds.), *Brookings Trade Forum, 2000.* Washington, D.C.: Brookings Institution, 2001.

Jacobson, Louis. "Compensation Programs." In Susan Collins (ed.), *Imports, Exports, and the American Worker.* Washington, D.C.: Brookings Institution, 1998.

Jacobson, Louis, Robert LaLonde, and Daniel Sullivan. "Earnings Losses of Displaced Workers." *American Economic Review* 83 (September 1993): 685–709.

Jaffe, Adam B., et al. "Environmental Regulation and the Competitiveness of U.S. Manufacturing: What Does the Evidence Tell Us?" *Journal of Economic Literature* 33 (March 1995): 132–163.

Jones, Charles I. "Economic Growth and the Relative Price of Capital." *Journal of Monetary Economics* 34 (December 1994): 359–382.

Jones, Charles I. "Comment on Rodríguez and Rodrik." In Ben S. Bernanke and Kenneth Rogoff (eds.), *NBER Macroeconomics Annual, 2000.* Cambridge: MIT Press, 2001.

Jones, Ronald W. *Globalization and the Theory of Input Trade.* Cambridge: MIT Press, 2000.

Josling, Timothy. *Agricultural Trade Policy: Completing the Reform.* Washington, D.C.: Institute for International Economics, April 1998.

Kahn, Matthew. "United States Pollution Intensive Trade Trends from 1972 to 1992." Working Paper, Department of Economics, Tufts University, February 2000.

Katz, Lawrence F., and Lawrence H. Summers. "Industry Rents: Evidence and Implications." *Brookings Papers on Economic Activity: Microeconomics,* 1989.

Keller, Wolfgang. "Do Trade Patterns and Technology Flows Affect Productivity Growth?" *World Bank Economic Review* 14 (January 2000): 17–47.

Keller, Wolfgang. "Trade and the Transmission of Technology." Working Paper, Department of Economics, University of Texas at Austin, March 2001.

Kim, Euysung. "Trade Liberalization and Productivity Growth in Korean Manufacturing Industries: Price Protection, Market Power, and Scale Efficiency." *Journal of Development Economics* 62 (June 2000): 55–83.

Klenow, Peter, and Andrés Rodríguez-Claire. "Quantifying Variety Gains from Trade Liberalization." Working Paper, University of Chicago, September 1997.

Kletzer, Lori G. "Job Displacement." *Journal of Economic Perspectives* 12 (Winter 1998): 115–136. (A)

Kletzer, Lori G. "Trade and Job Displacement in U.S. Manufacturing: 1979–1991." In Susan Collins (ed.), *Imports, Exports, and the American Worker*. Washington, D.C.: Brookings Institution, 1998. (B)

Kletzer, Lori G. "Trade and Job Loss in U.S. Manufacturing, 1979–1994." In Robert Feenstra (ed.), *The Impact of International Trade on Wages*. Chicago: University of Chicago Press for the NBER, 2000.

Kletzer, Lori G. and Robert E. Litan. "A Prescription to Relieve Worker Anxiety." International Economics Policy Briefs. Washington, D.C.: Institute for International Economics, March 2001.

Krishna, Pravin, and Devashish Mitra. "Trade Liberalization, Market Discipline and Productivity Growth: New Evidence from India." *Journal of Development Economics* 56 (August 1998): 447–462.

Kristof, Nicholas D. and Sheryl WuDunn. "Two Cheers for Sweatshops." *New York Times Magazine*, September 24, 2000, pp. 70–71.

Krueger, Alan B. "International Labor Standards and Trade." In Michael Bruno and Boris Pleskovic (eds.), *Annual World Bank Conference on Development Economics 1996*. Washington, D.C.: World Bank, 1997.

Krueger, Anne O. "Free Trade is the Best Policy." In Robert Z. Lawrence and Charles L. Schultze (eds.), *An American Trade Strategy: Options for the 1990s*. Washington, D.C.: The Brookings Institution, 1990.

Krueger, Anne O. (ed.). *The Political Economy of American Trade Policy*. Chicago: University of Chicago Press, 1996.

Krueger, Anne O. "Free Trade Agreements as Protectionist Devices: Rules of Origin." In James R. Melvin, James C. Moore, and Raymond Reizman (eds.), *Trade, Theory and Econometrics: Essays in Honor of John S. Chipman*. New York: Routledge, 1999.

Krueger, Anne O. "NAFTA's Effects: A Preliminary Assessment." *The World Economy* 23 (June 2000): 761–775.

Krugman, Paul. "Competitiveness: A Dangerous Obsession." *Foreign Affairs* 73 (March-April 1994): 28–44.

Krugman, Paul. "Growing World Trade: Causes and Consequences," *Brookings Papers on Economic Activity* 1, (1995): 327–362.

Krugman, Paul. *Pop Internationalism*. Cambridge: MIT Press, 1996.

Krugman, Paul. "Ricardo's Difficult Idea: Why Intellectuals Don't Understand Comparative Advantage." In Gary Cook (ed.), *The Economics and Politics of International Trade*, Vol. 2 of Freedom and Trade. London: Routledge, 1998.

Krugman, Paul. *The Accidental Theorist*. New York: Norton, 1998.

Krugman, Paul, and Robert Z. Lawrence. "Trade, Jobs, and Wages." *Scientific American* 270 (April 1994): 44–49. Reprinted in Krugman (1996).

Krugman, Paul, and Alasdair Smith. *Empirical Studies of Strategic Trade Policy.* Chicago: University of Chicago Press, 1994.

Kull, Steven. *Americans on Globalization: A Study of U.S. Public Attitudes.* University of Maryland, Program on International Policy Attitudes, March 28, 2000.

Lawrence, Robert Z., and Robert E. Litan. *Saving Free Trade: A Pragmatic Approach.* Washington, D.C.: The Brookings Institution, 1986.

Lawrence, Robert Z.,and Matthew J. Slaughter. "International Trade and American Wages in the 1980s: Giant Sucking Sound or Small Hiccup?" *Brookings Papers on Economic Activity* no. 2 (1993): 161–211.

League of Nations. *World Economic Survey.* Geneva: League of Nations, 1933.

Lechter, Max. *U.S. Exports and Imports Classified by OBE End-Use Commodity Categories, 1923–1968.* Washington, D.C.: GPO, 1970.

Lee, Jong-Wha. "Capital Goods Imports and Long-Run Growth." *Journal of Development Economics* 48 (October 1995): 91–110.

Lerner, Abba P. "The Symmetry between Import and Export Taxes." *Economica* 3 (August 1936): 306–313.

Levine, Ross, and David Renelt. "A Sensitivity Analysis of Cross-Country Growth Regressions." *American Economic Review* 82 (December 1992): 942–963.

Levinsohn, James. "Testing the Imports-as-Market-Discipline Hypothesis." *Journal of International Economics* 35 (August 1993): 1–22.

Levinsohn, James. "Employment Responses to International Liberalization in Chile." *Journal of International Economics* 47 (April 1999): 321–344.

Levinsohn, James, and Wendy Petropoulos. "Creative Destruction or Just Plain Destruction? The U.S. Textile and Apparel Industry Since 1972." Working Paper, Department of Economics, University of Michigan, June 2001.

Levy, Philip I. "A Political-Economic Analysis of Free Trade Agreements." *American Economic Review* 87 (September 1997): 506–519.

Lindsey, Brink. "The U.S. Antidumping Law: Rhetoric versus Reality." *Journal of World Trade* 34 (February 2000): 1–38.

Lindsey, Brink, Daniel T. Griswold, and Aaron Lukas. "The Steel 'Crisis' and the Costs of Protectionism." Trade Briefing Paper, Center for Trade Policy Studies. Washington, D.C.: The Cato Institute, April 16, 1999.

Lindsey, Brink, Mark A. Groombridge, and Prakash Loungani. "Nailing the Homeowner: The Economic Impact of Trade Protection of the Softwood Lumber Industry." Trade Policy Analysis No. 11. Washington, D.C.: The Cato Institute, July 2000.

Lipsey, Robert E., and Fredrik Sjöholm. "Foreign Direct Investment and Wages in Indonesian Manufacturing." NBER Working Paper No. 8299, May 2001.

Lizza, Ryan. "Silent Partner: The Man Behind the Anti-Free Trade Revolt." *The New Republic* 222 (January 10 2000): 22–25.

Low, Patrick. *Trading Free: The GATT and U.S. Trade Policy.* New York: Twentieth Century Fund, 1993.

Lowe, Jeffrey H. "An Ownership-Based Framework of the U.S. Current Account, 1982–98." *Survey of Current Business* 81 (January 2001): 44–46.

McKinsey Global Institute. *Manufacturing Productivity.* Washington, D.C.: McKinsey & Co., October 1993.

Macaulay, Thomas Babington. *The Complete Writings of Lord Macaulay.* Volume 18: Speeches and Legal Studies. Boston: Houghton, Mifflin, 1900.

Magee, Christopher. "Administered Protection for Workers: An Analysis of the Trade Adjustment Assistance Program." *Journal of International Economics* 53 (February 2001): 105–125.

Maggi, Giovanni. "The Role of Multilateral Institutions in International Trade Cooperation." *American Economic Review* 89 (March 1999): 190–214.

Maggi, Giovanni, and Andrés Rodríguez-Clare. "The Value of Trade Agreements in the Presence of Political Pressures." *Journal of Political Economy* 106 (June 1998): 574–601.

Mansfield, Edward D., Helen V. Milner, and B. Peter Rosendorff. "Free to Trade: Democracies, Autocracies, and International Trade." *American Political Science Review* 94 (June 2000): 305–321.

Marshall, Alfred. *Official Papers of Alfred Marshall.* Edited by J. M. Keynes. London: Macmillan, 1926.

Maskus, Keith. "Should Core Labor Standards Be Imposed Through International Trade Policy?" World Bank Policy Research Paper No. 1817, August 1997.

Maskus, Keith. *Intellectual Property Rights in the Global Economy.* Washington, D.C.: Institute for International Economics, 2000.

Mayer, Jane, and Jose de Cordoba. "Sweet Life: First Family of Sugar is Tough on Workers, Generous to Politicians." *Wall Street Journal.* July 29, 1991.

Mayer, Wolfgang. "Theoretical Considerations on Negotiated Tariff Adjustments." *Oxford Economic Papers* 33 (March 1981): 135–53.

Mayer, Wolfgang. "Endogenous Tariff Formation." *American Economic Review* 74 (December 1984): 970–985.

Mazumdar, Joy. "Imported Machinery and Growth in LDCs." *Journal of Development Economics* 65 (June 2001): 209–224.

McCallum, John, "National Borders Matter: U.S.-Canada Regional Trade Patterns." *American Economic Review* 85 (June 1995): 615–23.

Melitz, Marc. "The Impact of Trade on Intra-Industry Reallocations and Aggregate Industry Productivity." Working Paper, Department of Economics, Harvard University, November 1999.

Messerlin, Patrick A. *Measuring the Costs of Protection in Europe.* Washington, D.C.: Institute for International Economics, May 2001.

Milazzo, Matteo. *Subsidies in World Fisheries: A Reexamination.* World Bank Technical Paper No. 406. Washington, D.C.: The World Bank, 1998.

Mill, John Stuart. *Principles of Political Economy.* London: Longmans, 1909.

Mill, John Stuart. *The Letters of John Stuart Mill.* Edited by Hugh S. R. Elliot. New York: Longmans, Green, 1910.

Mitra, Devashish. "Endogenous Lobby Formation and Endogenous Protection: A Long-Run Model of Trade Policy Determination." *American Economic Review* 89 (December 1999): 1116–1134.

Montesquieu. *The Spirit of the Laws,* translated by A. M. Cohler, B. C. Miller, and H. S. Stone. New York: Cambridge University Press, 1989.

Montgomery, Mark. "Reassessing the Waste Trade Crisis: What Do We Really Know?" *Journal of Environment and Development* 4 (x 1995): 1–28.

Moore, Michael O. "Rules or Politics? An Empirical Analysis of ITC Antidumping Decisions." *Economic Inquiry* 30 (July 1992): 449–466.

Moore, Michael O. "Steel Protection in the 1980s: The Waning Influence of Big Steel?" In Anne O. Krueger (ed.), *The Political Economy of American Trade Policy.* Chicago: University of Chicago Press, 1996.

Moore, Michael O. "Antidumping Reform in the United States: A Faded Sunset." *Journal of World Trade* 33 (August 1999): 1–17.

Moore, Michael O. "VERs and Price Undertakings in the WTO." Working Paper, George Washington University, 2000.

Morris, Julian. "International Environmental Agreements: Developing Another Path." In Terry L. Anderson and Henry I. Miller (eds.), *The Greening of U.S. Foreign Policy.* Stanford: Hoover Institution Press, 2000.

Moser, Peter. *The Political Economy of the GATT.* Grusch: Verlag Ruegger, 1990.

Mussa, Michael. "Government Policy and the Adjustment Process." In Jagdish Bhagwati (ed.), *Import Competition and Response.* Chicago: University of Chicago Press, 1982.

Nader, Ralph (ed.). *The Case Against Free Trade: GATT, NAFTA, and the Globalization of Corporate Power.* San Francisco: Earth Island Press, 1993.

Nelson, Douglas. "The Political Economy of Trade Policy Reform: Social Complexity and Methodological Pluralism." *Journal of International Trade and Economic Development* 8 (March 1999): 3–26.

Olson, Mancur. *The Logic of Collective Action.* Cambridge: Harvard University Press, 1965.

Oneal, John, and Bruce Russett. "The Classical Liberals Were Right: Democracy, Interdependence, and Conflict, 1950–1985," *International Studies Quarterly* 41 (June 1997): 267–294.

Oneal, John, and Bruce Russett. *Triangulating Peace: Democracy, Interdependence, and International Organizations.* New York: Norton, 2000.

Organization for Economic Cooperation and Development. *The OECD Jobs Study: Facts, Analysis, Strategy.* Paris: OECD, 1994.

Organization for Economic Cooperation and Development. *Trade, Employment, and Labour Standards: A Study of Core Workers' Rights and International Trade.* Paris: OECD, 1996.

Organization for Economic Cooperation and Development. *Agricultural Policies in OECD Countries: Monitoring and Evaluation 2000.* Paris: OCED, 2000. (A)

Organization for Economic Cooperation and Development. *International Trade and Core Labour Standards.* Paris: OECD, 2000. (B)

Orme, William A., Jr. *Understanding NAFTA: Mexico, Free Trade, and the New North America.* Austin: University of Texas Press, 1996.

Palmeter, N. David. "National Sovereignty and the World Trade Organization." *Journal of World Intellectual Property* 2 (January 1999): 77–91.

Panagariya, Arvind, Shekhar Shah, and Deepak Mishra. "Demand Elasticities in International Trade: Are They Really Low?" *Journal of Development Economics* 64 (April 2001): 313–42.

Pareto, Vilfredo. *Manual of Political Economy.* Translated by Ann S. Schwier. New York: Augustus M. Kelley, 1971.

Passell, Peter. "Economic Scene: Protecting America's Shores from those Chinese Crawfish." *New York Times,* August 28, 1997, p. D-2.

Pastor, Robert A. *Congress and the Politics of U.S. Foreign Economic Policy, 1929–1976.* Berkeley: University of California Press, 1980.

Pastor, Robert. "The Cry-and-Sigh Syndrome: Congress and Trade Policy." In Allen Shick (ed.), *Making Economic Policy in Congress.* Washington, D.C.: American Enterprise Institute, 1983.

Pavcnik, Nina. "Trade Liberalization, Exit, and Productivity Improvements: Evidence from Chilean Plants." NBER Working Paper No. 7852, August 2000. Forthcoming *Review of Economic Studies.*

Pecorino, Paul. "Is There a Free-Rider Problem in Lobbying? Endogenous Tariffs, Trigger Strategies, and the Number of Firms." *American Economic Review* 88 (June 1998): 652–660.

Perkidis, Nicholas, William A. Kerr, and Jill E. Hobbs. "Reforming the WTO to Defuse Potential Trade Conflicts in Genetically Modified Goods." *The World Economy* 24 (March 2001): 379–398.

Petrin, Amil. "Quantifying the Benefits of New Products: The Case of the Minivan." NBER Working Paper No. 8227, April 2001.

Potters, Jan, and Randolph Sloof. "Interest Groups: A Survey of Empirical Models that Try to Assess Their Influence." *European Journal of Political Economy* 12 (November 1996): 403–442.

Preeg, Ernest H. *Traders in a Brave New World: The Uruguay Round and the Future of the International Trading System.* Chicago: University of Chicago Press, 1995.

Prusa, Thomas J. "Why Are So Many Antidumping Petitions Withdrawn?" *Journal of International Economics* 33 (August 1992): 1–20.

Prusa, Thomas J. "The Trade Effects of U.S. Antidumping Actions." In Robert C. Feenstra (ed.), *The Effects of U.S. Trade Protection and Promotion Policies.* Chicago: University of Chicago Press, 1997.

Prusa, Thomas J. "Cumulation and Antidumping: A Challenge to Competition." *The World Economy* 21 (November 1998): 1021–1033.

Prusa, Thomas J. "On the Spread and Impact of Antidumping Duties." NBER Working Paper No. 7404, October 1999.

Reich, Robert B. "Keynote Address." In *International Labor Standards and Global Economic Integration: Proceedings of a Symposium.* Washington, D.C.: U.S. Department of Labor, 1994.

Reid, Peter C. *Made Well in America: Lessons From Harley-Davidson on Being the Best.* New York: McGraw-Hill, 1990.

Reinert, Kenneth A. "Give Us Virtue, But Not Yet: Safeguard Actions Under the Agreement on Textiles and Clothing." *The World Economy* 23 (January 2000): 25–56.

Revenga, Ana L. "Exporting Jobs? The Impact of Import Competition on Employment and Wages in U.S. Manufacturing." *Quarterly Journal of Economics* 107 (February 1992): 255–284.

Richards, Bill. "Shaky Numbers: Layoffs Not Related To NAFTA Can Trigger Special Help Anyway." *Wall Street Journal,* June 30 1997, p. A1.

Rivera-Batiz, Luis A., and Paul M. "Economic Integration and Endogenous Growth." *Quarterly Journal of Economics* 106 (May 1991): 531–55.

Roberts, Mark J., and James R. Tybout. *Industrial Evolution in Developing Countries: Micro Patterns of Turnover, Productivity, and Market Structure.* New York: Oxford University Press for the World Bank. 1996.

Roberts, Donna. "Preliminary Assessment of the Effects of the WTO Agreement on Sanitary and Phytosanitary Measures Trade Regulations." *Journal of International Economic Law* 2 (December 1998): 377–405.

Roberts, Donna, and Kate DeRemer. *An Overview of Technical Barriers to U.S. Agricultural Exports.* Economic Research Service, U.S. Department of Agriculture, Staff Paper AGES-9705, March 1997.

Robertson, David. "Civil Society and the WTO." *The World Economy* 23 (September 2000): 1119–1134.

Rodríguez, Francisco, and Dani Rodrik. "Trade Policy and Economic Growth: A Skeptic's Guide to Cross-National Evidence." In Ben S. Bernanke and Kenneth Rogoff (eds.), *NBER Macroeconomics Annual, 2000.* Cambridge: MIT Press, 2001.

Rodrik, Dani. "Optimal Trade Taxes for a Large Country with Non-atomistic Firms." *Journal of International Economics* 26 (February 1989): 157–167.

Rodrik, Dani. "The Political Economy of Trade." In Gene M. Grossman and Kenneth Rogoff (eds.). *Handbook of International Economics,* Vol. 3. Amsterdam: Elsevier Publishers, 1995.

Rodrik, Dani. "Labor Standards in International Trade: Do They Matter and

What Do We Do About Them?" In Robert Lawrence et al., *Emerging Agenda for Global Trade: High Stakes for Developing Countries*. Washington, D.C.: Overseas Development Council, 1996.

Rodrik, Dani. "Democracies Pay Higher Wages." *Quarterly Journal of Economics* 114 (August 1999): 707–738.

Roland-Holst, David, Kenneth Reinhart, and Clinton Schiells. "North American Trade Liberalization and the Role of Non-Tariff Barriers." In U.S. International Trade Commission, *Economy-Wide Modeling of the Economic Implication of an FTA with Mexico and a NAFTA with Canada and Mexico*. USITC Publication 20436. Washington, D.C.: USITC, 1992.

Romer, Paul. "New Goods, Old Theory, and the Welfare Costs of Trade Restrictions." *Journal of Development Economics* 43 (February 1994): 5–38.

Rosenberg, Nathan. "Some Institutional Aspects of the 'Wealth of Nations.'" *Journal of Political Economy* 68 (December 1960): 557–570.

Rotemberg, Julio J. "Commercial Policy with Altruistic Voters." NBER Working Paper No. 7984, October 2000.

Sachs, Jeffrey D., and Andrew Warner. "Economic Reform and the Process of Global Integration." *Brookings Papers on Economic Activity* (1995): 1–95.

Sampson, Gary P. *Trade, Environment, and the WTO: The Post-Seattle Agenda*. Washington, D.C.: Overseas Development Council, 2000.

Samuelson, Paul A. *The Collected Scientific Papers of Paul A. Samuelson*. Vol. III. Cambridge: MIT Press, 1972.

Sazanami, Yoko, Shujiro Urata, and Hiroki Kawai. *Measuring the Costs of Protection in Japan*. Washington, D.C.: Institute for International Economics, January 1995.

Schattschneider, E. E. *Politics, Pressure, and the Tariff*. New York: Prentice Hall, 1935.

Scheve, Kenneth F., and Matthew J. Slaughter. *Worker Perceptions and Pressures in the Global Economy*. Washington, D.C.: Institute for International Economics, March 2001. (A)

Scheve, Kenneth F., and Matthew J. Slaughter. "What Determines Individual Trade-Policy Preferences?" *Journal of International Economics* 54 (August 2001): 267–292. (B)

Schnietz, Karen E. "The Institutional Foundation of U.S. Trade Policy: Revisiting Explanations for the 1934 Reciprocal Trade Agreements Act." *Journal of Policy History* 12 (November 2000): 417–444.

Schoepfle, Gregory K. "U.S. Trade Adjustment Assistance Policies for Workers." In Alan V. Deardorff and Robert M. Stern (eds.), *Social Dimensions of U.S. Trade Policies*. Ann Arbor: University of Michigan Press, 2000.

Schott, Jeffrey J. *The Uruguay Round: An Assessment*. Washington, D.C.: Institute for International Economics, 1994.

Scott, Robert E. "NAFTA's Pain Deepens: Job Destruction Accelerates in 1999 with Losses in Every State." Washington, D.C.: Economic Policy Institute Briefing Paper, November 1999.

Scott, Robert E., and Jesse Rothstein. "American Jobs and the Asian Crisis: The Employment Impact of the Coming Rise in the U.S. Trade Deficit." Economic Policy Institute Briefing Paper, January 1998.

Shin, Hyun Ja. "Possible Instances of Predatory Pricing in Recent U.S. Antidumping Cases." In Robert Z. Lawrence (ed.), *Brookings Trade Forum, 1998.* Washington, D.C.: The Brookings Institution, 1998.

Smith, Adam. *An Inquiry into the Nature and Causes of the Wealth of Nations.* Oxford: Clarendon Press, 1976.

Smith, Adam, *The Correspondence of Adam Smith.* Oxford: Clarendon Press, 1977.

Smith, Adam. *Lectures on Jurisprudence.* Oxford: Clarendon Press, 1978.

Spinanger, Dean. "Textiles beyond the MFA Phase-Out." *The World Economy* 22 (June 1999): 455–476.

Srinivasan, T. N. *Developing Countries and the Multilateral Trading System.* Boulder, CO: Westview Press, 1998.

Staiger, Robert W., and Frank A. Wolak. "Measuring Industry Specific Protection: Antidumping in the United States." *Brookings Papers on Economic Activity: Microeconomics,* (1994): 51–103.

Steil, Benn. "'Social Correctness' is the New Protectionism." *Foreign Affairs* 73 (January/February 1994): 14–20.

Stigler, George J. "The Theory of Economic Regulation." *Bell Journal of Economics and Management Science* 2 (Spring 1971): 3–21.

Stigler, George J. "Free Riders and Collective Action: An Appendix to Theories of Economic Regulation." *Bell Journal of Economics and Management Science* 5 (Autumn 1974): 359–365.

Stolper, Wolfgang F., and Paul A. Samuelson, "Protection and Real Wages," *Review of Economic Studies* 9 (November 1941): 58–73.

Suomela, John W. *Free Trade versus Fair Trade: The Making of American Trade Policy in a Political Environment.* Turku, Finland: Institute for European Studies, 1993.

Swagel, Phillip. "Union Behavior, Industry Rents, and Optimal Policies." *International Journal of Industrial Organization* 18 (August 2000): 925–947.

Sykes, Alan O. "Protectionism as a 'Safeguard': A Positive Analysis of the GATT 'Escape Clause' wth Normative Speculations." *University of Chicago Law Review* 58 (Winter 1991): 255–305.

Sykes, Alan O. "Antidumping and Antitrust: What Problems Does Each Address?" In Robert Z. Lawrence (ed.), *Brookings Trade Forum, 1998.* Washington, D.C.: The Brookings Institution, 1998.

Tasca, Henry J. *The Reciprocal Trade Policy of the United States.* Philadelphia: University of Pennsylvania Press, 1938.

Tempest, Rohn. "Barbie and the World Economy." *Los Angeles Times.* September 22, 1996, p. A-1.

Tonelson, Alan. "Beating Back Predatory Trade." *Foreign Affairs* 73 (July/August 1994): 123–135.

Tornell, Aaron. "Time Inconsistency of Protectionist Programs." *Quarterly Journal of Economics* 106 (August 1991): 963–974.

Tornell, Aaron. "Rational Atrophy: The U.S. Steel Industry." NBER Working Paper No. 6084, July 1997.

Trefler, Daniel. Trade Liberalization and the Theory of Endogenous Protection: An Econometric Study of U.S. Import Policy. *Journal of Political Economy* 101 (February 1993): 138–160.

Trefler, Daniel. "The Long and Short of the Canada-U.S. Free Trade Agreement." National Bureau of Economic Research Working Paper No. 8293, May 2001.

Tybout, James R. "Manufacturing Firms in Developing Countries: How Well Do They Do, and Why?" *Journal of Economic Literature* 38 (March 2000): 11–44.

Tybout, James R. and M. Daniel Westbrook. "Trade Liberalization and the Dimensions of Efficiency Change in Mexican Manufacturing Industries." *Journal of International Economics* 39 (August 1995): 53–78.

U.S. Bureau of Census. *U.S. Commodity Exports and Imports as Related to Output, 1961 and 1960.* Washington, D.C.: GPO, 1963.

U.S. Bureau of the Census. *Historical Statistics of the United States, From Colonial Times to 1970.* Washington, D.C.: GPO, 1975.

U.S. Bureau of Census. *U.S. Commodity Exports and Imports as Related to Output, 1993 and 1992.* Washington, D.C.: GPO, September 1995.

U.S. Bureau of the Census. *Statistical Abstract of the United States, 2000.* Washington, D.C.: GPO, 2001.

U.S. Department of Commerce, International Trade Administration. *United States Sugar Policy: An Analysis.* Washington, D.C.: GPO, April 1988.

U.S. Department of Commerce, Office of Inspector General. "Import Administration's Investigations of Steel Industry Petitions," Report No. TTD-5541-4-0001, December 1993.

U.S. Department of Energy, Energy Information Administration, *Petroleum Supply Annual 1998.* Washington, D.C.: GPO, 1998.

U.S. General Accounting Office. *Sugar Program: Changing Domestic and International Conditions Require Program Changes.* RCED/93/84. Washington, D.C.: GAO, 1993.

U.S. General Accounting Office. *Sugar Program: Supporting Sugar Prices Has Increased Users' Costs While Benefiting Producers.* RCED/00/126. Washington, D.C.: GAO, June 2000.

U.S. General Accounting Office. *World Trade Organization: Issues in Dispute Settlement.* NSIAD-00-210. Washington, D.C.: GAO, August 2000.

U.S. House of Representatives, Committee on Ways and Means. *Hearings: North American Free Trade Agreement (NAFTA) and Supplemental Agreements to the NAFTA.* Washington, D.C.: GPO, 1994.

U.S. House of Representatives, Committee on Ways and Means. *Overview and Compilation of U.S. Trade Statues: 1997 Edition.* Washington, D.C.: GPO, June 1997.

U.S. International Trade Commission. *The Economic Effects of Antidumping and Countervailing Duty Orders and Suspension Agreements.* Investigation No. 332–344. Publication 2900. Washington, D.C.: USITC, June 1995.

U.S. International Trade Commission. *Likely Impact of Providing Quota-Free and Duty-Free Entry to Textiles and Apparel from Sub-Saharan Africa.* Investigation 332–379. Publication 3056. Washington, D.C.: USITC, September 1997.

U.S. International Trade Commission. *The Economic Effects of Significant U.S. Import Restraints.* Second Update 1999. Investigation No. 332–325. Publication 3201. Washington, D.C.: USITC, May 1999. (A)

U.S. International Trade Commission. *Production Sharing: Use of U.S. Components and Materials in Foreign Assembly, Operations 1995–1999.* USITC Publication 3265. Washington, D.C.: USITC, December 1999. (B)

U.S. International Trade Commission. "Value of U.S. Imports for Consumption, Duties Collected, and Ratio of Duties to Values, 1891–2000." March 2001.

U.S. Tariff Commission. *Operation of the Trade Agreements Program, July 1934 to April 1948, Part 1. Summary.* Washington, D.C.: Government Printing Office, 1948.

U.S. Trade Representative. *2000 Trade Policy Agenda and 1999 Annual Report.* Washington, D.C.: USTR, 2000.

Viner, Jacob. *Studies in the Theory of International Trade.* New York: Harper, 1937.

Viner, Jacob. *Essays on the Intellectual History of Economics.* Princeton: Princeton University Press, 1991.

Vogel, David. "The Environment and International Trade." *Journal of Policy History* 12 (January 2000): 72–100.

Wacziarg, Romain. "Measuring the Dynamic Gains From Trade." *World Bank Economic Review,* 15 (September 2001), forthcoming.

Wallach, Lori, and Michelle Sforza. *Whose Trade Organization? Corporate Globalization and the Erosion of Democracy.* Washington, D.C.: Public Citizen, 1999.

Watson, James L. *Golden Arches East: McDonald's in East Asia.* Stanford: Stanford University Press, 1997.

Winters, L. Alan, and Won Chang. "Regional Integration and Import Prices: An

Empirical Investigation." *Journal of International Economics* 51 (August 2000): 363–378.

World Bank. *World Development Indicators, 2000.* Washington, D.C.: The World Bank, 2000.

World Resources Institute. *World Resources.* Washington D.C.: World Resources Institute, 1999.

World Trade Organization. "Report of the Panel: EC Measures Concerning Meat and Meat Products (Hormones), Complaint by the United States." WT/DS26/R/U.S. August 18, 1997.

World Trade Organization. *Annual Report, 1998.* Geneva: WTO, 1998.

World Trade Organization. *Trade Policy Review: United States, 1999.* Geneva: WTO, September 1999.

World Trade Organization. *The Legal Texts: The Results of the Uruguay Round of Multilateral Trade Negotiations.* New York: Cambridge University Press, 1999.

World Trade Organization. *International Trade Statistics, 2000.* Geneva: WTO, 2000.

World Trade Organization. *Annual Report, 2001.* Geneva: WTO, May 2001.

Yoon, Carol K. "Simple Method Found to Increase Crop Yields Vastly." *New York Times*, August 22, 2000.

Zeiler, Thomas W. *Free Trade, Free World: The Advent of GATT.* Chapel Hill: University of North Carolina Press, 1999.

Zeile, William J. "U.S. Affiliates of Foreign Companies: Operations in 1998." *Survey of Current Business* 80 (August 2000): 141–158.

Zeile, William J. "U.S. Intrafirm Trade in Goods." *Survey of Current Business* 77 (February 1997): 23–38.

Index

Boldface numbers refer to figures and tables.